Living a Life That Matters

Living a Life That Matters
A Memoir of the Marquis de Lafayette

David M. Weitzman

Liberty Flame

ISBN: 978-1-935736-02-8

Cover design: Jeff Brandenburg
Interior page design: Jeff Brandenburg
Editor: David Colin Carr
Map design: Ronnie Seats

Cover: Portrait of Gilbert Motier the Marquis De La Fayette as a Lieutenant General, 1791 (1834).

Published by Liberty Flame, an imprint of Lone Wolf Consortium
www.loverofliberty.com

First printing, 2015
Printed in U.S.A.

Dedication

This book is dedicated to Bea Bragg who encouraged me to write; my wife Kathy who supported my efforts; my children Kate, Martin, Gwendolyn, Laura, Gabrielle, Lisa and Danielle and my grandchildren, Caelan, Donya, Darius, Madeleine, Abigail, William and Zaina, and my brother Donald and friend Rem.

Freedom is never voluntarily given by the oppressor;
it must be demanded by the oppressed.

—*Martin Luther King, Jr.*

Freedom is never more than one generation away from extinction.
We didn't pass it to our children in the bloodstream. It must be
fought for, protected, and handed on for them to do the same.

—*Ronald Reagan*

We hold these truths to be self-evident: that all men are created equal;
that they are endowed by their Creator with certain unalienable
rights; that among these are life, liberty, and the pursuit of happiness.

—*Thomas Jefferson*

Contents

Prologue

I am a very old man who, a few months ago, did a very imprudent thing. A good friend of mine was killed in a duel, and on a damp and chilly day I followed his bier to the gravesite to speak at his funeral. By the time I had finished the eulogy, my throat was sore and my hands were quaking like autumn leaves. At home afterwards, the cold set up camp in my aged bones like troops gathering arms and provisions for an invasion. My doctors tell me that I have now contracted pneumonia. Most of my precious time is spent bundled in thick blankets, coughing and spitting blood, while my beloved grandchildren force me to drink endless cups of broth and copious amounts of quinine.

Though I am tired and irritable, I review my journals for the hundredth time to finish my memoirs. I hope to be able to draw them to a close in the near future, but there is a great deal to recount and muse upon. With my lungs impaired by years in prison and the war wound that has disturbed my gait for more than half a century, this is likely my last opportunity to instill in my descendants my passion for freedom. It is my hope that they will be devoted guardians of liberty by appreciating my struggles to loosen the shackles of the world I was born into seventy-six years ago.

It feels odd to have lived so long that my life and deeds have entered the annals of history. I must offer here some details of the battlefields I stepped onto in order to convey those aspects of my life that I consider most important. Please forgive small and large inaccuracies—I have no time to consult with librarians or historians, so I depend on my notes, journals, letters, and memory—whose accuracy surprises the rare visitors who lived these times with me.

My point is not to write exacting accounts. Much of that has been recorded in great detail and from a perspective far broader than my in-the-field experience. Rather I invite you to see over my then-unstooped shoulder as my life unfolded and my wisdom evolved, in order to appreciate the world I bequeath you in the best condition I have been able.

As even calendars, those markers of time's passage, have changed radically during my lifetime, so have units of measure and exchange. Therefore I have employed the contemporary usage of my old age, and trust my future editors to update these for their own readers.

•—◆—•

With my birth three-quarters of a century ago, besides physical characteristics I inherited my nationality, occupation, social status, and religion, all by dint of feudal law. I was born a Frenchman, a soldier, a nobleman, and a Catholic. France at the moment of my first breath was the largest and most dominant power in Europe, with a population twice Britain's. For hundreds of years the House of Bourbon had ruled by whim and wile. Louis XV sat upon the throne he had inherited at age five from his great grandfather, Louis XIV, the self-declared Sun King.

Though a lesser nobleman, I inherited the right to hunt, to wear a sword, to possess land that brought me feudal rights and dues, and exemption from certain taxes. And I was precluded from business or commercial ventures. I was eligible for—nay, bound to—specified ecclesiastic, civic, or military positions in service of the king. My father and most of my ancestors had chosen the military, so by family tradition I was obligated to become a soldier.

Before I could think or reason, my religion had been chosen for me, for everyone in France was Catholic by law. Other religions were subjected to persecution, prosecution, and even death.

I did not yet know that there were neither democracies nor republics in Europe. In the world of my birth, few people had any say in their governance. Revolution was unthinkable in 1757. Even the rights of a wealthy nobleman who might have the ear of the king were not guaranteed, fully subject to their monarch's moods and strategies. What was called law was merely the tyrant's will used to violate the personal territory of individuals.

Yet, some movement was shifting the underpinnings of the world. Merely months before my birth, Jean-Jacques Rousseau had written in *The Social Contract* that for all but a king, "man is born free, and everywhere he is in chains." Those chains were imposed by the king and Church on everyone—and I was taught to revere those who had fashioned my chains. And as Voltaire observed, "It is difficult to free fools from the chains they revere."

Fortunately, my arranged marriage let me into the home of a mother-in-law who illuminated those invisible chains that had been wrought link by link to deprive us of our most fundamental birthright. She taught me to question my childhood beliefs.

I have devoted nearly sixty years liberating myself, my family, and the family of man from the chains inflicted upon our thought, speech, and writing to provide for everyone the basic entitlements our Creator endowed us with. For my part in helping start the ball of liberty rolling, Voltaire called me the "hero of two worlds," and the emperor of Austria called me "the most dangerous revolutionary." Yet as my friend Thomas Jefferson predicted, "This ball of liberty . . . is now so well in motion that it will roll round the globe, at least the enlightened part of it, for light & liberty go together."

Because of my involvement—along with many others I was graced to speak with and fight beside—the life I inherited has dramatically changed. In 1834 a legislature allows me a non-violent forum to serve my electorate. I am a citizen of America as well as France. I am no longer a nobleman, but a commoner. And I am a deist who helped sever France from its identity with the Catholic Church.

My three adult children know much about the circumstances of my life. But most of my grandchildren only know me as an old man who bounces them on gangly knees. It brings me great sadness that they never had the opportunity to be nurtured and guided by their grandmother. I want them to understand the small role that Adrienne and I played in bringing about the changes that have bettered their birthright. It is my hope that this memoir will motivate them to keep the ball of liberty in motion, for the forces of enchainment may seem quiescent, but I cannot imagine them ever completely vanquished. The thousands of letters and papers, in addition to my daily journals that Adrienne preserved, I am having stored for them in the attic of La Grange, their ancestral home.

I force myself to write, slowly and carefully, despite gasping for air. My shaking spatters ink across the page as I bequeath them the story only I can tell.

PART I

The Vicissitudes of Childhood

1757–1777

CHAPTER 1

Chavaniac

1757–1768

THREE HUNDRED YEARS BEFORE CHRIST my Gallic ancestors settled in the Auvergne, an isolated mountainous region
in south central France that remains among the most sparsely
populated in all of Europe. In the fourteenth century my namesake,
Gilbert Motier, served as an officer in the French army. The king held
him in such esteem for his service that he granted him the noble title of
marquis and gave him a large piece of imperial territory—a *march*—
which Motier was entrusted to fortify and defend against invasion.
He called his march *La Fayette*, which in the Occitan dialect of the
Auvergne means "little beech tree."

From the top of the hill where he established his homesite, he
looked out over rolling meadows, dense virgin forests, and the outline
of extinct volcanoes in the distance. From the local black volcanic rock,
the new marquis de la Fayette had built a small château flanked by
four watchtowers. He called his new estate *Chavaniac*. The rocky soil,

unsuitable for farming, was leased to herders of sheep and cow. Since that time his family lived a quiet rural life supported by rents and taxes, unless called upon by their king to fight for God and country.

Many generations later my father, Michel Louis Christophe Motier, was born in the château in 1731, and raised to be a soldier. Six years later my mother, Marie Louise Jolie de la Rivière, was born in Paris and raised to be a wife and mother.

Her Paris was the most populous, cosmopolitan city in Europe—center of the arts, sciences, and philosophy. Her aristocratic parents, extremely affluent and influential, were related by blood to the king. From an early age she was on familiar terms with his family and life at Versailles, the royal residence. Her father Joseph Yves Thibault Hyacinthe, marquis de la Rivière and duke de Noailles, was one of the prestigious musketeers—the elite cavalry soldiers responsible for protecting the monarch when he left the royal residence. To insure that my grandfather would always be nearby to protect him, the king assigned him his own quarters in the palace. The proximity made him one of the king's closest friends.

It was expected in feudal France that a wealthy nobleman produce an heir to his fortune. So when my mother was seventeen, the duke deemed his daughter ready for childbearing and set about finding her a husband. My father, who had been sent to Paris to military school to further his career, was found suitable to provide the duke an heir to his fortunes.

I cannot guess the specific circumstances that moved the duke to enter into a marriage contract with the significantly less affluent, land-poor, and relatively unimportant Motier family in the far away Auvergne, but there is little doubt the Motiers were induced to sign the marriage contract by the exceptional dowry offered.

A week before the wedding, my paternal grandparents traversed the 250 muddy or dusty miles by carriage. They stayed just long enough to participate in the ceremony, and returned immediately to the remote seclusion of the Auvergne with their son and new daughter-in-law.

My mother had never been beyond the countryside around Paris and knew no one in the Auvergne, including her husband. The few people there spoke a unique dialect that made it difficult for outsiders like my mother to meet new people.

In the dreary old manor house she lived with two much older women—her husband's widowed mother and his sister, my unmarried aunt Madeleine. As considerate as they may have been, they were likely insufficient companionship for an urbane young woman. And as a noblewoman, she was precluded from most activities except trying to produce a male heir for the de la Rivière fortune and the Motier estate.

Once she succeed in becoming pregnant, I suspect she had little to do except prepare clothes and accommodations for her new infant, fret about the real possibility of death during childbirth, and wait until I forced my way into the world. On September 6, 1757 her water broke and she began experiencing the intense pain that brought me forth to my destiny. To everyone's relief, mother not only survived the ordeal, but so did I, considerately continuing the Motier lineage. My happy parents celebrated by bestowing upon their heir an appropriately convoluted noble appellation—Marie-Joseph Paul Yves Roch Gilbert du Motier.

Three years before I was born France was at war in America, the conflict with the British confined mostly to Canada and the Ohio River Valley. A year prior to my birth, the war had escalated to Europe when Prussia allied with Britain and Austria allied with France, setting off the Seven Years War.

Shortly after my birth, my father, a colonel in the French Grenadiers, was ordered by the king to serve him and God in western Prussia. Neither God nor king prevented him from being struck by a British cannonball near Minden. I unfortunately inherited the noble title of *marquis de la Fayette* at the age of two, and his untimely death deprived me of ever knowing my father, the camaraderie of siblings, and indirectly deprived me of my mother.

When mother learned he would not be returning to Chavaniac, she left me in the old chateau in the care of my father's mother Catherine and her two daughters. At twenty-two she was not prepared for the responsibilities and demands of a baby. Lonely and likely bored, she was eager to return to her family and the excitement of Paris and Versailles. Having done all she could to meet the obligations of marriage, she left.

For the next decade my grandmother Catherine and her daughters Madeleine and Charlotte fed, clothed, educated, and oriented the only male in their lives to the limited world they knew, providing me with a loving home and great affection. Charlotte's daughter Louise, one year older than me, was my playmate and, essentially, a sibling.

When I turned five, my grandmother arranged for me to attend the rural church-run one-room schoolhouse in Le Puy-en-Velay, the main (yet small) village of the province, notable primarily for the volcanic pipes standing grandly in the center of town. Because it was some twenty miles from Chavaniac, I did not go very often. Eventually Grandmother hired a Jesuit priest to instruct me at home in the practical subjects of mathematics and proper French. To learn Latin, he made me read the memoirs of the great Julius Caesar which described his conquests of Gallic tribes nearly two millennia earlier. The first words of Latin I learned were, "Gallia est omnis divisa in partes tres." (All Gaul is divided into three parts.)

Volume Seven described the heroics of Vercingetorix, chieftain of the Arverni, my Gallic ancestors. In 52 B.C. he organized the various local tribes to defeat the mighty Julius Caesar near Gergovia and in several other battles. These tales were about my region and a local hero I could identify with. Besides being educational, the military tactics fired the imagination of a young boy with little else to do, for most local boys, sons of shepherds or cowmen, were busy helping their fathers and had little time for play nor use for education. My cousin Louise and I played soldiers—dueling with wooden swords, racing pine branch horses, and battling the Roman legions or evil British redcoats.

Shortly after I turned eleven, my grandmother called me into her room. She had received a letter. Her face was grim. My mother was moving me to Paris, and a carriage was already on its way to fetch me.

Grandmother was instructed to pack all my belongings, for the move would be permanent.

Since leaving me in Grandmother's care, Mother had merely visited Chavaniac briefly each summer to supervise her estate. Though always friendly, her brevity gave little opportunity to bond, so I was angry about her sudden interest in me.

The idyll of childhood was abruptly terminated. I was brokenhearted.

CHAPTER 2

First View of Paris

1768

THE DEPARTURE WAS PAINFUL. My grandmother and aunts were distraught—their darling little soldier whom they had nourished and nurtured was being sent toward war, as his father disastrously had been. Cousin Louise was saddened to realize that I would be absent from the rest of her life. For my part, I felt helpless, ripped away from family, home, and friends.

For a full week I was bounced and jostled, cooped up alone in a carriage. Even the beauty of harvest fields and autumn woods did not improve my disposition. I knew little about the people I would be living with, and most of what I knew about the city I was being sent to was from Caesar's *Commentaries*—and no doubt the city had changed from the tiny Parisii trading settlement on an island in the middle of a river which Caesar had easily conquered. Romans subsequently expanded it with temples, palaces, and baths into the town of Paris. As

I was approaching many hundreds of years later, the outlying colony was larger than Caesar's Rome.

When the coachman announced our approach, all I could see was a thick stone wall that appeared to encircle a sizable expanse and the dirt road aimed toward one of several portals. Entering the dark tunnel magnified the clanking of the carriage wheels over cobblestones. The racket and pitch finally roused my excitement.

We emerged onto a street crowded with wooden shacks that seemed to grow out of each other. The stench made me gag. Beggars besieged the carriage, but the driver slowed neither for them, nor dogs and chickens, nor the blur of people milling or running or pushing carts. The filth and poverty were shocking.

The houses grew increasingly substantial, mostly two stories of masonry, as the carriage approached the Seine. As we continued eastward, the roads grew wider, the houses grander, the air less noxious. The river seemed to slice the city in half, itself forced in half by an island dominated by a massive cathedral. We rode the southern embankment past a covered bridge crammed with carriages, shops, and people. Along the edge of the river well-dressed people strolled with children and dogs.

The carriage entered a landscaped park with flower-filled gardens and stately trees, and stopped in front of an imposing three story granite structure with grand wings on either end. A servant standing by the entrance announced the arrival of our carriage, and my mother and an elderly gentleman came out to greet me.

Mother, beautiful in a simple, long dress, called, "Come, my dear Gilbert, give me a hug." I admit to feeling conflicted—glad to be invited into her life finally, while resentful of losing my only home. I clasped her upper arms gently and extended a formal kiss on each cheek. She introduced me to my grandfather Joseph, the marquis de la Rivière who had met me only once years ago when he came to the Auvergne with Mother for a few weeks. I barely remembered him. He expressed his pleasure at my safe arrival, commenting that I had grown taller than he since we last met. He appeared strong and animated—a dashing man with shoulder-length black hair, piercing chestnut eyes, and a small moustache.

I followed them up the white marble staircase to mother's apartment on the second floor of the west wing of the Luxembourg Palace. It was so cultured and sophisticated compared to the austere castle of Chavaniac.

Frescoes spanned the ceiling and prominent Frenchmen of all ages hung on walls illuminated by hundreds of candles in crystal chandeliers. Mother led me through a pair of tall carved oak doors opened by elegant servants and through lushly furnished rooms until we reached the spacious great room, where an ancient man was resting before a stone fireplace. Mother introduced me to my great-grandfather, Charles Yves Thibault, the marquis du Paulmy, comte de la Rivière. Though withered and weak with age, he stood and welcomed me to Paris and especially into our family residence. We gathered in front of the hearth while servants brought in my traveling chests. Both gentlemen seemed genial and interested—especially in my continuing the family tradition in the military, joking that my unusual height and bright red hair would make me an easy target.

A servant announced that dinner was ready and we adjourned to the dining room for a meal unlike any in the Auvergne—chateaubriand smothered in foie gras, truffles in wine sauce, greens and vegetables au gratin, sweet baguettes, and red wine that warmed my innards. How many meals have I eaten since, yet this burst of luxury is still remembered. When I thought I could eat no more, a hot soufflé Grand Marnier was served. I was no longer at Chavaniac, where baked meat was served on earthenware by servants in peasant garb. After dinner we withdrew to the living room where a servant offered me a crystal glass of cognac on a small silver tray.

The next morning I was awakened by loud knocking. Several immaculately dressed servants carried in armloads of clothing and a note from my mother that they were to assist in dressing me for appearing at court. They measured and altered until the clothes fit properly—a long white linen shirt, silk cravat, lavishly embroidered white linen waistcoat, long blue coat trimmed with lace at collar and sleeves, narrow breeches fastened at the knees and edged with rows of lace, white silk knee stockings, and black shoes with silver buckles and high red heels. They applied thick white powder to my bright hair, makeup to my blemishes, and handed me a tricorne hat trimmed with braid—with instructions not to be worn, merely held. The fuss and my new finery both were uncomfortable. My life in the Auvergne was well concealed.

When the servants were satisfied, I waited impatiently in the dining room for Mother. Her own revamping must have begun during the night, well before I was awakened. Her dress jutted widely from both hips. Her hair was sculpted into a tall comical mound decorated with jewels and ribbons of silk. Her face was coated with heavy white powder which contrasted with the red applied to her cheeks and lips and to the round black beauty mark. I was curious how she would be able to perform the normal functions of everyday life, and curious why she would spend so much time and money to attire us in such discomfort. The servants hurriedly brought in our breakfast—coffee with hot milk and a warm, crisp baguette with butter and preserves. I already missed the leisurely breakfast of Chavaniac with fruit and cheese. Mother could not sit because of her cumbersome skirt, and needed help through the succession of doorways out to our carriage whose low bench was constructed to accommodate her fashions. The width of her dress took up her entire seat and intruded on the space across where I was sitting.

Safely settled, she signaled the coachman. The team of white geldings pulled the carriage out to Versailles. The heavily rutted road passed through twelve miles of dense forest, which thinned to a formal park with gardens, tree-bordered paths, lakes and falls cascading down marble Neptunes, and vases and statuary. Commanding the gardens, the palace was divided into three sections—the central three-story building framed by two wings dwarfed the Luxembourg Palace. Mother explained that this enormous edifice was the family residence of just one man, albeit inhabited by thousands of guards, servants, mistresses, as well as noblemen, their families, and staff. It was impossible for me to grasp. Imposing guards bore elongated rapiers and man-height staves topped with axe blades. The French and Swiss Guards wore distinctive uniforms—and either was preferable to the senseless vain one I was being forced into wearing to serve my mother.

Once on the ground, Mother strode swiftly past the guards and entered the palace as if she owned it. She hurried through a labyrinth of ornate rooms—one with a billiard table, another with round felt tables for cards or chess, and one for musical entertainment. I was stunned by the spectacle—paintings, sculptures, huge mirrors, marble walls, and ceilings with angels and naked women. Mother appeared to give no notice to either the magnificence or the smell, proceeding resolutely into the main hall lit by carriage-size crystal chandeliers reflected in the tall mirrors covering both long walls. She continued into the king's apartment, directly to the Salon of Apollo where a platform covered by a Persian carpet held aloft the eight foot high silver throne upholstered in red velvet, in which the resplendent king was seated. He looked bored. Without waiting for his command, Mother approached the monarch of my country, curtsied, smiled, and began chatting as if he were an old friend or neighbor, informing him that she wished to introduce him to her son who had finally arrived in Paris.

I had never been in the presence of royalty, nor was I even comfortable being introduced to adults. I was afraid that I might do something inappropriate and embarrass Mother. The king smiled and greeted me warmly, then turned to my mother to praise her striking young son. In my discomfort, I simply grinned and looked nervously about the room filled with fancifully dressed courtiers. Mother took me around, making introductions. We had happened to arrive at Versailles on one of three evenings a week when the king allowed his supporters admission to his apartments, free to mill about, play cards, chess, billiards, and music, and partake of refreshments in the Salon of Abundance.

Those first weeks in Paris and Versailles I was exposed to many new things, from the mighty royal court to pitiable street beggars, from Enlightenment thought to self-indulgent decadence. I enjoyed being with my charming, energetic mother—whether at court, over dinner, riding her horses through the Tuileries or along the banks of the Seine, traveling out to Versailles, or strolling about the capital. She was kind, educated, and clever.

After a few stimulating weeks, Mother informed me that she had wonderful news—she had enrolled me in one of the most prestigious schools in France, the Collège du Plessis de Louis-le-Grand, an annex of the Sorbonne. I would be starting soon.

I was concerned that my bright red hair and a strange dialect would be ridiculed by wealthier, more sophisticated, urban peers. Mother escorted me to the school to introduce me to the headmaster. He welcomed me graciously, informed me of my classes, and had one of the senior boys show me to my room. My height stood out, but the boys were welcoming and shared my interest in learning new things. My teachers required me to read the works of popular French writers like Diderot, Montesquieu, Rousseau, Voltaire, and Abbé Raynal, who attacked false or antiquated concepts that enslaved the mind. I admired their insight and willingness to risk imprisonment for their beliefs—soldiers fighting with a pen.

I was a diligent student and continued especially to enjoy Latin. I had to reread Caesar's nine years of trying to subdue the French tribes, and was again intrigued by the Gallic fight for independence, which inspired me to hope that someday I too would lead a life worthy of telling, I won the school prize for Latin composition and began keeping a detailed journal.

CHAPTER 3

Twin Tragedies

1770

ONE DAY I WAS CALLED into office of the headmaster. I was nervous I had been caught in some adolescent transgression, for earlier in the day I had objected to what I perceived as the unfair punishment of a friend. Instead the headmaster informed me that my mother had taken ill. His demeanor gave me no cause for concern and he informed me that the best doctors in Paris were treating her. A few weeks later I was again summoned. The headmaster's face was tense and knew immediately that something was wrong. When he told me that my mother had passed away, I was stunned. I felt extremely guilty that I had not been with her during her illness.

I was permitted to leave school immediately. My grandfather was in shock. He had lost his only child, despite obtaining the best doctors in Paris to treat her. I watched a strong musketeer wither like a rose in a vase. He cried frequently, wandered the rooms all night, hardly ate and rarely spoke. I was disappointed to lose someone whose company I enjoyed now and then, but he grieved his closest companion. I escorted my grandfather and great-grandfather to my first funeral, watched as my mother was lowered into the damp ground. An orphan now, my only relatives in Paris were two old men I hardly knew. I felt deserted, this time without the adoring care of the women at Chavaniac.

I returned to my training, but I could not focus on studies. I wanted to be alone and was easily annoyed. Two weeks later, when the headmaster called me in, I was irritated that he was bothering me. He seemed distracted and agitated. He put his hand on my shoulder. My grandfather had passed away. I was sure he meant my great-grandfather Charles, not the lion among men who would likely die defending the king. But my grandfather had simply disintegrated from his loss. Charles was appointed my legal guardian until I reached the age of majority, twenty-five. If he lived another dozen years, we would become thoroughly acquainted. But he was so fragile that I had difficulty imagining him being selected—for his height, handsomeness, and decorative value—to serve in the Black Musketeers, the prestigious military company on their famous black stallions.

Nevertheless he was lucid and wise, capable of assisting and supervising me as well as controlling my finances. Several weeks after his appointment, he asked me to join him at the Luxembourg Palace to discuss our arrangement. The presence of my mother and grandfather lingered there like a scent, but little noise and no laughter and reduction of staff left our rooms feeling dry and hollow as a fallen tree. My guardian told me that the attorneys representing the estates of both my mother and grandfather reported that each had left most of their vast estates to me—numerous properties, thousands of acres of land, several farms in Brittany, business investments in the West Indies, and a great deal of money. The comte, in an intimate tone, confided that I was now one of the richest bachelors in France—a subject I had not yet considered. I had gone from being a boy in my grandfather's house to owning it. At thirteen it suddenly felt imperative to think earnestly about my future and career. When I returned to the Collège du Plessis I became even more conscientious and introspective.

Just prior to my fourteenth birthday, without consulting me my guardian made a major career decision for me—he had enrolled me in the junior unit of the Black Musketeers he had once commanded. He considered this a coveted career opportunity—the only way to catch the king's eye and perhaps enable me to join a cavalry unit in the Royal Household. However desirable this might be, it would require me to transfer to the Royal Military Riding Academy near Versailles, the most prestigious military school in France, to learn advanced military skills and strategy along with the three sons of the heir apparent to the French throne and sons of the king's ministers, generals, and other aristocrats.

I was ripped away again from all those I knew. Initially I felt ill at ease by the instabilities of adolescence, but I quickly made friends and adapted to my new routine. However all the cadets were required to appear for routine inspection before the king, and I did not take well to being frequently at the palace.

Versailles was always crowded, with thousands of noble families in residence with their retinues, plus many more visiting each day. The king alone had 5000 personal servants and 9000 soldiers insuring his protection. Besides those with apartments in the palace, another 5000 nobles living in the town of Versailles frequented the court. I did not fit well in court. I did not like the courtly flattery, small talk, drinking, gambling and promiscuity, and the seeming preference of style over substance, but most importantly the palace was crowded, smelly and filled with dissembling people.

Bathing was generally frowned upon for medical reasons because physicians had warned that unhealthy miasmas floating in the air, entering the body through the skin when hot water opened the pores, made people more vulnerable to disease.

Mingling with the heavy smell of unbathed bodies and the generous sweet fragrances used to mask their stench was the nauseating stink coming from the hundreds of chamber pots which desperate aristocrats used to relieve bursting bladders and other body functions. The repelling odors permeated the building and clung to clothing and wigs.

I was also repelled by the constant flattery and fawning. The courtiers struck me as shallow, undignified, devious, and tasteless—including the king and his retinue. It was apparent that the king was less interested in the affairs of state than in the numerous beautiful women in his court. His new official mistress and primary sexual consort was Jeanne Béçu, comtesse du Barry—the king's *maîtresse-en-titre*. Rumor and gossip, circulated like the omnipresent stench, confirmed that the king had given her an apartment directly below his own quarters. A vertical shaft and moving chair operated by royal servants brought his majesty directly to her boudoir, unobserved. For her royal services, each day the royal mistress displayed a different necklace, bracelet, or ring set with precious stones. If Madame du Barry was indisposed or the king preferred diversity, he had many unofficial mistresses conveniently nearby, each with her own apartment at Versailles, a comfortable royal purse, and frequent gifts.

It was also rumored that he maintained at great taxpayer expense his personal underage brothel in the Hermitage Building in the Deer Park, a remote corner of Versailles that no one was allowed to enter. I heard rumors that in her day Madame de Pompadour had directed the royal valet to procure ten-year-old girls from poor families for the pleasure of the king, in order to cement her influence over him.

It bothered me that nobles and clergy regularly at court did nothing to stop his depravity or extravagances. I felt strongly that the people of France deserved a leader more concerned with their welfare. Yet as a gawky adolescent, the most compelling reason to avoid being at court was personal—some of the young women teased me about my bright red hair, mimicked my awkward gait, or ridiculed my inelegant dancing.

Not long after my fourteenth birthday, I received a letter from my guardian that he had made another business decision intended to improve my career opportunities. He had hired an attorney to arrange a suitable marriage for me to insure an heir to the Lafayette estate, and increase that estate with a suitable dowry and the assets of my bride. In short order he had located an excellent prospect from a well-known, extremely influential, and very affluent family.

During a school holiday, I went with a friend to Chavaniac to visit my grandmother, aunts, and cousin. There I received a letter from

Charles informing me that the negotiation of the contract of marriage had been concluded to his satisfaction and, as required for all contracts involving nobility, submitted to the king for his approval. Louis had already signed it. I was now bound for life to a girl I had never seen and knew nothing about. The girl's father, the influential and wealthy Fifth Duke of Noailles and Ayens, Jean-Louis-Paul-François, had agreed to give me an appointment to his personal army regiment, the Noailles Dragoons, including command of a light cavalry battalion as a captain when I turned eighteen—and a large dowry that included generous land holdings. I was in an excellent position for a flourishing military career. At the time that seemed much more important than the financial or social considerations—or even the girl herself.

In early April my guardian received an invitation from the duke's wife, Henriette d'Aguesseau, inviting us to their home in Paris to meet their family. The comte and I rode from the Luxembourg apartments on the left bank to the duke's home, the Hôtel de Noailles, on the right bank directly across from the Tuilleries gardens. Needless to say, I could hardly wait to see the young woman who had been chosen to share my home, life, and bed, and bear my heir and other offspring.

Our carriage traversed the length of the rue St. Honoré passing the Tuileries on our right. Looming on my left, the three story building occupied the entire block—a stately affair with elaborately framed windows and statues between them. The horizontal stripes of light and dark stone gave both a feeling of floating and enormous breadth at the same time, rather like an invulnerable warship. The entrance to the Hôtel de Noailles, the Paris residence of the Noailles family, was carpeted in a subdued maroon. Two smartly uniformed servants escorted Charles into the building and led us through a series of rooms, refined and tasteful—far more so than the gaudy extravagance of Versailles. Though palatial, it was welcoming and comfortable.

While we waited in an antechamber for the arrival of the family, I felt shy about being judged by the illustrious duke, despite the contract's finality. The double doors were opened to a dozen handsomely attired people including several young girls. The duke introduced himself, bowed with a genuine smile, and introduced his wife and each of his daughters: Louise, Adrienne, Antoinette, Paule, and Angelique; plus his brother and several cousins. Two girls were of marriageable age, but I had not yet heard the name of my betrothed. Both looked pleasing enough, but I was not smitten by either. The duchess personally introduced my guardian to the younger, Mademoiselle Marie Adrienne Françoise de Noailles, and then introduced me. I bowed and forced my cracking voice to express my pleasure. She curtsied, made eye contact, and decorously faded back into the family. She was short and thin with a round pale doll-like face, big blue eyes, long lashes, tiny full lips, and button nose all framed by curly brown hair. She was far from ugly, but I was not attracted by her appearance. We couldn't have been more mismatched physically—I was a foot taller, had already reached puberty, and was developing the broad shoulders of a military carriage.

The duke and duchess spoke mostly with Charles, giving the children little opportunity to talk among each other for most of the day. Adrienne spoke only in response to adults, but I was impressed with her intelligence, confidence, and poise. As our visit was being terminated, the duchess took my great-grandfather's hand to acknowledge her pleasure with the contract, but expressed concern that we were yet too young for marriage. She suggested that the wedding be postponed for at least two years to give us time to mature, but she invited me to live with their family until the ceremony. This would give her daughter time to mature and get to know me.

The duchess made clear that Adrienne was not yet informed of the arranged marriage, and I was cautioned not to disclose that information. During our return to the Luxembourg Palace Charles did not ask my approval of the arrangement.

I moved my belongings settled into the Noailles' townhouse in Versailles. During the week I was occupied with training to be a soldier and my duties at court. On weekends and holidays I slept in my new home and adapted to the ways of the family. Henriette was in charge of the extensive households, both in Versailles and Paris, a daunting task that included the children, staff, menu, and invitations to guests The duchess—who insisted that I call her Henriette—was amiable, unpretentious, and very kind in trying to make me part of their life. With my own quarters, I rarely saw Adrienne except at meals, on walks, and lessons with Henriette. When I was in the presence of Adrienne, we were always chaperoned by her mother or other adult female.

During Henriette's last pregnancy, she had contracted smallpox and miscarried the son who would have been heir to the Ayen estate. The illness left her sterile, badly disfigured, and distanced from her husband. During her illness, she was not concerned about herself, but feared that her dying would harm her children. After she recovered, and with her husband's increased absences, she discharged her daughters' Jesuit tutor to devote herself to educating her children. She invited me to participate, but I spent all week at school and doubted the value. With no public or private schools for girls, the only other education available to them was in convents which instructed on religious doctrine and the womanly arts.

I was fascinated by Henriette's educational technique, as well as her conduct. Like Socrates, Henriette would challenge us to think critically, a process that initially I found irritating. At the Riding Academy my teachers lectured or assigned books by experts whose revered wisdom was rarely questioned. At the Academy we memorized and were frequently examined to see what we had retained. By contrast, Henriette bombarded us with questions.

Henriette had been educated in a convent school. However her paternal grandfather, Henri François d'Aguesseau, was a lawyer, chief prosecutor, and three times chancellor whom Voltaire called "the most learned magistrate France ever possessed." He instilled in her an analytical mind determined to examine and question everything. She passed on that skepticism, tolerance, and respect for analysis. Her grandfather's death left her a wealthy heiress at fourteen, and her father removed her from the convent school to prepare her for marriage. She was tutored at home by her step-mother in music, painting, embroidery, sewing, history, and literature, and encouraged to read

Enlightenment authors who challenged ideas grounded in tradition and faith—authors who advanced the scientific method, skepticism and intellectual exchange, while opposing superstition, intolerance and abuse of power by both Church and state.

Even though she believed passionately in the good and moral wisdom in parts of the Bible, she wanted her daughters to realize its illogical, irrational, and absurd passages so they would think for themselves. She agreed with Voltaire that "those who can make you believe absurdities can make you commit atrocities," and was painfully aware that her Church had promulgated inquisitions and crusades of mass slaughter, condoned slavery and the massacre of the Protestant Huguenots, and still sanctioned the torture and execution of slaves despite the prohibition against killing.

I learned to cast doubt on the veracity of a statement or the logic of a phrase, and was drawn into her competitions. Her thought-provoking lessons kept Adrienne and me grappling with issues after lessons concluded. Why had God created humans, then drowned them in a flood? Why would God damn us for using the capacity for pleasure that God had endowed us with? Henriette asked us to reconcile the first accounts of creation in the Pentateuch—Genesis 1:1 in which God created animals before Adam and Eve—and a version beginning Genesis 2:4 in which God created Adam, then the animals, then Eve. She pointed out the dissimilar genealogies of the seed of Adam in Matthew and Luke; disparate narratives of the flood where animals enter the ark in couples but also in seven-folds. She asked us to justify why an all-loving God would permit, even encourage, the killing of children and the rape of women in Deuteronomy, why God would permit fathers to sell their daughters as sex slaves or the burning of witches or punish children for the sins of their first father, Adam.

While I was growing up in Chavaniac, it never occurred to me to question what I was told by an adult. We rarely discussed politics or religion, and the Age of Enlightenment had not yet found its way down to the Auvergne. In Henriette's informal classes, we sat in front of a crackling fireplace on a freezing Parisian night as an informal family gathering after dinner, wrestling with these challenges. The discussions caused Adrienne religious doubts, leaving her reluctant to receive communion—which angered her father. But Henriette permitted her daughter to delay her communion until she was ready—which was not until our first wedding anniversary.

Henriette herself was deeply religious, attending mass almost every day. But she knew that the clergy who performed the work of the Church were merely human and often succumbed to frailties contrary to their lofty pontifications. She wanted her daughters to see that the Church was a business that was not always managed ethically.

Henriette not only talked about being a good Christian, she worked at it. She took her children to hospitals and prisons to tend to the sick and help the unfortunate, as well as raised funds for the needy.

Her instruction and conduct opened my eyes to the impact of the Church on France and the fairness of our political system. Thanks to Henriette we came to revere the idea that everyone was entitled to freedom of their conscience and to abhor the intolerance of the Church.

I had been living contently as one of the family for two years when Adrienne's older sister Louise was married. As the oldest unmarried daughter, Adrienne was next in line. Shortly after the ceremony Henriette informed her that her father had entered into a contract of marriage—and that she had been promised to me. I was later informed that Adrienne offered no opposition, for we had grown quite fond of one another. The wedding of a daughter of such an influential duke would be attended by the king, his brothers, many ministers, and his important noble friends. To properly plan and orchestrate this major public event, sufficient time was required. Henriette set the ceremony a year hence.

The wedding was a grand affair in the chapel of the Hôtel de Noailles. The vicar general of Paris pontificated in holy fashion, and finally the party broke loose in every corner of the house. Adrienne and I danced formally, both nervous about the change in our relationship. Late in the evening everyone escorted us to our matrimonial chamber singing bawdy songs, giggling, and showering us with flower petals. Henriette had considerately chosen a large room for our nuptial suite. The celebrants practically pushed us in. The fragrance of flowers was magnified by the heat of the fireplace. Numerous candles flickered nervously, causing light to dance across the walls and ceiling. Henriette had done well to evoke the great mystery we were about to enter.

Adrienne smiled, excused herself, turned shyly away, and slid behind a large silk screen in the corner of the room. I could hear her removing clothing, so I went over to the bed and began removing my own and climbed quickly under the covers to anxiously await my bride. When she appeared, she looked lovely covered only in a thin pale pink shift. I watched her move around the room blowing out candles. By firelight she scampered into our bed and covered herself.

We were both uneasy, hesitant to initiate any movement toward the other, apprehensive we might do something to offend or that might make us look foolish to the other. We were both naïve—shy, nervous, and tentative—but willing, if not ready, to assume the duties society expected of us to consummate our marriage. In our ignorance we were not clear precisely how to initiate the expected activity.

My heart was racing and I felt warm all over, so I moved towards her timidly, not to appear aggressive and frighten her. I was rewarded for my courage. She turned to me and embraced me. Emboldened, I moved to kiss her, and felt the shock of our lips touching softly. Our first kiss was polite and respectful, but it welcomed me to profound pleasure.

Initiation into such intimate experience changed our ways of seeing the world and each other, opening up feelings for the other that neither of us had previously felt. We were now a couple. We had come together in trust, thanks to Henriette's wisdom of bonding us as siblings and intellectual peers. For the first time I felt I was falling in love.

CHAPTER 4

Starting My Career

METZ, 1775

S HORTLY AFTER OUR WEDDING Louis XV died of smallpox. His nineteen-year-old grandson Louis-Auguste was crowned Louis XVI. He had attended the Riding Academy with me and been present at my wedding. He had known my father-in-law for most of his life, so the new king retained him as protector of the royal person. At the duke's request, Louis appointed me to his personal regiment, with the rank of lieutenant. My career was budding, and I was pleased.

As a result of my new appointment, however, the following summer I received orders from the minister of war to report for duty with my father-in-law's company, a cavalry regiment stationed in Metz, 200 miles northeast of Paris, near the Austrian Netherlands border. I was sad to be leaving Adrienne, yet excited about my career.

I reported to the Dragoons in Metz, was assigned accommodations, advised of my duties, and introduced to my fellow officers. That evening at the dinner welcoming those training to become officers and participating in the annual training exercise, we met our celebrated commander, Marshal Charles-François de Broglie, marquis de Ruffec, the governor of Metz. After dinner I introduced myself to the general as Lieutenant Gilbert Motier, marquis de Lafayette. Broglie was pleased to meet me, for he had admired my father whom he had fought with in Prussia, as well as my uncle. He was sorry for my loss, but happy that I was following my father's career and invited me to come to him for assistance any time I felt the need. Broglie struck me as very kind.

The next day my training began. They evaluated my horsemanship first, then were directed in squadron and regimental training with shooting, saber, and field exercises, and a course in how to prepare a troop of recruits.

Long days of repetitious training and routine were broken by a letter from Adrienne—she thought she was pregnant. I responded that I loved her and could not believe the unanticipated news would move me so deeply. I wanted to return to Paris to be with her, but my orders required I remain with my regiment. I expected that in time this training at Metz would be to our mutual benefit. I hoped I would make her and the baby proud.

Twice a day over meals I came to know my fellow officers and our commander. Broglie frequently spoke of his experiences in the Seven Years War against the British, including the loss of several close friends. He felt personally humiliated by the British victory, and embarrassed that France had lost Canada, Louisiana, Senegal, and the colonies in India. He admired the colonists in America who wanted to break away from oppressive British rule. He encouraged us to take part in the colonial quarrel, both to advance our careers and to restore the honor and glory of France by driving "les rosbifs" out of North America. Given Broglie's hostility toward the British, it was a great surprise when all his officers were invited to a dinner honoring the Duke of Gloucester, brother of the British king.

We expected fireworks between the British royal and our commander, but Broglie gave a laudatory introduction, and the duke thanked him, a fellow Freemason, for his kind words and hospitality. He spoke about the Masonic ideals of equality and the rights of man, noting that a Freemason aids his fellow man without self-interest and told us the motto of all Masons—liberty, equality, fraternity. He related events in America and regaled us with stories about the colonists. He told of a recent skirmish in the village of Concord, a score of miles west of the Massachusetts colony's main port. Farmers and shopkeepers had boldly taken up hunting muskets against British troops and formed a makeshift governing body and militia to oppose the policies of George III. Despite a lack of military training, artillery, or the capacity to make weapons, their hubris included a declaration of war against the mighty ruler of the seas.

To command their venture, they had selected a surveyor and tobacco farmer from Virginia whose only military experience was limited to serving with neither pay nor distinction in the colony's militia during the French and Indian War. Though Washington was perhaps the wealthiest man in the colonies, he was risking his life, property, and reputation by openly defying King George's force, knowing he could be tried and hung for treason.

Most Americans remained loyal to Britain, but the duke thought it was not feasible for England to be embroiled in another distant war. The nine years of the Seven Years War had drained the empire's resources, and these American colonies produced very little revenue compared to the colonies in the West Indies, Africa, and India. They were not worth the manpower and capital of another lengthy entanglement. Moreover it would leave those important possessions vulnerable to the aspirations of foreign powers—meaning the French, Spanish, and Dutch, though he was too polite to name them. It struck me that if the British devoted troops and equipment to North America, it might weaken them sufficiently for France to recover Canada, India, and Africa, as well as Minorca. With sufficient personnel, money, and the proper military tools the colonists could keep the British preoccupied while France, supporting the colonists, might be able to drive the British out of North America. The colonials were like my hero Vercingetorix. I admired their pluck and identified with their desire for freedom.

With my duty in Metz completed in the late fall, I returned to the Hôtel de Noailles. Adrienne radiated motherhood, and I doted. On December 15 she gave birth to a baby girl whom we named Henriette to honor Adrienne's beloved mother and my mentor. Our infant, tiny and fragile, required constant attention from Adrienne and all the women in the household. Of little help, I set about exploring the discord in America through reading and salons, where the latest controversy concerned the six notorious volumes of *Philosophical and Political History of the Institutions of Trade of the Europeans in the Two Indies*. The author, Abbé Guillaume Raynal, was a Jesuit who had renounced the priesthood. The books criticized colonialism, the feudal and absolutist systems, and the Catholic Church. They railed against slavery, and supported the revolution in North America. Few had read the treatise until the king and Church banned it and ordered all copies burned. When suppressing the book failed, the king tried to arrest Raynal—which only popularized his work—but he fled for Belgium.

Raynal's belief in freedom of religion called for less control by the Catholic Church and urged kings to disassociate themselves from Church hierarchies. In open opposition to the Church, he opposed slavery, and joined the Freemasons despite the 1738 Papal Bull banning all Catholics from Masonic activities. French Freemasonry had separated itself from the idea of a religious ideal, and established its goals as generally humanistic. I liked the sympathies of Raynal and the compassion of the Freemasons, so I asked Broglie to introduce me into his Freemason Lodge and sponsor my membership. I had no reservations about the oath I took to act toward others in accordance with the principles of absolute liberty of conscience and human solidarity.

In June I received a letter from the minister of war removing me from active service, an insurmountable roadblock to my career. The financial drain of the protracted global war with Britain had left France with a budget crisis exacerbated by salaries continuing to be paid to officers of the Seven Years War, though there was no longer need of their service. I was among many middle-rank officers who had received promotions through monetary or political position without serving in war. We were doomed to languish without hope for advancement or honoring our ancestors—we would have to look outside France if we wanted to advance our careers and be of service.

When the Seven Years War had ended badly for the French, Louis XV began seeking means to return their lost colonies in North America. With the king intent on recovering France's lost colonies in America, He instructed Broglie, head of his private diplomatic service, to send someone to America to ascertain the public sentiment of the colonists. Broglie had asked de Kalb to determine if France could induce the colonists to take up arms against the British. De Kalb crossed the ocean and travelled the colonies extensively. His encouraging report resulted in Broglie and the king secretly funneling weapons, money, and supplies to the colonists through a dummy trade company established by Foreign Minister Charles Gravier, comte de Vergennes, and Connecticut businessman Silas Deane. *Roderique Hortalez & Co* secretly transported muskets, cannons, cannon balls, gunpowder, bombs, mortars, tents, and enough clothing for 30,000 men to Connecticut via the ostensibly neutral Dutch island of St. Eustatius.

I was confident that Broglie would be excited about my plan, but he refused to encourage me. He had mourned my uncle's death in Italy, and was still distressed by witnessing my father's death at Minden. He would not be accessory to the destruction of my lineage. I was impressed with the depth of his feelings toward my father and an uncle I had never heard of, and forced me to reflect on the balance of service, courage, and risk. Yet he did not deter me from thinking about sailing to America.

I happened to be at court in August when word was received that fifty-six representatives of the thirteen American colonies had published a collective statement declaring independence from the British Crown. I had no idea how many colonists these delegates actually represented, but I think everyone believed that the British army would have little difficulty squashing a handful of truculent discontents, and that the treasonous signers would soon be suspended by the neck. Even the royalists were amused by the colonists' brash declaration, and hoped they could humiliate King George. Marie Antoinette was so delighted that she ordered champagne for everyone present.

A few months later Broglie introduced me to Silas Deane, a representative of the new government. He had been sent to Versailles to meet with his old colleague to assure him that the colonies were moving toward total separation and to urge Vergennes to send funds for militiamen, weapons, gunpowder, uniforms, shoes, and canteens, as well as enlist a few highly trained staff officers, engineers, and experienced artillerymen. Deane was pointed with concerns about the competency of French officers, because the Seven Years War had demonstrated that many noblemen did not merit their rank, lacked battle experience, and were merely interested in glory and personal gain. Congress also was distrustful after the French and Indian War, adamant that French troops would try to replace one oppressive ruler with another.

A few weeks later translation of the declaration of the American rebels was on display at Versailles. I joined the crowd gathered around the long scroll. Unlike the tedious terminology of government documents, the language inspired me with its simple beauty and universality. I copied the declaration in my journal so I would never forget these words:

> *All men are created equal, that they are endowed by their Creator with certain unalienable Rights, that among these are Life, Liberty and the pursuit of Happiness. That to secure these rights, Governments are instituted among Men, deriving their just powers from the consent of the governed, That whenever any Form of Government becomes destructive of these ends, it is the Right of the People to alter or abolish it.*

The concept that the people had a right to abolish a government was novel as the bible condemned anyone who resists authority, and our kings and their clergymen had declared that the powers of the monarch were derived directly from God, who decided the form and actions of government. The beauty of the document persuaded me that I had a righteous responsibility to support those seeking to alter their government in order to ensure a voice in their laws.

It was a truly innovative concept in the era of absolute rulers for God to authorize all men to claim happiness—by force if necessary—and their right to liberty. My profound appreciation of those radical views was not widely shared by others at court. Despite hatred of the British, most of the aristocracy did not approve of egalitarianism, nor even in liberty for everyone. They had no faculty for contemplating the overthrowing of any monarch, even their enemy George III. When asked for his opinion of the declaration, Louis responded, "I am a royalist by trade, you know."

The beauty of the document persuaded me that I had a righteous responsibility to support those seeking to alter their government in order to ensure a voice in their laws. As Caesar had said nearly 2000 years earlier, "Alea iacta est." The die has been cast—he would cross the Rubicon, and I would cross the Atlantic.

I returned to Paris to tell Adrienne of my decision. My enthusiasm was clear, but she was not pleased with my objective, and she opposed my leaving her and our sick baby. She was pregnant again, and she wanted the father of her children to be with her. She asked me to consider the great personal and financial risk, as well as the impact my death would have on our family. I would be lucky to even make it to America alive, given routine devastation by disease, starvation, storms, shipwrecks, and pirates. If I survived, I might be severely injured or taken prisoner. She reminded me of the impact on me of my father dying in a foreign war. I was proposing to risk my children living fatherless. Even if I returned home from this impetuous undertaking, the financial hardship would be extreme for our family. In my absence she would worry constantly—both about my well-being and the management of the family and our affairs. She wanted to be with me, dreading that she might never see me again.

When the duke learned of my plan, he was furious. He accused me of deserting his daughter and grandchild and of dishonoring France to help fanatical foreign traitors. He had no patience with my "moral duty." He went directly to the king to stop me. The British Ambassador, having gotten wind of the matter, complained to Louis about allowing a wealthy nobleman to be embroiled in overthrowing George III. The British king would likely activate a hostile response.

Louis could not afford an open war with Britain. He immediately issued an order forbidding any soldier in his service from taking part in the rebellion in America, and he ordered me to appear before him. He not only denied my request to go to America, he commanded me to immediately join a regiment in Marseille, with the warning that disobeying his orders would lead to the Bastille. Witnessing this tongue lashing, my father-in-law was satisfied. Yet despite the king's admonition, every day I continued planning for the possibility.

Some weeks later, I happened to see an unconventional foreigner at court, distinctive among the lavishly attired legions by his simple clothing and unkempt hair beneath a flat furry hat that resembled a dead animal. I was informed that this bespectacled elder was another representative of the rebel government helping Deane win support for the American cause. Mr. (the formal title he preferred) Benjamin Franklin, who had brought his sixteen-year-old grandson William to serve as his secretary, was also distinctively cheerful and plain in manners.

Unlike Mr. Deane who was all business, Mr. Franklin avoided finances and politics while in court, rather regaling pretty ladies with risqué anecdotes, witticisms, and tales about his fascinating inventions, or strumming a guitar and indulging his passion for chess. His French was limited, his accent difficult to understand, and I spoke no English at all. However we were able to converse in Latin with help from a bilingual courtier. I was eager to talk to him about America, and learn a few words of English.

Not long after we met, Mr. Franklin invited Adrienne and me to the house he was renting in Passy, a small village just outside the walls of Paris. Although he was merely a lodger, Franklin had set up a printing press and a small lab, and organized a dinner with Abbé Raynal as guest of honor. Ben, I learned, was a Freemason—along with many of the leaders of the rebellion, including Washington, Hancock, and Monroe. Conversation focused on the rebellion in America and slavery. Franklin disclosed that when he was running his printing business in

Philadelphia, he had owned a half-dozen slaves. However, he had freed them and now found slavery immoral and offensive. He was proud to be an active abolitionist and the only signer of the Declaration of Independence to have emancipated his slaves. My decision was made. If this old man could risk his life and leave family, friends, and business behind, I could do no less. Despite upsetting Adrienne and her father, and apprehensive about the consequences of disobeying the king, as a Freemason I had taken an oath to help those seeking liberty. I would seek a commission in the rebel army.

Although Louis had publicly denounced me and made a show of not supporting the rebels, he had been secretly funding them for years—though ensuring freedom was hardly his motivation. Deane was in need of supplies, weapons, and money, and he thought the colonists could use me to their advantage—though it was unlikely that I would obtain a battlefield commission, given my meager credentials. Deane assumed that I would not waste the time and incur the expense of traveling to America unless I were handsomely paid, and he was certain that the Continental Congress had no money for a salary nor even my passage. I assured him that if they would make me a major general, I would pay my way as well as the expenses of some twenty friends and fellow officers—and no salary was required. Still Deane was hesitant. Such a rank was unlikely for someone of my youth and lack of experience. With nothing to lose personally, and much to gain, he began preparing the enlistment contract.

I rushed home to tell Adrienne. Seeing that my mind was made up and trusting me, she reluctantly and secretly gave me her blessing. I immediately set about solidifying my plans, gathering funds, and securing a ship suitable to transport twenty officers, battle equipment, and the supplies to sustain us for the month-long crossing. Everything had to be done in secret.

Knowing Vergennes was willing to leave no stone unturned to weaken Britain's colonial empire, I sought his advice. Though reluctant to openly disobey the king's orders, he told me that Marie Antoinette was also willing to help, as long as it was done secretly—not easy at the court of Versailles—three people can keep a secret only if two of them are dead, Mr. Franklin had said. They would provide an agent and funds to purchase our ship, since I was a minor. I was responsible for finding it—a challenge because most vessels sailing from Europe were destined for the West Indies. With the British navy controlling all American harbors, French or Spanish ships sailing there were subject to boarding in search of contraband—like well-equipped French officers.

Vergennes suggested that to avoid suspicion, I proceed as if I were following Louis's orders, but instead search west along the Atlantic ports, and he offered to send de Kalb to assist in selecting and outfitting a ship. Because the king had spies, soldiers, and police in almost every port, my ship could not sail directly to America. And with the king of Spain as Louis's cousin and ally, I had to be circumspect even sailing out of a Spanish port.

I left Paris with only a few aides and servants, apparently bound for Marseilles, but heading southwesterly towards the ocean. We rode into a port and I strolled casually around the waterfront looking for the right ship. I was rewarded in Bordeaux with a suitable merchant ship called *La Clary* destined for Saint Domingue, as we called Haiti then. The owner was unwilling to change his plans—unless we purchased his cargo and paid his crews' supplies, as well as our own. Between a robber and an angry king, I had little choice. I sent a messenger to inform Vergennes of our good fortune, and he arranged for Broglie to buy *La Clary*.

While I had been in search of a vessel, news of the colonists' defeat on Long Island reached the king. Both he and my father-in-law, fearing that the British would quickly win the war, became even more concerned about antagonizing them. Increasingly suspicious of my activities, they amplified their search for me. Fortunately, friends at Versailles sent me a warning. I decided to misdirect them by going to London under the pretext of visiting my father-in-law's brother, the French Ambassador to Britain. I hoped this would convince them that I had given up plans to fight the British and help me escape suspicion while the ship was being readied.

I sailed directly to London. The ambassador welcomed me cordially, and to show me his importance, presented me to King George—who was an impressive four inches taller than I, with flame red hair. The ambassador escorted me about the great houses of London, took me to a ball at the house of Lord Germain, the Secretary for the Colonies, and to the opera where he introduced me to Major-General Sir Henry Clinton. The gossip and news of my social activities with the British elite were widely reported, convincing everyone in France that I had given up my self-indulgent scheme. Yet I sent a note to inform Adrienne:

> *Farewell my dear heart... I am always sorry to take leave of you. It is my fateful star that keeps me always on the move, so that I must blame myself when I see you only one-sixth as much as I would truly enjoy. But you know my heart, or at least its sincerity, and will believe me, I hope, always, when I assure you that it will love you for life, with the most steadfast and tender feelings. Hug our dear Henriette twenty times for me.*

When I heard that *La Clary* was ready to sail, I immediately returned to Paris. I arranged for my fellow officers to join me at Baron de Kalb's house, where we made our final plans. We left Paris at night, disguised and in small groups, and rode swiftly to Bordeaux. The king had suspected that I was in Bordeaux and sent agents to arrest me and seize the ship. Fortunately, before his orders could be served, we boarded hastily and sailed for the tiny port of Los Pasajes in Spain where I thought we would have less chance of discovery. While we were taking on last minute supplies, I paid the captain to change the name of the ship to *La Victoire*. On the morning of April 20, with the outgoing tide and a good wind, we set sail for the New World. Caesar may have crossed the English Channel to fight the tribal British, but I was crossing an ocean to challenge the mightiest military force of my time.

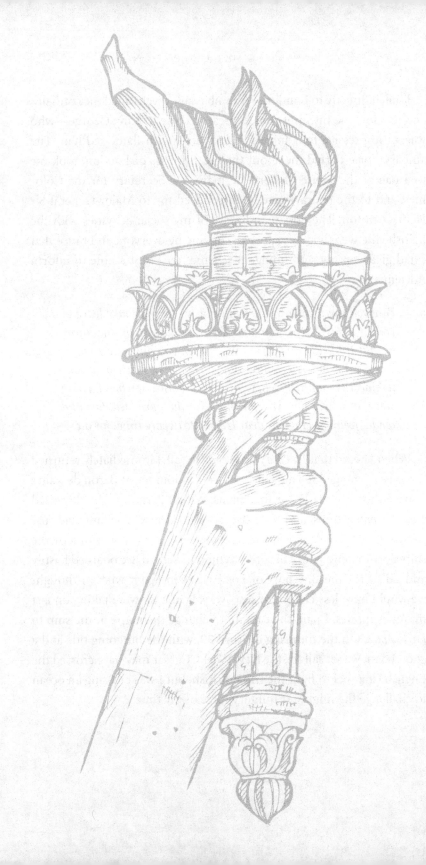

PART II

America

1777–1785

CHAPTER 5

The Colonies

1777

I HAD SAILED FROM DOVER TO CALAIS on a small ship across the narrow passage separating England from France—a crossing of just a few hours, and never out of sight of land. Though the ocean was larger, I thought it would be essentially similar—romantic and invigorating, fresh air, blue water, and the cheerful screeching of gulls. An adventure I eagerly was embarking upon.

Not so! Although our three-masted ship was much larger than the channel boats, it was still relatively small—and susceptible to waves and winds, in danger from faster predatory ships of pirates and privateers, to say nothing of British warships. We would be unable to anchor at ports secured by the British navy, so we aimed for an inconvenient isolated bay in South Carolina. After a week at sea most of the food I had purchased for the voyage had filled with mold and maggots. Only preserved food—sauerkraut, vinegar, and beer—survived very long.

Everyone on board shared their bunks, food, and bodies with rats, mice, cockroaches, bedbugs, fleas, and lice.

Much of the fifty-six days, I was nauseated with seasickness, weak from malnutrition, and confined to my hammock with no pressing task, except to learn English. My instruction came from de Kalb who generously bombarded me with English phrases day and night. Even when I was vomiting and had to run to the chamber pot, he forced me to converse in English.

Well or ill, I missed Adrienne and my tiny Henriette, and felt the weight of my sacrifice being off on this miserable journey. When the sea was calm and the day sunny, such as on June 6, I was able to write to Adrienne:

> It is from afar that I write to you, my Dear Heart, and to this cruel separation I must add the even more horrible doubt of when I can receive news from you. Have you forgiven me? Did you consider that in any case I had to be separated from you—or live without glory among people most opposed to my plans and to my way of thinking. If you knew all I suffered; the forlorn days which I spent sailing away from all that I love most in the world. Will I have to add to these sorrows the knowledge that you do not forgive me! Truly, my Love, I would then be worthy of pity.
>
> I should have already arrived, but the winds have cruelly betrayed me. I will not reach Charles town for another 8 to 10 days. It is in this city that I will disembark.
>
> I was rather sick during the first part of the trip and could have consoled myself with the fact that I was not the only one. I took care of myself in my own way and got better sooner than the others. I now feel about the same as if I were on land. Once ashore, I am convinced that my health will remain perfect for a long time.
>
> Please do not imagine that I will run any risk in my future activities. The position of general officer has always been

considered as an assurance of immortality. It is a service so different from what I would have done in France, as a colonel for example. The post of general officer is one of counseling only. Ask all the French general officers whose number is all the larger because they do not run any risk; as a consequence they are not eager to let others in as they do in other branches.

I will confess that at present we are in some danger for we could be attacked by British vessels and mine is not equipped to defend itself. But once we have arrived I will be perfectly safe. You see, my Dear Heart, that I am telling you everything. Trust me and do not worry without cause.

I will not journal my voyage for you. At sea, the days that follow one another look always the same: sky and water, water and sky, unceasing, unchanging. Fortunately, my good health allows me to keep busy. I share my time between military books and English ones. I made some progress in this language which is to become so necessary to me. Several kinds of birds can now be seen, which tells us that we are approaching land.

But let's now talk about more essential matters. Let's talk about you, about dear Henriette and her brother or sister. Henriette is so lovable that she makes me fond of girls. Whatever the sex of our new child, I will welcome it with much joy. Do not delay one instant to hasten my happiness by informing me of the birth. I do not know if it is because I now am a father twice that I feel more a father than ever.

Do write. You do not know the strength or tenderness of my feelings for you if you think that you can neglect anything that concerns you. As soon as I have settled down, you will often receive news.

My activities and life here will be quite different from those reserved for me in this futile trip. Defender of this freedom which I venerate, freer than anyone and coming as a friend to offer our help to such an interesting republic, I bring here my

integrity and good will only. No ambition, no personal inter-
ests. While working for my glory, I work for their happiness.

I hope that as a favor to me you will become a good American
citizen, a feeling for virtuous hearts. The happiness of America
is closely tied to that of humanity; America will become a
secure and honorable haven for virtue, tolerance and quiet
freedom.

Farewell my Dear Heart; darkness does not allow me to con-
tinue writing because, for the past few days, I have ordered
that no light be lit on my vessel. See how careful I am! Farewell
then. If my fingers were led by my heart, I would need no light
to tell you that I love you and will love you always.

The birds I had seen from the ship accurately announced the approach to land, and the excitement grew. When I heard one of the crew high atop the main mast shouting, "Land ahoy!" I was overcome with joy. I rushed on deck, though I still could not make out any land formations. Shortly I was able to see in the distance through the hazy humid air a thin sliver of gray shoreline. I had no idea where we were—and I did not care. I felt my first small victory—surviving the Atlantic crossing.

The captain sailed into a small bay at the mouth of the Pee Dee River, dropped anchor, and lowered the sails. I could not wait to disembark. According to the captain's charts, we were near the tiny village of Georgetown about thirty miles north of Charleston. We collected our belongings from the hold of our ship, placed them on deck, and climbed over the rails into waiting rowboats. The crew rowed us onto the shore, where we stepped onto American soil. My legs needed time to adjust to the firm unwavering surface. The warm sand soothed my damp feet. The bright sun felt good on my back. June 13 was a beautiful day, and the heat and humidity were healing.

While the rowboats returned to *La Victoire* for our trunks, I surveyed the area. Several small boats bobbed in the bay, each occupied by one or two men fishing. On shore a few men were repairing the hulls of small boats. I saw a white-haired black man dressed only in tattered cutoff pants bent over a small boat, scrubbing. Visible all over his back were large discolored welts. Slavery was outlawed in France—though not in her colonies—so I had never seen a slave. Raynal's words about the brutality of slavery had seemed remote and intangible, but this personal encounter brought home the cruelty of domination of another human being. The old man graphically imprinted the evils of slavery in my memory and on my heart.

We said adieu to *La Victoire*'s crew. We were all exhausted. Fortunately a curious elderly black man cautiously approached the disheveled, oddly dressed human cargo barking a strange language. De Kalb told him we were French, in need of a place to rest and eat. He led us up the river to a large house where he knocked loudly and spoke briefly. The owner spoke excellent French and introduced himself as Benjamin Huger. He was a descendant of French Huguenots, and an officer in the South Carolina regiment of the Continental Army. Recognizing our uniforms, he welcomed us into his home.

De Kalb explained that we were going to Philadelphia hoping to assist the colonists. Huger was pleased and invited us to spend the night. We accepted with gratitude and relief. He introduced us to his wife and three-year-old son Francis and ordered a domestic slave to prepare accommodations for all of us.

We stayed with his family for nearly two weeks, regaining our strength. We were undoubtedly an entertaining novelty—a change in their isolated farm routine. The major and his family twice a day fed us fresh vegetables, fruit, and recently slaughtered, unsalted meat from their farm. Mrs. Huger was an excellent cook. The Huger family gave me opportunities to practice what de Kalb had been teaching me. I wrote to Adrienne:

15 June

I have arrived my Dear Heart, and in very good health, at the house of an American officer and, by sheer good luck, a French vessel is setting sails. Imagine my joy! There is yet no interesting news to report. The countryside is open and there is no fighting, at least not much. Manners in this world are simple, honest and, in all things, worthy of the country where the beautiful word liberty resonates.

Farewell, farewell, my Dear Heart. From Charles town I will go to Philadelphia by land and then join the army.

Isn't it so my Heart that you still love me?

—Lafayette

Huger told me that the fastest, easiest, and cheapest way to Philadelphia was by ship, but as French soldiers carrying weapons we could not risk being detained by British troops. Huger understood our problem, but was able to find only two horses and carriages. Some in our group volunteered to walk to Charleston or look for small local boats to take them there. In Charleston, I purchased sufficient food, water, and supplies to sustain us for our 650 mile trip up to Philadelphia.

My caravan started out with four carriages and several outriders, but the only road going to Philadelphia was little more than a narrow overgrown path, amply supplied with deep ruts and fallen trees. Much of our time was spent clearing roads and figuring out how to cross the numerous steams and rivers. We lost two of our carriages to broken axles during the four weeks it took to reach our destination. I had been told that Philadelphia was the largest city in the colonies, yet it had no defensive walls and there were no guards securing the road leading into it. I was surprised that it was merely a large village of 40,000 people. We could see a bell tower and steeple in the distance and headed toward that beacon, discovering that it sat atop our goal—the Pennsylvania colonial legislature building where the Continental Congress was meeting. We settled into the City Tavern, which had enough rooms to accommodate all of us.

The next morning, refreshed by a good night's sleep, a sponge bath, a shave with lather and hot water, and wearing our best clothes, we walked from Second Street down to Fifth and Chestnut. We told the clerk who we were, why we were there, and showed him the enlistment papers signed by Deane. A French-speaking congressman came out to meet us, James Lovell, chairman of the newly formed Committee on Foreign Applications—who, I found out later, was the leader of the anti-French faction.

Informed that we had come to receive commissions, Lovell responded brusquely that the Continental Army had no need for foreign officers. I told him that their representative Silas Deane had already signed an agreement on their behalf giving me a commission as Major General. Lovell was adamant that Congress would not recognize Deane's commission. A delegate nearby was more diplomatic—Congress appreciated our coming, would consider the matter further, and would inform us when they had reached a decision.

That night at the City Tavern we chanced to strike up a conversation with one of the delegates. I asked why eager volunteers were not embraced enthusiastically. I learned that many of the delegates had either fought in or been impacted by the French and Indian War, and they held resentment toward the French for stirring up the Indians. Many of the French officers, as well as adventurers from Prussia, Spain, Holland, and Austria who had sought employment in the army had made false claims of rank, experience, and abilities—and their limited English was not useful for commanding American fighters. Moreover, even if a foreign officer were better trained and more qualified, many colonists felt it unfair for ranking positions to go to foreigners over available American officers. This information did not leave me optimistic about receiving a commission.

After waiting nervously for a decision, we were finally summoned and escorted to the delegates hall. I was apprehensive, afraid to have to return home and face imprisonment. I was shown the supportive letter from Deane:

> *His noble lineage, his connections, the high dignities exercised by his family at this Court, his ample possessions in this Kingdom, his personal worth, his celebrity, his disinterestedness, and above all his zeal for liberty of our Colonies have alone influenced me in promising to him in the name of the United States, the aforesaid rank of Major General.*

Franklin had also sent a letter urging the delegates to give me an appointment, if only honorary, for it would facilitate him raising the desperately needed financial and military assistance which Congress had sent him to France to obtain. Besides noting a close personal relationship with the king and queen of France (embellishing that I was a favorite dancing partner of Marie Antoinette), Franklin reinforced the urgency by informing Congress of my financial position and that of my wife's father. Yet Commander in Chief Washington had recommended to Congress that they give no commissions to French officers—and his word undoubtedly carried great weight.

The delegates were polite but reserved, hospitable but not friendly, and definitely not eager to embrace us even though we had already risked our lives, spent months at great cost and personal discomfort to advance a cause for liberty not even our own. Our fate was now in their hands. While Congress spent several days arguing over us, we explored the town, which was unlike Paris in dress and the diversity of race, language, heritage, and religion. English, Germans, Scotts, Irish, Huguenots, blacks, and Indians had built churches for Lutherans and Reformed, Mennonites, Amish, German Baptist Brethren or "Dunkers," Schwenkfelders, Moravians, Catholics, and Jews. Freedom of expression prevailed, no doubt influenced by Mr. Franklin. They had a fire company, circulating library, hospital, paper money, and postal system.

They agreed to give me a commission in the Continental Army, but were opposed to granting the rank of major general, since this was the rank below commander in chief and I was merely the age of a lieutenant, had no experience in war, and was not fluent in English. Moreover they would not be able to use the services of any of the other officers who had come all this way from France, except for the two engineers whose services were desperately needed. De Kalb informed them most forcefully that unless both he and I received the commissions from Congress that Deane had promised us, we would return to France to sue Deane, which would not be looked upon with favor by the king. Congress understood that would alienate their only ally and sole means of support. They reluctantly agreed but were adamant that they could not pay us.

With de Kalb acting as my interpreter, I told them that I would pay the salary of de Kalb and all of my friends, as well as myself. They quickly agreed to let them remain with me, as they had nothing to lose. I now had one highly vulnerable foot in the door, but it was clear that I would be a figurehead, a titled flunky with no responsibilities, under the close supervision of a higher-ranking officer. The other officers would have no assignments. We agreed, as it was preferable to returning in disgrace to France.

Congress ordered us to report the next day to the temporary location of the Continental Army at the Moland Farm in Bucks County, Pennsylvania, thirty miles north of Philadelphia.

CHAPTER 6

War and its Politics

AUGUST 1777

T HE UNENGAGED GARRISON AT Metz was as close to war as I had been before. Moland House, the army's temporary headquarters, was a frenzy of activity. Farmers, dressed in rags not much better than the peasants in my fief of Fayette, were energetically carrying and building and digging. There was a sense of order, despite 15,000 soldiers having arrived earlier that day. I had stepped into the vortex of the rebellion, with the king's forces on their way to Philadelphia to crush the declared capital.

An armed sentry escorted us into the stone farmhouse, and an aide directed us to a large room to await the arrival of our supervising officer. Presently, a tall, elderly man in the uniform of a high-ranking officer— a distinguished blue coat, white wool waistcoat, and breeches—quietly entered the room. He was a patrician soldier of my height, broad shouldered and muscular. At his side was his aide, an officer about my age who spoke fluent French and acted as our interpreter. With my eyes on the general, I told the young man my name and purpose, and showed them my commission from Congress. The aide introduced himself, Lieutenant Colonel Alexander Hamilton, and my supervising officer, General George Washington. The general said nothing, but sat stiffly gazing at me, appearing displeased by being saddled with the burden of supervising a wealthy French aristocrat seeking glory and fame, while he was preparing to engage the enemy.

Noticing the Freemason pin on Washington's vest, I told him I was also a Freemason. Later he told me he had been a Mason since his early twenties and had achieved the highest basic rank of Master Mason—which explains why he softened, viewing me as his fraternal brother and trusting my motivation for coming to America to offer my services. Through Hamilton he thanked me for wanting to help the colonist cause and appreciated my efforts to get to Pennsylvania. He asked me to sit, had another aide bring us tea, and inquired about my military service. I mentioned my training, friendship with Broglie, and the inspiration engendered by the Declaration of Independence.

He had Hamilton inform me that he hoped I would understand that he was extremely busy preparing to prevent the British from capturing Philadelphia and arresting the Continental Congress. He had neither the time to train or personally supervise foreign officers, and if they did not speak English, they could be of little use to him, especially if inexperienced. Moreover he wanted my companions to know that it was unlikely we could ever get a field command. For the present he could only use us to do clerical work, though it was clearly beneath the station of a major general.

I told him that I would be happy to serve in any way he deemed useful. With our preliminary introductory talk concluded, I expected to be shown to our billet, but was delighted when General Washington took additional time to walk me to his private quarters and introduce me to his wife Martha, a delightful woman full of life. The general summoned another of his many aides to introduce me to the rest of his staff.

I was taken to meet the General's steward and his wife and daughter, a French cook, a kitchen-woman, the washerwoman, and Washington's valet and body-servant, his slave William Lee. After meeting several dozen aides, my fellow French officers and I were taken to a house where we would be billeted. The graciousness of my reception was the more impressive in the midst of preparing for battle. At dinner I felt that the officers were sizing me up as a competitor and foreigner whose English was poorer than the soils of the Auvergne.

Just after daybreak, Hamilton took me to the staff dining area for a brief breakfast, then to a large tent in which several young men were bent over small writing desks with goose quill pens, writing furiously. Hamilton led me to a desk with stacks of papers, quills, a bottle of ink, a blotter, and a candle. I was to make two copies of each document, place the second in the "Letter Book" and give the original to a senior aide for the General's signature or correction. If corrected, I would have to rewrite it. I began copying, and continued non-stop until the sun set, though the pile of paperwork never seemed to diminish. My fingers cramped, my back hurt, and my eyes were heavy well before mid-afternoon when Hamilton escorted me to Washington's headquarters for dinner. Washington required his personal staff—Alexander Hamilton, John Laurens, and eight other volunteer and paid officers—to join him for dinner every day to gather and disseminate information and to assess it, as well as discuss personalities and issues. After two or three hours, I returned to copying documents until about 7:30.

With these meetings, informal discussions, and the many thousands of words I copied, my English improved quickly. I learned the names of people and places, as well as about the war prior to my arrival, our present circumstances, much about my supervisor, why the army was at Moland House, and our strategic situation. The tone and contents provided information about Washington's relationships, whom he liked and whom he tolerated, and his goals and needs.

Hamilton and I worked closely together. He was witty, charming, and insightful—highly respected by everyone for his intellect and intensity at work. When he learned of the skirmish in Boston, he and many other students from King's College had joined a New York volunteer militia company. Subsequently, he formed an artillery company and was with Washington and Nathanael Greene in the campaigns around New York. Hamilton was now Washington's chief of staff, his most valuable assistant. He handled all of the general's many letters to Congress, colonial governors, and the most powerful generals in the Continental Army. He drafted many of Washington's orders and letters at the latter's direction, and even had the authority to issue orders from Washington over his own signature.

In July 1775, as newly elected commander in chief, Washington assumed command of the Massachusetts militia. He set about surrounding the British in Boston to block their overland access to supplies. The British navy evacuated, but prepared for an attack on York Island (as Manhattan was called then).

Washington ordered his second in command, Charles Lee, to raise troops and take command of the defense of York Island since they had no navy to support them. But General Lee had urged him to abandon New York. Washington, however, led 20,000 troops towards Manhattan to reinforce Lee.

British General Howe, with 10,000 men on Staten Island and awaiting an additional fifteen thousand, initiated peace negotiations with John Adams and Benjamin Franklin. When the attempt failed Howe moved his army south of where Washington had taken up a defensive position at Brooklyn Heights. The British victory was decisive, and Washington retreated to Harlem Heights, and then to a better defensive position at White Plains. The armies clashed again, and Washington was forced to retreat into New Jersey.

Thousands of forlorn militiamen, fearing a prompt British victory, deserted. A third of the remaining force were non-professional militiamen—poor farmers or tradesmen with almost no military training, no uniforms, and armed with their own hunting rifles. Unprepared for the bitter cold, many left at the end of their enlistment commitment. Washington's army dwindled rapidly to fewer than five thousand.

With morale deteriorating, the capture of his second-in-command Charles Lee, and the confidence of the public ebbing, Washington proposed an audacious surprise attack on the Hessian garrison at Trenton, which required crossing the icy Delaware River. Just as morale collapsed, a new aide, a British corset maker working for Major General Nathanael Greene, wrote an inspirational piece on a drumhead. Washington was so moved by Thomas Paine's writing that he ordered all his officers to read it to their troops. The opening line, "These are the times that try men's souls," so inspired them that they followed Washington across the treacherous river on Christmas day. By capturing 900 Hessians, for the first time colonial forces proved they could defeat a European army of regulars.

With bad weather, so many prisoners, and their much-needed equipment, Washington was still at Trenton a week later when General Lord Cornwallis arrived at Princeton with 9000 men. Washington could not find boats to escape back across the Delaware River, but he evacuated and circled around Cornwallis. He drove back three British regiments, then fled before Cornwallis himself could arrive. With troops exhausted, freezing, and undernourished, he retired to his winter encampment at Morristown. The British, having suffered two defeats in ten days, returned to the safety of York Island. The two victories raised morale and men began to enlist. By April Washington had attracted enough men to engage the British when Cornwallis resumed chasing him.

During the winter, British General William Howe planned two campaigns—one on the rebel capital of Philadelphia, and the other to control Newport, Rhode Island as a base for future operations against Boston. On July 23 Howe ordered the two hundred and sixty vessel British fleet to transport him and 17,000 British and Hessian troops to take Philadelphia.

I had arrived in Philadelphia on July 31 with no knowledge of what had been transpiring. While I was meeting with Congress, its president John Hancock demanded that Washington take steps to protect Congress, with the British fleet fifty miles south of the capes at the entrance of Delaware Bay. However, subsequent intelligence informed Washington that the ships carrying General Howe's army had not sailed into Delaware Bay, but had continued south, possibly towards Charleston, South Carolina. Unsure of Howe's intentions, Washington halted his army at Moland farm to camp on August 10 to ascertain more intelligence. I arrived later that day.

After eleven days dispatches informed Washington that British ships had entered Chesapeake Bay to disembark troops for Philadelphia at Head of Elk, Maryland. While Washington was prepared to defend the Continental Congress, I received a letter from Adrienne informing me that on July 1 she had given birth to Anastasie Louise Pauline du Motier. I was much relieved that she and the baby had survived childbirth.

On August 23 we began leaving camp for Head of Elk. I was elated when Washington asked me to join him and his large contingent of officers and aides at the front of 20,000 troops.

The most direct road between Head of Elk and Philadelphia crossed the wide and deep Brandywine Creek. As we were approaching Head of Elk, Washington's intelligence indicated that the most likely crossing was at Chadd's Ford. We beat the British there on September 11 and Washington put the bulk of his forces at Chadd's Ford. Instead of launching a full-scale attack against the defenses at Chadd's Ford, General Howe used only a small contingent to attack there, and sent most of his army in a flanking maneuver on Washington.

When Washington realized his mistake, he sent General John Sullivan to bolster his eastern side. Seeing this as an opportunity, I asked Washington's permission to go with Sullivan. Sullivan and I were immediately immersed in my first taste of the reality of war. I saw horses shot and men skewered by metal blades. I heard screams of agony and witnessed blood spurting from bodies. I was scared, but remained composed as a militia brigade armed only with hunting rifles was trying to hold the center against British troops charging with fixed bayonets. I spurred my horse through the dense smoke and jumped off to show the colonials how to fasten bayonets to their rifles, and exhorted them to hold their position. Musket balls were flying all around me. One went through my hat, another through my coat, one hit my left leg. I was in severe pain and losing blood. I feared I would lose consciousness. I owe my longevity to an aide who put me back on my horse and guided me off the hill.

Seeing an officer wounded caused the brigade to panic. They broke ranks in chaos, catching me up in their panicky flight. After withdrawing twelve miles eastward with the British in hot pursuit, I rose in my saddle and halted their retreat. Shortly after we stopped, Washington rode up and took charge. Seeing my wound, he ordered that I be taken without delay to the medical aid station at nearby Bennett Farm.

An aide tied me to my saddle and led my horse. I managed to hold the reins of consciousness long enough to prevent overzealous surgeons from amputating my leg. They cleaned and bandaged my wound. I was transported by carriage into Philadelphia where a surgeon removed the musket ball, then transported by wagon seventy miles north to the military hospital in Bethlehem, Pennsylvania. Though in and out of consciousness over those ten days, and weak from loss of blood, I imagined myself home with Adrienne and our tiny daughters, refusing to let a British missile take down another Motier.

CHAPTER 7

My First Command

SEPTEMBER 1777

MISSIONARIES OF THE MORAVIAN CHURCH ran the hospital that Washington had commandeered. Though the oldest Protestant Church was established in many parts of Europe, the power of the Catholic Church in France had left me unaware of these gentle people. Their treatment and doctors' orders did not permit me to walk, so I lay in bed with ample time to read and write. I wanted to inform Adrienne of my injury before she received inaccurate reports—though I avoided saying I had almost lost a leg my first month of service with the rebels. I also had ample time to contemplate the cruel consequences of war, for there were many wretched young men missing arms or legs, their lives ruined. Others, mortally wounded, cried out in pain and begged for death's mercy. I felt nothing like a hero, merely lucky to be alive.

Though the Moravians took excellent care, Washington sent his personal physician, Doctor Cochran, to "care for him as though he were my son, for I love him in that way." I was deeply moved that the commander in chief left camp to visit a Frenchman and humble aide. He said he was impressed with reports of my courage and skills at Brandywine, that I had behaved gallantly and bravely under extreme personal circumstances. On his second visit he informed me that he had decided to give me my first battlefield command. I was moved by his show of trust—and more impatient to be released.

I learned from the patients, staff, and visitors that Brandywine had been a military disaster—nearly half of Washington's army had been killed, wounded, or captured. All of the artillery horses were killed, and most of the cannons left behind. Many soldiers deserted and the Continental Congress had hastily abandoned Philadelphia before the British marched triumphantly into the capital unopposed.

Howe had quartered part of his troops at Germantown outside Philadelphia. Washington took advantage of out-manning them and attacked. But between the descent of heavy fog and intoxication of one of his generals, Washington suffered major casualties again. I soon heard rumors that General Thomas Conway, whom I had been trying to assist at Brandywine, had written to Congress and other officers blaming Washington for the loss at Brandywine, disparaging his commanding officer's handling of the battle, and supporting General Horatio Gates, the hero of the battle of Saratoga. Conway, however, was angry because after the defeat at Brandywine, he had written to Congress requesting a promotion from brigadier general to major general. Washington had opposed it to avoid dissension in the ranks.

When I received a communiqué from General Washington asking me to join him as soon as possible at his headquarters outside Philadelphia, I was conflicted. Though my leg was still too sore to wear a boot, and I would have trouble mounting a horse, I was restless and anxious to take charge of my first battlefield command, as well as to alert Washington to the threat to his command. Even though my doctor had not discharged me, and against his advice, I left the hospital and rode as quickly as I could down to Washington's headquarters.

I reported promptly to General Washington, who greeted me with fatherly concern. I assured him I was fine, appreciative of his personal attention, and ready to assume command responsibility. He assigned me to Nathanael Greene who had fought alongside him in every battle of the war. Greene was to protect Fort Mercer in New Jersey, which prevented British ships from bringing supplies up the Delaware River to their huge army around Philadelphia. General Howe had already taken Fort Mifflin on the Pennsylvania side of the river.

His recent intelligence suggested that Cornwallis and 5000 troops were heading toward Fort Mercer. To verify this information, he gave me command of 350 light cavalry. Routine scouting seemed like an easy mission, so I was in high spirits as I proudly led my troops out of camp.

When I thought we were sufficiently close to the British camp, I sent a few scouts ahead to explore. One came galloping back, having seen forward movement of about four hundred Hessians separated from the main body of British troops. Excited with the prospect of actually engaging an enemy, I led my men with drawn sabers, and surprised the forward pickets of Hessians. Galloping at full speed we bore down on those nameless men. The thundering hooves and snorting of steeds mingled with the urging shouts of riders, the whines of gunshots, and nauseating screams of the injured. I plunged my saber into another human. Though horrified, I was also aware these were mercenaries who had voluntarily sold their services to fight battles not their own. They had made a choice. I had no time, in the reality of fighting for my cause and for my own life, to imagine what my victim might have thought in the face of death.

We killed twenty Germans and wounded twenty more. As they retreated we gave chase, but an overwhelming force of British grenadiers provided covering for their escape. With night falling, and with Cornwallis' superior numbers, I withdrew back to camp with eighteen prisoners, and reported to Greene that I had only lost one man.

Greene was buoyant with our success, and together we continued to follow Cornwallis until we learned that the commander of Fort Mercer, rather than lose the garrison to a British assault, had abandoned it. With the British in control of their supply route, there was nothing more we could do. With the weather turning colder, Greene decided to join Washington at Valley Forge. I welcomed the opportunity to rest and for my wounded leg to mend.

We led our soldiers over snowy trails the forty miles to Valley Forge, twenty-five miles northwest of Philadelphia—far enough to prevent a surprise attack, but close enough to allow our troops to defend Congress now settled in York, Pennsylvania. Washington had chosen an easily defensible location between Mount Joy and Mont Misery, with the Schuylkill River to the north.

The ground was frozen and covered with snow. Long marches around New Jersey and Pennsylvania by Washington's soldiers had destroyed their shoes, and bloodstained footprints in the snow pointed our way. A crude encampment had been quickly thrown together. The six foot square canvas tents were thin and cracked—little protection against the weather. These were replaced in the first six weeks by wooden shelters with oak slab roofs covered with earth. But dampness and crowding led to filth and disease. The commander in chief's own hut was barely worthy of the poorest farmer. Greene and I were assigned a large officers' tent until better accommodations could be constructed. On our arrival, Washington informed me that with success against the Hessians, Congress had awarded me a commission as a major general.

Provisions were scarce because of the weather. Nearby farmers had families to feed and would not sell to us because Continental paper money was nearly worthless. Some were caught sneaking grain into Philadelphia because the British army paid in gold. Other farmers were hoarding in order to earn higher profits in the spring. Nathanael Greene had published in the *Pennsylvania Packet* newspaper and on flyers the food we needed: "Fresh Pork, Fat Turkey, Goose, Rough skinned Potatoes, Turnips, Indian Meal, Sour-Croute, Leaf Tobacco, New Milk, Cyder, and Small Beer." As the weather worsened and soldiers were reduced to eating fire cakes—moistened flour baked on a stone among coals—Greene sent men out to round up cattle and other items.

We were only prevented from starving by the courageous action and generosity of sympathetic Oneida Indians who brought several hundred 70-pound bushels of heavy corn 200 miles from northern New York. The soldiers were so hungry that they had to be restrained from eating uncooked dried corn which would have bloated them. These Oneida were the first dark skinned men with fierce-painted faces, scalp-lock hair, and shaved bodies that I saw.

An Oneida woman stayed with us to show the troops how to cook the corn. To show his appreciation for her help, Washington offered the woman money, but she refused. However Martha brought her a shawl, bonnet, and hat that she had purchased in Philadelphia, which pleased the woman.

Each passing night of hunger and cold engendered desertions, illness, and death. Morale was low and my fellow French officers beseeched me to return with them to France, despairing of success against the British army. I would have happily escaped these miserable conditions to see my wife and children, but merely wrote to her on January 6:

> *What a date, My Dear Heart, and what a country from which to write in the month of January! It is in a camp in the middle of woods; it is fifteen hundred leagues from you that I find myself buried in midwinter. Not too long ago, we were separated from the enemy by a small river; now we are seven leagues away from them and it is here that the American army will spend the winter in small barracks hardly more cheerful than a jail. I do not know if the general will decide to visit our new abode; should he, we would show him around. The bearer of this letter will describe to you the pleasant place which I seem to prefer to being with you, with all my friends and amidst all possible pleasures.*

In all sincerity, My Dear Heart, don't you think that strong reasons forced me to this sacrifice? Everyone has been encouraging me to leave; honor told me to stay.

Many foreigners, whose help was turned down and whose ambition was not served, created powerful intrigues and, with all sorts of tricks, they tried to turn me away from this revolution and its leader. If I leave, many Frenchmen, who are useful here, would follow my example.

General Washington would really be unhappy if I told him that I was leaving. His trust in me is deeper than I dare say. In the place he occupies, he is surrounded by flatterers and secret enemies. He finds in me a trustworthy friend in whom he can confide and who will always tell him the truth. Not a day goes by without his talking to me at length or writing long letters to me. And he is willing to consult me on most interesting points.

The abasement of England, service to my homeland, the happiness of Humanity whose interest it is to have a completely free country in the world, all these reasons contributed to my not leaving, precisely when my absence could have been harmful. In addition, after a small success in Jersey, the General, following the unanimous wish of the Congress, asked me to take an army division and to train it as I saw fit, as well as my mediocre means would allow.

What pleasure I will have to kiss my two poor little daughters and to have them ask their mother's forgiveness. Do not believe me insensitive or ridiculous enough to think that the sex of our new child has diminished in the least the joy of her birth. The next one will absolutely need to be a boy.

Several generals are having their wives come to the camp. I am really envious, not of their wives, but of their happiness to be able to see them. Farewell, farewell. Love me always and do not forget the unhappy exile who thinks of you with renewed tenderness.

Shortly after finishing that letter, one of Washington's aides came to fetch me. I wanted to tell him my concerns regarding congressional attempts to replace him as commander. The Board of War had already taken actions in that direction by promoting Conway to major general despite Washington's objections, and had subsequently made Conway inspector general of the army and sent him to review the camp at Valley Forge. Since Conway was the most outspoken individual in the movement to replace him, I urged the general to go to York and defend himself before Congress. Washington thanked me for my concern, informed me that he already had been made aware of the situation, and had taken steps to deal with it. Then he changed the subject to pressing issues in the camp.

The next day he sent a short note:

> I have no doubt that everything happens for the best; that we shall triumph over all our misfortunes, and shall in the end be ultimately happy; when, my dear Marquis, if you will give me your company in Virginia, we will laugh at our past difficulties and the follies of others.

Despite his optimistic tone, I went to York on his behalf in the freezing cold. I addressed Congress pretending to be official spokesman of the French court, brazenly cautioning the delegates that France regarded Washington as one and the same as the American cause, warning them that my friend the king of France could not even conceive of another commander.

I was sure Louis would not care as long as France's enemy was weakened and France given advantage. However fallacious, it had the intended consequences—Congress kept Washington as titular commander in chief. However they gave the power to determine the course of the war to General Horatio Gates by making him President of the War Board—effectively Washington's superior despite his lower rank.

In addition, certain members of Congress had plotted with Gates to win me over to their side. Gates appointed me commander in chief of the Northern Army, a rank equal to Washington's, and ordered me to lead an invasion of Canada. It was a unique opportunity for a French officer to regain his country's lost colony. My command would be subject only to Congress and the Board. Although this sudden bestowal of power was enticing and the prospect of instant fame and glory tantalizing, I was immediately distrustful of Congress' and Gates' motives. Also I did not consider an invasion of Canada in the middle of winter a good idea.

My meeting with Gates did not satisfy my misgivings, so I returned to Valley Forge to tell Washington that I considered the machinations of Congress an insult to him, and was doubtful of its success. Washington agreed, however he urged me to take the position but insist that Gates give me specific written details of his plans, including the size of the force he would be providing me. I copied the president of Congress on my letter to Gates, being clear that I could not agree to lead the campaign unless I could depend on Gates to provide adequate troops, weapons, equipment, and supplies.

At Washington's urging, I returned to York to accept my new commission. However, before my arrival, Congress appointed Conway as my second in command. I vigorously objected and told Congress that I would resign my appointment unless Baron de Kalb replaced Conway. Congress had no choice—as a volunteer I could return home in a huff and jeopardize French support for their cause. I demanded that Congress add the condition that I remain subordinate to Washington, and that all orders to me, whether from Congress or the Board, be issued only through Washington and that I would respond only through Washington.

Those issues resolved, Congress requested that I travel without delay to Albany, which Gates had selected as the staging area for the expedition, assuring me in writing of ample troops, munitions, and adequate equipment and supplies would be waiting when I arrived. I left York with Baron de Kalb and a small band of troops.

Slowed by deep snowdrifts and icy streams, it took two weeks to traverse the 300 miles. We arrived on February 17 to discover that there

were neither sleighs nor snowshoes—essential to a winter campaign—
and a severe shortage of food and weapons, and only half the promised
troops. I dispatched a letter to the president of Congress complaining
about the deception, and this letter to Washington:

the 19th February, 1778.

*I have consulted everybody, and everybody answers me that
it would be madness to undertake this operation. I have been
deceived by the board of war; they have, by the strongest
expressions, promised to me one thousand, and (what is more
to be depended upon) they have assured me in writing, "two
thousand and five hundred combatants, at a low estimate."*

*Now, Sir, I do not believe I can find, "in all," twelve hundred
fit for duty, and most part of those very men are naked, even
for a summer's campaign.*

*I have sent to congress a full account of the matter; I hope
it will open their eyes. What they will resolve upon I do not
know, but I think I must wait here for their answer.*

*Your Excellency may judge that I am very distressed by this
disappointment. My being appointed to the command of the
expedition is known through the continent, it will be soon
known in Europe. I am afraid it will reflect on my reputation,
and I shall be laughed at. My fears upon that subject are so
strong, that I would choose to become again only a volunteer,
unless congress offers the means of mending this ugly business
by some glorious operation.*

*I think your Excellency will approve of my staying here till
further orders, and of my taking the liberty of sending my
dispatches to congress by a very quick occasion, without
going through the hands of my general; but I was desirous to
acquaint them early of my disagreeable and ridiculous situation.*

With the greatest affection and respect, I have the honor to be.

I sent aides to York and Valley Forge to deliver the letters. Given weather conditions, I knew a response would not be forthcoming for weeks. I decided to enlist the nearby Oneida Indians to send warriors down to Valley Forge in the spring to help Washington when fighting resumed. They had already sent food, but because they fondly remembered working with the French, they promised to send Oneida warriors down to Valley Forge.

Six weeks with neither more supplies nor response from Congress, I felt it pointless to remain. I angrily trudged back to York. On receiving my correspondence, Congress too had become suspicious of the whole affair and agreed that it would have been foolish to proceed with the invasion. They formally canceled the invasion and passed a resolution praising my prudence in abandoning such a futile mission. They removed Gates from the Board of War, assigned him to a desk job in the Eastern Department, and quickly reappointed Washington as commander in chief. Washington immediately replied that he would only accept his appointment on condition that Congress also appoint Nathanael Greene as quartermaster general.

Neither of us understood why Washington would consider making his most trusted general a business functionary, merely responsible for contacting civilians to procure provisions. Greene joked that "Nobody ever heard of a Quarter Master in history." Yet he trusted Washington implicitly, and accepted his appointment on condition that he retain the right to also command troops in the field.

When I arrived at Valley Forge on April 8, the camp had been transformed. An unemployed Prussian drill instructor had arrived in full military attire with his tall Irish wolfhound Azor, bearing a letter introducing him as Baron Friedrich Wilhelm von Steuben, "Lieutenant General in the King of Prussia's service." The aide informed Washington that the baron spoke only German and was volunteering his services. Von Steuben informed Washington he had been deputy quartermaster at headquarters for the Prussian Army and had served as aide-de-camp to Frederick the Great.

Appalled by the camp's lack of basic hygiene, he demanded complete reorganization. No one had bothered to build latrines, so troops relieved themselves wherever the urge struck them, even near the kitchen. Von Steuben asked permission to have military engineers build latrines on the opposite side of camp from the kitchen area, and urged Washington to order the men to use them.

Engineers laid out 2000 huts in parallel lines along military avenues. Von Steuben insisted on strengthening our defenses by building miles of trenches, five earthen forts (redoubts), and a state-of-the-art bridge over the Schuylkill River. The army had also built log cabins, located supplies, constructed makeshift clothing and gear, and was cooking at least subsistence meals. The camp was nearly overflowing with uniforms, shoes, cattle, vegetables— and rum. Morale had drastically improved. I saw the shrewdness of appointing Greene quartermaster.

While construction was going on, von Steuben had begun preparing a military training manual in French, which was translated into English by his secretary and aide-de-camp. Alexander Hamilton edited the text and Captain Pierre (who preferred to be addressed as *Peter*) l'Enfant provided illustrations.

With the help of his French-speaking aide, von Steuben first trained a model company of forty-seven men, followed by a general training to shape the soldiers into a unified, effective fighting machine. He personally demonstrated every move, and with his untraditional willingness to work directly with the men, he taught the troops an efficient method of firing and reloading weapons, installing and using bayonets, and Prussian drill techniques far more advanced than the Brits'.

He pared down the officers' staffs of personal servants and insisted that officers drill with their men. In addition to improving their chances of survival, his training broke the winter boredom. One could feel a sliver of confidence and optimism growing in camp. By the end of April, Washington recommended to Congress that von Steuben replace Greene as quartermaster general and promote Greene to major general.

I had been in constant communication with Washington while I was away from camp and kept him aware of my efforts in his behalf. He appreciated my reports, was impressed by the courage and maturity of my decision to abandon the Canadian campaign, and honored my efforts to defeat the conspiracy to replace him, despite pressure from my fellow French officers to return home with them.

Though de Kalb commented on the French officers' incessant intrigues and endeavors to malign each other, he remained aloof from them but close to me. Rather than trying to find a better way to integrate non-English speaking officers into American divisions, I established several "corps d'étrangers" which enabled us to use many outstanding foreign cavalrymen, giving the Continental army several battalions of European professionals to counter the British Hessians.

With spring sunshine and snow melting rapidly, everyone was anticipating the imminent engagement with the British. One day in early May, Silas Deane's brother rode into camp bearing letters from Paris. We learned that in early February France had signed the Treaty of Amity and Commerce, formally recognizing American independence. Four days after the French ambassador informed the British government of the Treaty, Great Britain had declared war on France, and the following month Spain had declared war on Britain. Washington had suddenly acquired two powerful allies with warships and experienced professional troops. He and his officers were ecstatic. I was particularly pleased that Louis had finally committed to the war, and grateful that France was our ally. My identity with the revolutionaries was no longer split.

Deane had also brought a letter from Adrienne—my baby daughter Henriette had died. I felt extremely remorseful, but helpless to bring solace to Adrienne, the baby, or myself. But Adrienne also reported that my conduct at Brandywine had reached France, and that Ben Franklin and John Adams had taken time from their diplomatic duties to call on her to express America's gratitude. Even my father-in-law sent a letter forgiving me for going to America and assuring me that the king was now praising me, despite disobeying his order. I was grateful that the duke had taken the time to write—it would make my eventual return to France less risky.

I wrote Adrienne to tell her I loved her and wished I were there to commiserate. I did not say that I was anticipating the breaking of camp to begin a major campaign.

That night at dinner I told Washington about my daughter's death and how much I appreciated the busy American representatives in Paris going out to Versailles to publicly thank my wife. He asked if I wished to return to Paris to console her—but by the time I arrived my presence would be anti-climactic, only exacerbating a healing wound.

The next day Washington came to my tent and asked me to accompany him to the stable. We often rode together for pleasure, for we both loved horses. While we walked, he reiterated his sympathy for the loss of my daughter and his appreciation for my tactical skill, my loyalty, and for bringing France in as our ally. He stopped briefly in front of each horse to pet their muzzles—Blueskin, his bluish-gray, part-Arabian parade horse; Nelson, his calmer, venerable old sorrel which he rode in battle; and Magnolia, his Arabian racehorse. Then he stopped in front of the stall of his highly-prized chestnut courser, sixteen hands high, muscular, deep-chested, with strong haunches and bold carriage. The stallion's face had a wide white blaze down the middle. Its long black mane and tail shimmered from grooming. He wanted me to have his horse. I was deeply honored and appreciative, knowing that for him there was no more useful or personal present. He put his hand on my shoulder. I felt we would remain friends forever.

Washington and I had grown very close—like I imagined I would feel toward my father—yet I also felt camaraderie with many who shared the harsh winter at Valley Forge and the sacrifice that each was making for the cause of liberty. 2500 soldiers had died of disease, malnutrition, or exposure. I personally knew many of them. It would have been worse but for von Steuben's sanitation regulations—which limited the deaths from influenza, typhus, typhoid, pneumonia, and dysentery. In Barbados Washington had contracted smallpox which left him pockmarked and sterile. His orders to inoculate troops undoubtedly saved countless more lives. We also lost thousands through desertions.

To boost morale even further, Washington arranged with Martha's help a farewell extravaganza, beginning with a Grand Parade of the troops around the camp while cannons and muskets were fired in salute. He asked von Steuben, Greene, and myself to lead the parade— my first opportunity to ride the stallion Washington had given to me. After the feast the women entertained us all with a play. When Washington announced breaking of camp in the morning, the troops responded raucously, their approval echoing across the fields. Morale was soaring.

Nine days later the Oneida warriors rode into camp looking fierce in war paint, feathers, bows and arrows, riding pinto horses bareback. Morale was boosted further when two of Washington's most experienced generals, Benedict Arnold and Charles Lee, who had been out of service, entered the camp. Arnold had reinjured his left leg at Saratoga and been recuperating. He was applauded by the men who had served under him. General Lee, the army's second-in-command captured by the British in New Jersey, had been released in a prisoner exchange. We were now at full strength.

CHAPTER 8

Barren Hills

1778

S TUCK IN PHILADELPHIA AND UPSET by London's lack of support for his campaigns against the rebels, General Howe sent a letter of resignation. His close friend Major John André organized a grand farewell party for May 18 with fireworks and dancing until dawn. Washington's spies discovered that Howe intended to capture me to teach the French a lesson for meddling in British affairs. He and his brother Richard, the admiral, even had a special frigate outfitted to take me back to England in chains. He was so confident that he sent invitations to the ladies in the city to dine with me the night following my capture.

The morning of the party, Washington sent me out with a small force to determine British movements. He gave me 2200 troops and specific instructions against taking a stationary position that could enable Howe to encircle and overwhelm me—and make good his bragging. At dawn we crossed the icy Schuylkill River heading towards

Philadelphia. When I came to Barren Hill, about half way between the two camps, the plateau seemed an ideal location to watch the one road that led directly to the city. Despite Washington's warning, we set up a post on the summit, certain in the defensive nature of my position and convinced that I had several avenues of escape. With the guards I posted about the perimeter and miles of visibility, I was confident there would be no problem.

The wily Howe, intent on capturing me, had set a shrewd trap and stealthily encircled me from three positions. The guards failed to discover the British troop concealed by the density of the forest. We were surrounded by 16,000 of the world's best equipped, best fed, best trained, well-rested troops, commanded by one of Britain's best generals. Outmanned eight to one, the only possible avenue of escape lay at the bottom of a steep ravine and across the broad river, swollen with snowmelt.

I ordered a few small patrols, including the fifty Oneida warriors, into the woods to feint a counterattack, making the British think that we intended to stay and fight. While my men scurried around creating the impression of a much larger group, the rest of us slipped quietly down the ravine, hearing our rear guard's shots seeming to come from everywhere. The British had wasted valuable time chasing imaginary enemies.

Though we reached the river, some of the men announced they could not swim. I encouraged them not to panic and ordered my troops to link arms and help each other across. With discipline and self-control we managed to cross the river without losing a man, our first field test of what von Steuben had worked to instill. Safely across, we gathered wood and set fires to dry ourselves and our clothes, and to warm up.

At daybreak we marched back to camp where I immediately reported to Washington. He was not pleased, reminding me I would have been paraded around London like a zoo animal, to say nothing of jeopardizing a third of his force. I waited silently for further rebuking. "But you escaped!" he said, and poured us a drink to toast my accomplishment.

Shortly, the Oneida warriors returned—they had harassed the British back towards Philadelphia. The celebration was ours, not Howe's!

Howe was replaced as British commander in chief by his second in command, Lieutenant General Sir Henry Clinton, who had soundly defeated Washington at the Battle of Long Island. With France entangled in the rebellion, High Command in London was concerned that Philadelphia was vulnerable to attack or blockade, so Clinton was ordered back to Manhattan as his main base of operations, since it was defensible by the superior British navy.

Lacking enough ships to transport 15,000 troops and 3000 loyalists plus horses, supplies, and belongings, Clinton prepared to march people and supplies a hundred miles to the northern most point of New Jersey, Sandy Hook, from where the British Navy could easily ferry them to Manhattan.

Summer was well underway with temperatures over a hundred by the time Clinton completed his evacuation. Our scouts reported that 1500 British carriages were spread out over twelve miles of rutted roads, protected only by scattered pockets of troops. This gave us an extraordinary opportunity to attack. Concerned about heat stroke and the health of our men and horses, we were acutely aware of the importance of obtaining drinkable water—as would be the British. Washington ordered bridges burned and trees felled across the roads, and sent patrols ahead to muddy wells and creeks. This slowed the British and gave us time to find the optimal location for a full-scale attack.

At Monmouth Courthouse, thirty-five miles south of Sandy Hook, with logistics favorable, this was Washington's opportunity. However, Washington's most experienced general, Lee, argued that American soldiers lacked the discipline and experience to engage the British in conventional warfare, so "embarking on an all-out attack was highly absurd, and the advantages to be gained by victory were not to be put in competition with the evils that might result from defeat." Twelve of his generals agreed, arguing that it was pointless to risk engaging numerically superior forces when we could expect ample French help in the near future. Only Greene, Hamilton, Wayne, and I were in favor of an immediate attack, and Washington agreed.

Normal protocol required that he appoint his most senior and experienced officer to command the advance. But Lee refused to take the command, being uncooperative and condescending to his superior officer. Instead of directly confronting Lee, Washington appointed me to lead the attack, with Alexander Hamilton as my second in command. We accepted the honor eagerly, believing that there was more than enough intelligence to achieve a significant victory.

Before we could leave camp, Lee stormed into Washington's tent, insulted that "this French boy" was given his command and demanding that it be returned to him. Washington refused. Hamilton and I entered the tent, concerned that the tension between the two generals would escalate. I offered to return the command to Lee. Washington grudgingly gave in, but ordered Hamilton and me to go with Lee and do whatever was necessary to secure victory.

Washington ordered Lee to attack Cornwallis' troops that were protecting the flank of the rear in order to delay the carriage train long enough for Washington's army of 10,000 to arrive. We rode off at the head of 5500 men, but Lee, fearful of being ambushed, was overly cautious. He ordered no reconnaissance, failed to keep in contact with Washington, and had no plan of attack. When we belatedly made contact with the British, Lee did not press his attack aggressively—nevertheless sending word to Washington that nothing was wrong. Hamilton and I, believing Lee was intentionally deceiving his superior, each sent corrective dispatches to Washington.

Washington rode out to corroborate our information. Seeing that Lee's troops had not attacked the British as ordered, he screamed obscenities at Lee in front of his troops, and ordered him to strike immediately. Lee, mortified to have been reprimanded in front of his troops, assured Washington that he would launch an offensive without further delay.

Washington returned back to the main body of troops and Lee met with the generals of the advanced guard—Wayne, William Maxwell,

Charles Scott, and me—but he was unable to flesh out a plan or give any coherent order. His delay allowed the British ample time to prepare for battle. When Lee did move, he gave orders and counter-orders, resulting in a disorganized attack. Wayne was attacking vigorously with a prospect of victory when Lee ordered him to pull back. A dutiful soldier, Wayne obeyed. We sent a request to Washington to appear on the field immediately. Meanwhile Lee ordered a retreat—which rapidly became a rout when Cornwallis ordered a counterattack. Washington's advance stopped the retreat. Washington rode his horse close to Lee, relieved him instantly of his command, and personally took over Lee's troops and led a ferocious frontal attack.

I had never seen Washington risk his life. Surrounded by redcoats with bayonets, he swung his sword amidst flying musket balls. He was possessed, and so utterly fearless that three of his aides-de-camp were badly wounded trying to force him to safety. His reckless actions seemed to be securing victory, but darkness was descending and hundreds of men had already died from heatstroke. We had no choice but to look for a place to lie down and ready ourselves for another attack after dawn.

Washington found a level, dry place under a broad tree, spread his mantle and motioned for me to join him. It was gratifying to be singled out to share a moment alone with the General. It confirmed to me that I provided him the solace that intimacy can offer. We rested for a while without saying a word, then shared our skimpy rations of salted meat, fetid water, and stale bread. We lay down side by side, watching the stars as we recounted bits of the combat and Lee's extraordinary conduct.

When the rising sun awakened me, the general was already up and eager to renew the attack. Staff was called together and scouts sent out to reconnoiter. They returned much too quickly to tell us that the British had slipped silently away in the middle of the night, putting a six hour gap between us and their rear guard. With our troops exhausted, parched, and many wounded, there was no point in pursuing. Washington conceded, angry that Lee had cost us a golden opportunity.

Yet that afternoon Washington received a dispatch from one of his scouts that the first French warships had sailed into Delaware Bay. He immediately saw an opportunity to salvage victory. Washington sent aides to request that Admiral Charles Hector, comte d'Estaing, sail immediately for New York harbor to stop the British ferry fleet. But by the time he arrived, Clinton's hordes had already reached the safety of Manhattan. D'Estaing considered engaging the smaller British fleet, but his warships were too large and could not clear the Sandy Hook sand bar, so d'Estaing anchored to block the entrance to the harbor, and requested further instructions from Washington.

Washington, irate that success had slipped through his fingers, immediately instigated Lee's court-martial. Lee was found guilty and Congress relieved him of all command for one year, eventually dismissing him from the service.

That was little consolation—we had lost the moment. The British achieved a defensible base of operations for both army and navy, along with control of the Hudson River Valley. This effectively cut off all of New England from further participation in the war. At least the British had vacated Philadelphia. Washington moved his weary troops in to occupy the city, appointing his trusted friend Benedict Arnold as military commander, and turned his attention to the two other locations where the British might be attacked.

CHAPTER 9

The Battle of Newport

1778

THE BRITISH HAD STATIONED large numbers of troops on two islands well protected by the British navy—Manhattan and Newport, Rhode Island. Now that he had a small fleet at his disposal, Washington planned to attack both British sanctuaries. He would lead the attack on British headquarters, and sent Major General John Sullivan with 3000 troops to Fort Barton on the Rhode Island mainland to prepare for an attack at Newport on Aquidneck Island in Narragansett Bay. Orders were issued for additional militia from the surrounding colonies to reinforce Sullivan.

Sullivan stockpiled supplies while he was waiting for enough additional militiamen to attack. He would transport them from Fort Barton on unarmed flat-bottomed ferries to the northern end of Aquidneck Island in preparation for a siege. Washington dispatched Admiral d'Estaing to Newport to protect the transfer, and he sent me and Nathanael Greene, a Rhode Island native, to help Sullivan coordinate his attack with the French admiral.

Traveling on horseback, Greene and I left New Jersey and arrived before d'Estaing. Meanwhile the British fleet sailed out of New York chasing the French fleet, but d'Estaing wanted to avoid a fight. Then he discovered that the British had sunk ships to obstruct his entry to Narragansett Bay.

Sullivan, Greene, and I went out to meet with d'Estaing to advise him of plans. We asked him to clear a path to Newport harbor and move his ships closer to the British garrison in preparation for the attack.

Militia units from around New England streamed into Fort Barton. When Sullivan felt he had enough men, he ordered the crossing. The British retreated back to the safety of their garrison at Newport. While Sullivan was still ferrying militia, Lord Howe's fleet appeared off Newport. With a numerical advantage, d'Estaing, decided to engage Howe before more British ships could arrive. He sailed out to sea, and as the two fleets were maneuvering for position to engage, an intense storm erupted that severely damaged both fleets.

Howe sailed south to make repairs in New York. Before leaving for Boston for repairs, d'Estaing sailed up the Narragansett to inform Sullivan he would be unable to support him. I thought d'Estaing's explanation and apology were gracious and his dispatch considerate. But Sullivan had already begun siege operations and needed immediate naval support as well as the French troops on d'Estaing's ships. He asked us to go with him out to the flagship to plead with d'Estaing to support him, if only for two days.

Greene and I urged d'Estaing to delay his departure. He was personally willing to stay, but the captains of his other ships, fearing that a large British fleet would trap their battered ships and easily sink them, refused to remain.

The entire French fleet left for Boston—unaccountably taking their ground forces. Though Sullivan felt deserted, he futilely continued fighting for four more days. When it became obvious that they could not take Newport, militiamen started deserting. Sullivan was incensed—the abrupt departure of the French had forced him to abandon an attack that had taken weeks of planning and preparation. Sullivan blamed the French for the failure of his mission, and hastily drafted a belligerent order castigating d'Estaing, charging that the departure of the French fleet was treacherous and cowardly, contrary to the interests of the Continentals, harmful to the alliance between France and America, and injurious to French honor. All of his generals signed it, though I refused seeing that the document as an ill-considered condemnation of our only ally. Sullivan rashly sent an aide to Boston to deliver the document to d'Estaing. I sent a courier to Washington to inform him of Sullivan's lack of tact and diplomacy.

Militiamen who returned to Boston publicly expressed anger with the French, calling d'Estaing's withdrawal a cowardly desertion. Bostonians began denouncing and attacking all things French, and threatening to close the port of Boston to d'Estaing and all French ships. This would have caused an international incident and jeopardized the financial and military support by our only ally.

D'Estaing's withdrawal had clearly shown everyone—including the British—that naval support was indispensable to American success. Washington acted at once to restore harmony, sending Sullivan a courteous letter to calm his wrath, pointing out the indiscretion of his conduct, and dispatching Greene and me to Boston to apologize to d'Estaing on his behalf and encourage him to send his ships and troops back to Newport as soon as they were repaired. We also delivered a letter to his friend John Hancock who had returned to Boston.

Greene and I rode non-stop, covering the seventy miles in seven hours, and went directly to meet with Hancock. Washington asked his friend, fellow officer, and Freemason to personally intercede in the rioting and attacks on the French. He also asked him to intervene with the city's ship-fitters to repair the French fleet so the attack on Newport could be resumed.

Although General Hancock had signed the protest criticizing d'Estaing, he understood the diplomatic problem. He used his prestige and popularity with the citizens of Boston to make a public gesture of good will towards the French, and suggested we all go to d'Estaing to calm the situation.

Hancock ran a profitable shipping business in Boston. He had used his wealth and signature to support the colonial cause from the beginning, and was very popular in Boston. His mansion, highly visible on prestigious Beacon Hill, was so commanding that when the British held Boston, Lord Clinton had used it as his headquarters. Hancock made a conspicuous show of leaving in his recognizable carriage. As we rode slowly through the crowded streets toward the harbor, curious crowds followed. Hancock orchestrated a loud and conspicuous display of boarding d'Estaing's flagship, waving to the crowd and various reporters he had informed of his visit.

I introduced him to Admiral d'Estaing. Hancock greeted the French admiral with a Masonic handshake and apologized for any misunderstanding, expressing his appreciation for the Admiral's efforts. The Admiral responded warmly and invited us for tea.

Before leaving, Hancock invited the admiral to bring forty French officers to dine with Boston's leading citizens at his home on Beacon Hill. The Admiral agreed with pleasure. Hancock invited his influential friends and publicized the dinner widely, hoping that the conspicuous show of friendship between well-known community members and French officers would pacify hostile Bostonians.

At the end of the sumptuous dinner, Hancock toasted his French friend and colleague, and presented d'Estaing with a portrait of Washington. Hoping that the diplomatic crisis had been resolved, Greene and I left Boston to rejoin Sullivan. We arrived close to midnight to learn that Sullivan had begun ferrying his men back to the mainland. So far, only 1000 men had made it across. Greene and I boarded a flatboat returning empty to Aquidneck Island, for the British had left their garrison to attack the retreating Americans. Sullivan asked us to help by commanding his rearguard under the attack. Near the regiment I was helping, there was an all black unit, the African American Rhode Island Regiment, former slaves commanded by Colonel Christopher

Greene (no relation to Nathanael). I was impressed with their discipline and valor as they fought bravely to repulse professional Hessian soldiers. During the three hours it took to get everyone back to the mainland, the black solders' line was never broken, and none of them was injured. It was the first time I had seen black men face fire, act as a unit, and show their discipline, courage, and skills in battle. Having seen them only as workers or slaves, and disturbed that men could be so badly treated simply because of their skin color, I vowed to do something about this situation when the war was over.

As a result of our combined rearguard action, all troops returned unharmed. We were fortunate, for shortly after we withdrew, more than a hundred British ships carrying 5000 troops sailed into Newport harbor to reinforce the garrison. This effectively ended the opportunity to force the British out of Newport.

A freak storm had cost us a great opportunity. But fortunately a diplomatic catastrophe had been averted.

My experiences at Newport showed the need for a significant, reliable navy to attack any island or port. Without a navy, the war would come to an impasse—neither side had the capacity to deliver a knockout blow, and both sides were hemorrhaging men and money. It was clear to me, Washington, the Continental Congress, and the general public that time was running out. The diplomatic crisis in Boston had focused the importance of our alliance with France, so I began considering how I could help reinforce this crucial objective.

With a recent letter from my father-in-law saying that he had forgiven me and that I was welcome to return home, this was the moment to return to France to ask the king for additional naval support, money, and supplies. Besides I was eager to be with Adrienne.

Congress granted my request, but asked me to work with their minister plenipotentiary, Ben Franklin, to obtain the assistance, and reiterated once again that they did not want ground troops.

CHAPTER 10

Return to France

1779

ON JANUARY 11 I BOARDED the new American ship *Alliance*. The wind and water were freezing and turbulent. The crossing was unusually rough and seemed to take forever. We arrived in Brest four weeks later, but I still faced 370 miles of bumpy, snow-covered roads. I decided that before visiting my family, I would go first to Versailles to convey the urgent needs of the colonists. I arrived at the palace fatigued and disheveled, but went directly to request an audience with the king. Not only was I refused permission, but as punishment for having disobeyed his earlier order, the king placed me under house arrest for two weeks. This was not the hero's welcome I had envisioned.

I arrived back at the Hôtel de Noailles exhausted, cold, and upset. When I walked in, Adrienne was sitting peacefully in front of a cozy fireplace rocking Anastasie in her arms. She jumped up, put the baby in a crib, and threw herself around me. She felt incredibly good, smelled even better, and looked more beautiful than I remembered. But I felt self-conscious, having had no bath in some time, and wearing clothes that had not been cleaned in even longer.

Adrienne was grateful that I was not residing in the Bastille and appreciative of the King's lenient sentence. She was certain that we could find something to do during my punishment.

During my house arrest, we explored each other's changes over our two years apart. We had both been matured by external events—I had become a tested soldier, witnessed death and the horrors of war, been shot, and had killed. I had borne the burden of the lives and well-being of the soldiers under my command. I had endured ocean crossings and a different language and unfamiliar culture. She had brought forth life, nurtured our children, lost her first born, and been solely responsible for the family finances and businesses.

We gladly discovered that our passions had evolved. For two weeks we were together constantly. I discovered my delight with the curiosity, playfulness, and intelligence of our daughter. I could have happily been imprisoned with Adrienne forever, but I felt compelled to see the king. Neither Adrienne nor I wanted to be separated, so when she asked to accompany me to Versailles, I was delighted.

The king admitted me quickly. He praised my efforts on behalf of France, and my accomplishments against the British. He called for the attention of everyone. The American Congress had asked his permission to honor me upon my return to France. He motioned to William Franklin, who presented me with a gold-plated sword commissioned by the Continental Congress. The king was pleased that the colonists were honoring a Frenchman, and he restored me to my position in the King's Dragoons, even promoting me to *Mestre de Camp*—a colonel in the French army.

After the banquet, a note was delivered asking that I join the king in private. With us were his minister of state and chief adviser, the comte de Maurepas; his foreign minister Vergennes; and his director-general of finance Jacques Necker. They were interested in the status of the colonial conflict with the British and the economic circumstances of the colonists. I reported on d'Estaing's episode, and advised them that, had there been a naval fleet available, the colonists would have taken the British garrison. A sizeable fleet might even enable them to take British headquarters in New York. The Americans could not hope to win a war against the British without obtaining siege equipment. They lacked large muzzle-loading cannons, chamber-loading mortars, and howitzers capable of firing bombs—and anyone trained to use these. The insurgents were also desperate for the most basic supplies like uniforms, blankets, and money.

With sufficient ground troops and a large naval fleet, the Americans might be able to win the war. In any case their efforts would surely weaken the British. Either way the conflict would benefit France. The colonists, fighting for their freedom, were extremely motivated, and the overextended British could not afford to maintain the war and still protect all their profitable colonies in the West Indies.

The meeting was the first of many regarding this matter, and appeared to be fruitful, for they asked me to submit a written proposal. While working on it, I remained in frequent contact with both Washington and the Continental Congress.

In early May I received a March 18 letter from Washington's Morristown winter camp:

> *The oldest people now living in this Country do not remember so hard a winter as the one we are now emerging from. In a word the severity of the frost exceeded anything of the kind that had ever been experienced in this climate before. We are absolutely, literally starved. I do solemnly declare that I did not put a single morsel of victuals into my mouth for four days and as many nights, except for a little black birch bark which I gnawed off a stick of wood. I saw several men roast their old shoes and eat them, and I was afterward informed by one of the officers' waiters, that some of the officers killed a favorite little dog that belonged to one of them. The soldiers wore what laughingly could be called a uniform, and possessed a blanket*

thin enough to have straws shoot through it without discommoding the threads.

The winter was much worse than the one we had experienced at Valley Forge, and Washington told me that it was perhaps the lowest point of the war for him. Dispatch riders could not transit the snow-covered roads, so all communications were carried by men on snowshoes. Washington had been unable to write me as frequently as he normally did. The civilian government failed to supply his troops who were on the verge of starvation. There had been two separate incidents of soldiers mutinying, and a real threat of mass desertions. New York harbor had frozen over, with eight feet of ice trapping all shipping.

His letter was a reminder of my grave responsibility. D'Estaing had left for the West Indies, so the colonists were without a navy. In December Clinton launched a major campaign to capture Savannah, Georgia, a port closer to the valuable British colonies in the West Indies. Yet neither Congress nor Washington were requesting French troops. Franklin wrote me:

> *I do not hear of any intention to send any troops to our Country. I have no Orders to request Troops, but large ones for supplies. And I dare not take any farther Steps than I have done in such a Proposition without orders.*

It looked like the colonists' insurrection was a losing cause—a waste of time and money. However, by September Washington indicated that his position might be softening. Although he did not specifically request more troops, he wrote that he would "give me a cordial welcome if I landed at the head of a corps of gallant French." Knowing his concern about using French troops, I thought that if all French troops were under Washington's command and all French officers stood junior to American officers of equal rank, we might avoid potential problems.

Maurepas was particularly receptive to my plan. I was hoping that he and Vergennes would put me in charge of such a force, as I was eager to show the Americans that their prejudices against the French were not justified.

When I arrived back to the Hôtel de Noailles, Adrienne greeted me at the door, threw her arms around me, and led me to a private room. She had good reason to believe that she was again pregnant. I was delighted. This time I had the opportunity to be with her and watch the amazing transformation to her little body. Her face took on a maternal glow that drew me to warm myself with her presence. During the seven months I waited for Louis's decision, I was frequently able to put aside war and confrontation and enjoy serene moments with Adrienne and our Anastasie, to delight in our gardens and listen to the song of birds.

Adrienne's water broke on Christmas Eve. I was forced to listen helplessly as my tiny wife screamed in pain. But thanks to her midwife, our first son—my little soldier—came screaming loudly into an unfamiliar world. He appeared strong and healthy, and I was greatly relieved that Adrienne survived the ordeal. We named our future general *George Washington Lafayette.*

The week after our son's birth, I wrote Washington informing him of our good fortune and asking him to be our son's godfather. We received a prompt reply about four months later that he was honored to have been asked and proud to accept the privilege.

In a separate letter the general reported that all British troops had left Newport for New York to consolidate their hold. Also that it was getting harder to obtain supplies because American farmers were refusing to accept Continental money. It was clear that Washington was again referencing the importance of soon attaining supplies from the king.

This time the response from Maurepas and Vergennes was prompt—they were eager to send ground troops, and agreed with both my analysis and solution. They recommended to the king that he send the Americans everything I had requested as soon as possible. The king immediately approved it. I was ecstatic.

Arrangements began to send a large naval fleet and thousands of soldiers to America. Despite my hope to command the ground troops, the king appointed Lieutenant General comte de Rochambeau—admittedly twice my age and much more experienced. The entire convoy of thirty-two transports and cargo ships would be protected by seven ships of the line, four frigates, four flutes, a cutter, and a schooner. In addition to crews of 7000 sailors, the ships would carry 450 officers and 5300 men. The king had given the entire task force the code name *Expédition Particulière.*

In view of the hostility to French troops by Congress, Commander Washington, and many colonists, I suggested it would be extremely important for them to do nothing that might offend the Americans. The alliance, to be successful, would require that all Frenchmen be sensitive to the colonials' pride, and I recommended that both Admiral Ternay and General Rochambeau understand that they would always be under Washington's orders and their troops auxiliary to the Americans.

Because of my experience with Americans, Vergennes asked me to leave promptly for Newport so that when the Expédition arrived, the task of receiving the French forces would go smoothly. Housing, food, and medical facilities to accommodate thousands of men would be necessary without straining the colonists' capacity. And the colonists had to be prepared to receive their unexpected and uninvited guests.

I returned immediately to Paris to arrange for my departure. When I had secured passage, I notified the king, and he requested my appearance at Versailles for a farewell audience.

On February 29 Adrienne, Anastasie, and my little soldier went to Versailles with me. I appeared in the blue coat, white vest, and breeches of an American general, wearing the ceremonial sword and carrying a tricorne hat with the red and black plume of the Corps of American Light Infantry. Everyone at court was impressed, and pleased that I was representing France in such a dignified manner. Marie Antoinette complimented my uniform, congratulated me on being the youngest general in the American army, and made a fuss over Anastasie and our tiny George Washington. When we were about to leave, Louis took me aside and handed me a sealed message for General George Washington which I was to personally hand to him as soon as I was able.

I had high hopes that these French troops and warships would turn the tide towards victory and liberty. Fifteen months with Adrienne had been profound. I was able to explain to her why I felt willing to risk crossing an ocean to a bloody war for foreigners—I was fighting to free people so that our children and their children could secure their own rights. The liberty of the Americans would motivate, influence, and inspire others to seek freedom. Adrienne was fully supportive, and even the duke approved.

Vergennes had ordered a bright young man, Commissary Agent Louis-Dominique Ethis de Corny, to accompany me to assist in making arrangements for the arrival of Rochambeau. We arrived at the harbor of Rochefort and boarded the *Hermione*, a large three-masted gun frigate provided by the king. This time I was leaving France a hero, with the permission and blessings of the king. And Louis was sending with me 4000 blue coats faced with red collars, cuffs and lapels, and buff waistcoats and pants for the American army. We set sail for Boston on March 20.

CHAPTER 11

Returning to America with Good News

1780

ANOTHER HARROWING VOYAGE ALLOWED me little enjoyment beyond planning our arrival with de Corny and thinking about my family:

> *Farewell, farewell, my dear heart. Kiss our dear Anastasie thousands upon thousands of times; kiss our other child. How fortunate they are to see you. Why do I, dear heart, who am made so happy by you, always return unhappiness by leaving you? Ah! Forgive me! The sorrow I suffer punishes me for it. Farewell, farewell again. I would never have believed that it would cost me so much to leave. My dear heart, I feel at this moment that I love you still more than I ever thought. Farewell. Farewell.*

After five horrid weeks at sea, the *Hermione* finally limped into Boston harbor. I was drained and ever so glad to see dry, firm, steady land again. De Corny and I rested with John Hancock and by May 2 were ready to proceed to Washington's headquarters at the Ford mansion near Morristown.

We arrived on a beautiful spring day with the sun shining bright and flowers blooming everywhere. When Washington saw me riding into camp, he rushed out, excited by my return and the news of my heir, and we went to his tent to exchange information of what had transpired during the year we were apart.

He informed me that British warships had sailed out of New York harbor taking Clinton and Cornwallis down to Charlestown, leaving Hessian General Wilhelm von Knyphausen in command of New York. In March Clinton had laid siege to the South's biggest city and most important port. After six weeks of bombardment, the city fell and Major General Benjamin Lincoln was forced to surrender his 5000 troops—the biggest loss of war.

I informed him that I had conceived a plan that would permit him to use the foreign soldiers—that all French troops would be placed under Washington's command and all French officers would be subordinate to American officers of equal rank and Maurepas and Vergennes had agreed to my plan. I asked the general if he would accept French soldiers on American soil under those conditions. He admired my initiative, given our inability to communicate in a timely fashion that made it impossible for me to obtain his prior approval. He might consider troops under the conditions I proposed.

I offered him the sealed message Louis had given me. He read it and, with a broad smile, handed me the king's letter. His Royal Majesty Louis XVI informed Washington that he was now officially Commander in Chief of the United Forces of France and the United States, and the king commissioned Washington Lieutenant-General and Vice-Admiral of France who would soon command an expeditionary force scheduled to leave France on May 2.

The general appreciated my success with Louis and could barely contain himself. He thanked me repeatedly for this windfall. Washington immediately sent a dispatch rider to Congress to inform them of the imminent arrival of the Expédition Particulière.

We did not know when or where the Expédition would be arriving, but we began arranging for their needs, and hired spies to go behind enemy lines to determine British plans with regard to the French fleet. Congress established a special committee in charge of Franco-American cooperation. Armed with an official letter of introduction as well as a letter from Washington, de Corny set out for Rhode Island to establish a hospital in Providence.

On July 11 the *Expédition Particulière* sailed into Narragansett Bay. The sight of the billowing sails of the advancing French fleet and cannons of the warships caused the residents some anxiety. But thousands of well-groomed, handsomely uniformed, highly disciplined, elite French troops sprightly walking off their ships impressed even the most dubious citizens.

The news of the arrival of the French fleet was rushed to Washington's headquarters, and I went immediately to help de Corny welcome Rochambeau and Ternay, and ensure that the troops received a cordial reception. When I arrived I learned that the initial reception had gone very well. Despite overcrowding, sleeplessness, malnutrition, and illness during their two month ocean crossing, the officers had demanded that their troops remain disciplined while disembarking, and that they demonstrate their professionalism to the Americans. During the first week, close personal contact helped to overcome fear, prejudice, and hostility.

The townspeople, accustomed to pillaging both by the English and by their own troops, were extremely happy when the French commander made it clear that they would pay for everything they received in silver and gold coins. By the time I reached Newport, some routine problems had arisen out of cultural differences, social status, language, food, and religion, but nothing bordering on hostility.

Washington had no immediate use for the French troops, so Rochambeau decided to keep his army at Newport. However, if the two armies were to work together in the future, the two commanders needed to form a cohesive alliance. General Rochambeau and Admiral Ternay agreed to meet with Washington on September 20 midway, in Hartford, to become acquainted and to plan and coordinate strategy. To make a good impression in preparation for that first meeting, Washington asked Alexander Hamilton to draft a plan of attack on British headquarters.

Neither Rochambeau nor Ternay were enthusiastic about Washington's proposal, noting that the island was heavily defended by warships far outnumbering the seven French warships at Newport. Moreover, British ships in the West Indies or in Europe could be repositioned at any time, so without more ships of the line, neither Rochambeau nor Ternay thought there was much hope for success. While we were still discussing strategy, news came that the British fleet off the coast of Long Island had sailed into New York harbor, possibly on their way to attack the French fleet. Rochambeau and Ternay returned immediately to prepare their troops. But to carry out Washington's wishes, Rochambeau sent his son, one of his aides-de-camp, back to France along with Lt. John Laurens to ask the king for more naval support.

Washington, Hamilton, and I departed for our headquarters in Tappan, New York. Washington had arranged to meet his friend Benedict Arnold, commander of West Point, on the way. They had scheduled a breakfast meeting in Arnold's home in Fishkill, New York to discuss administrative details regarding the fort. But before we reached Fishkill, Washington received a dispatch compelling him to take care of some unanticipated business. As a courtesy, he sent Hamilton and me ahead to inform Arnold. As we rode, Alex gave me background on Washington's good friend. Washington had trusted Arnold to lead an invasion of Canada, appointed him military commander of Philadelphia after the British abandoned it, and had appointed him commander of the fort at West Point which strategically controlled the Hudson River, giving Arnold power over the gateway to Canada and New England from Albany to New York City. Washington knew Arnold as a courageous soldier, twice battle-wounded, who had distinguished himself through acts of intelligence and bravery—the renown hero of Fort Ticonderoga and largely responsible for the major victory at Saratoga. Washington felt their bond—both had suffered for the cause and risked a great deal, yet had been subject to jealous conspiracies against them from plotting generals and petty politicians.

The Arnolds lived on the eastern shore of the Hudson, across from West Point. His second wife Peggy invited us to join them for breakfast and while we were eating, one of Arnold's aides rushed in out of breath, handed Arnold a letter, and whispered in his ear. Arnold excused himself, announcing he had to go immediately to West Point to prepare for Washington's arrival, and asked his wife to join him upstairs.

Neither of them returned to the table. About thirty minutes later, when Washington arrived, Hamilton and I went upstairs to look for them. When I pushed open the bedroom door, Peggy fell to the floor in a faint. We revived her with a damp cloth.

Washington finished his breakfast, thanked Peggy for her hospitality, and we proceeded to West Point. Washington was upset that Arnold was not present to greet his superior officer—a serious breach of protocol—and the officer in charge told us that Arnold had not been there all morning. We were surprised to see the stronghold's fortifications in disrepair, and waited impatiently for Arnold to arrive to explain the fort's deterioration.

Some hours later, the head of Continental Army Intelligence, Major Benjamin Tallmadge, rushed in and reported that General Clinton's Adjutant General, Major John André, had just been arrested, and a map of West Point found in his boot. Tallmadge believed that an associate of André had sent a letter to Arnold warning him of André's arrest. Arnold knew he must flee or be arrested as a traitor. By now he was aboard the British warship *Vulture* safely sailing for New York City.

Washington was confident that his friend was principled and honorable, not a traitor plotting to surrender a strategic military fort to the enemy. When the reality struck him, he retired to a darkened room and sat with his head in his hands, tears rolling down his cheeks. He turned to me and whispered, "Whom can we trust now?"

With André in custody, Washington ordered him brought to Tappan and held at the Old '76 House to await trial for spying. He assigned Hamilton—and only him—to watch André, trusting no one else. Washington wanted Arnold so desperately that he sent a message to Clinton offering to spare the life of his aide and friend André in exchange for Arnold. Clinton refused. Unable to bring Arnold to justice, Washington made immediate arrangements for André to be tried. I served on that jury along with eleven senior officers, including von Steuben. The trial was presided over by Nathanael Greene.

We found him guilty of being behind American lines "under a feigned name and in a disguised habit," and ordered that "Major André, Adjutant-General to the British Army, ought to be considered as a spy from the enemy, and that agreeable to the law and usage of nations, he ought to suffer death."

With the trial of André concluded, Washington immediately convened the same officers at a second military court to try Benedict Arnold. Again we heard evidence, unanimously found him guilty of treason, and also condemned Arnold to death.

André realized the fate of a spy but appealed to George Washington not for his life, but requesting merely the respect due an officer by being executed by firing squad. Washington denied him this final privilege. With dignified deportment, André bravely refused the blindfold, placed the noose around his own neck, and was hung from a tree. Washington held little animus against André, believing him to be "an accomplished man and gallant officer," and "more unfortunate than criminal." He blamed Arnold for the treachery. A few weeks later, Washington appointed Nathanael Greene the new commander of West Point, and ordered him to immediately correct the many deficiencies that had been observed.

CHAPTER 12

The War Moves South

1780

A FEW MONTHS LATER, WASHINGTON received reports that Arnold, promoted to general, had sailed from New York heading south to where the British had begun a major offensive campaign after capturing Savannah and Charleston. Clinton returned to New York leaving General Cornwallis in command of Charleston with instruction to take control over the Carolinas, assuming loyalist militias would gladly join the modest force of British and Germans. The victory at Charleston had already led thousands of loyalists to join the British.

Cornwallis sent Banastre Tarleton with a primarily loyalist regiment to pursue the remaining Continental Army in the south. In May, Tarleton found about 400 raw Continental recruits from Virginia near Waxhaw, South Carolina. Tarleton attacked with cavalry and the Continentals threw down their arms and raised a white flag. Tarleton's men gave no quarter to their surrender, carrying out indiscriminate carnage, even stabbing the wounded where they lay.

News of Tarleton's violation of protocol spread rapidly. Thousands of colonists opposed Tarleton's brutality, and thereby Britain's. "Over-mountain men" from the frontiers beyond the Appalachian Mountains formed volunteer militias while the Continental Army began to reform at Charlotte, North Carolina.

With these new recruits, General Gates took command of a cross-road just north of Camden, South Carolina, which was key to controlling the Carolina backcountry. Though numerically superior, Gates suffered 2000 casualties. Baron de Kalb's horse was shot out from under him. Before he could get up, he was shot three times and bayo-netted repeatedly. Cornwallis rode up and ordered de Kalb's wounds dressed by his own surgeons, but I was told that de Kalb responded, "I thank you, sir, for your generous sympathy, but I die the death I always prayed for: the death of a soldier fighting for the rights of man." Three days later my friend and mentor died.

During the battle Gates mounted a swift horse and left his troops behind. He was pursued by Tarleton's cavalry for some twenty miles before they drew rein. Gates took refuge sixty miles away in Charlotte, enabling Cornwallis to take thousand of prisoners and seize his seven guns and all baggage trains—and remove further threat to the British in South Carolina.

Congress had selected the generals who lost Savannah, Charleston, and Camden, without consulting the commander in chief. Fearing the entire south would soon be lost, they decided to let Washington select the next commander for the region.

Though Washington had just sent Nathanael Greene to replace Arnold at West Point, stopping Cornwallis was far more important. He immediately appointed his most trusted general as Commander of the Southern Department—covering Delaware to Florida. Greene, now effectively second-in-command of the entire Continental Army, was ordered to North Carolina.

Because of the British command of the seas, Greene marched over-land, which allowed him to stop in Philadelphia to ask Congress for weapons, wagons, horses, and money for the men he hoped to recruit.

He left November 4 with meager supplies. At Head of Elk he recruited militiamen, carpenters, blacksmiths, wheelwrights, and harness markers, and proceeded to Virginia to protect warehouses and foundries. To ensure the movement of supplies destined for the south, Greene left behind his second-in-command, the able quartermaster von Steuben.

Greene reached the backwater village of Charlotte and took command of the thousand ragged, hungry Continentals and 1200 militiamen who comprised his feeble army. Two decisive victories—at King's Mountain and Cowpens, North Carolina—greatly boosted morale and recruitment and dealt a significant blow to loyalist support for Cornwallis. I was starting to see that those "loyal to the crown" were merely loyal to power, at least in the south.

Cornwallis concentrated on destroying Greene's main army in order to attract more militia. In the north, freedom was a stronger principle than success. Greene did not dare engage the much larger army that was advancing, but his troops were local. They knew the remote rural area, were able to live off the land, and had less to carry. To maximize mobility, Greene divided them and ordered both sections to retreat into the backcountry towards the Dan River.

With Tarleton having lost his light infantry at Cowpens, Cornwallis was thus forced to divide his army, and to destroy his own baggage train in order to speed pursuit. Unfamiliar with the wilderness and its numerous waterways, his troops could not forage enough to adequately feed so many men. Running out of supplies, his soldiers grew weaker. Greene's skillful withdrawal across the Dan River into Virginia drew the British even further from their supply lines. Unable to pursue Greene across the Dan because local militiamen had commandeered every available boat, Cornwallis focused on simply feeding his desperate troops.

Reinforced by new militiamen, on March 15 Greene re-crossed the Dan River and encountered Cornwallis near Guilford Courthouse. While Greene suffered a tactical defeat and was forced to retreat, Guilford was a Pyrrhic victory for Cornwallis, for a third of his army lay dead or wounded on the field, and his scattered troops were out of food, water, and ammunition, and were shaking with malaria. Reduced to 2000 soldiers, Cornwallis was forced to abandon plans to conquer the Carolinas. He marched the remnant of his army to the nearest source of supplies and food—the port at Wilmington, North Carolina—with Greene sniping at his heels.

When Clinton reached New York in June, he immediately redirected supplies to Cornwallis. He also found there a very experienced general who was not in charge of any army—Benedict Arnold. And Virginia, the breadbasket of the colonies, had warehouses packed with food, high-value tobacco, weapons, and supplies, and foundries manufacturing weapons.

In December Clinton sent Arnold with 1200 men to Virginia to capture these, both to supply Cornwallis and prevent goods from reaching Greene. The Royal Navy took Arnold to the mouth of the James River, and by the afternoon of January 4 Arnold was sailing upstream on smaller ships. He landed his forces at Westover and brazenly marched into Richmond to seize the militia's weapons, take or burn the tobacco, and capture Governor Thomas Jefferson. When plantation owner William Armistead, purser of the Continental Army responsible for managing their worthless paper money and the real currency of tobacco, learned of Arnold's arrival in Virginia, he sent urgent dispatches to Jefferson requesting militia to protect the valuable stores and to General Washington to inform him of Arnold's incursion.

Washington ordered me to Virginia immediately to protect the supplies, promising me 1200 French troops from Newport. Additionally, while I was there I should capture and immediately hang Arnold. I left Peekskill with 1200 militiamen from New England and New Jersey on February 20, eager to confront the traitor.

My troops were upset to leave their families and farms and march 300 miles without pay. To prevent them from mutinying, I stopped in Baltimore and bought them clothes, haversacks, eating utensils, canteens, axes, blankets, tinderboxes with flint, and personal items. The men were appreciative of my concern, and that I paid with my own French coins. Meanwhile Jefferson was preparing Richmond for an attack by moving all military provisions to a foundry five miles out-side town. But with Arnold's unexpectedly rapid approach, Jefferson abandoned the provisions and fled to Charlottesville.

Arnold burned the Richmond foundry and marched towards the new storage facility at Westham. When he discovered that von Steuben was protecting the facility, he chose not to engage, returned to Rich-mond, and sent a dispatch to Jefferson offering to spare the new capital in exchange for the tobacco. Jefferson refused to communicate in any way, so Arnold ransacked Richmond, returned to his ships, and sailed to Portsmouth, which he proceeded to fortify—to lessen the chances of being captured and hung.

From Annapolis, I sent word to von Steuben that I was on my way. We sailed down Chesapeake Bay and up the York River to the port of Yorktown, marching up the Virginia peninsula to Williamsburg where we joined Steuben on March 17 to wait for my French reinforcements.

The next day we learned that the British navy had engaged the French fleet near Cape Henry at the southern entrance to Chesapeake Bay and forced them to return to Newport. I would have no French reinforcements.

Despite damage, the British fleet was able to deliver 2,600 rein-forcements under General William Phillips to Portsmouth, adding to Arnold's 3,000 troops. I decided that it was pointless to proceed and I could serve Washington better by returning to his headquarters. My troops were delighted to be returning home safe and out of harm's way.

When we arrived April 8 at Head of Elk I received a dispatch from Washington directing me to return to Virginia immediately and put myself under the command of General Greene, to help him prevent Phillips and Arnold from marching south to join Cornwallis in the Carolinas.

Some of my troops deserted, but I could not afford to waste time chasing them. The rest of us reached the wide and formidable Potomac River on April 20. I was expecting the British to try to prevent me from crossing over into Virginia, but there was no resistance. Scouts ascertained they were marching rapidly towards Petersburg, a valuable military depot for both local militia and Continental forces—more important to Phillips than my little band of militiamen.

To get to Petersburg quickly I had to force-march my troops and leave our artillery, heavy equipment, and sick behind. As we neared Richmond, von Steuben and Muhlenberg were retreating north from Phillips' attack.

I entrenched my army on a hill overlooking the city and took command of a small corps of Virginia militiamen. I spread 2000 troops in a long front on the hill to appear that I had many more, hoping to gain time for reinforcements. British troops paused at the Appomattox River and could see that I had the high ground across the river with more troops than they anticipated. Phillips withdrew towards Portsmouth.

Two personal letters reached me from Washington that had been written in late April. "My friendship for you makes me desirous of having you near me." He wished me to return. If I continued on to Virginia, "it will become my duty to go there in person." I was affected deeply that my dear friend cared so much for me.

But I was particularly eager to engage Phillips and Arnold because of an intense dislike for both men. Phillips had commanded the artillery at the battle of Minden where my father died. Though there was nothing personal, Arnold's betrayal disgusted me, having suffered with him in Valley Forge. With a chance of capturing him, I decided not to return to headquarters, especially with Cornwallis marching to join them to establish British control over the warehouse and foundries in Virginia, as well as Chesapeake Bay. They would then be positioned to trap Washington between their huge army marching north from the head of the Chesapeake Bay and their forces in New York.

As Cornwallis marched north, loyalists and other hangers-on followed the British army like a scourge of vultures, plundering every farm and plantation along the way, driving off horses and cattle, and forcing slaves to come along with them. News of this month-long devastation preceded Cornwallis' arrival in Petersburg.

On May 8 I received a dispatch from Greene giving me independent command of all the troops in Virginia in order to stop Cornwallis from pillaging the colony and returning to the Carolinas. While waiting for the arrival of Wayne's reinforcements, I learned that his troops had mutinied and he would be delayed and that Cornwallis' army had begun entering Virginia.

Suddenly the war had focused on Virginia. With Washington and Rochambeau far away and Greene in the Carolinas, I was commanding the only Continental army in the colony. I was in my tent planning strategy when a sentry came in holding a scruffy black boy by the arm. The boy claimed to have a letter from William Armistead.

I knew Armistead, owner of one of the largest plantations in New Kent County. He was close friends with many wealthy coastal plantation owners including Jefferson and Washington, and his daughter had married Martha Washington's brother, William Dandridge.

I was suspicious that this dirty, ragged slave could possibly know such an important person, and had not forgotten Washington's warning about utilizing blacks. If I ever had to, I should use only free men— and never give them arms. He warned me not to accept their word that they were free, since many a master presented a slave to the recruiter as a free man in order for the slave to serve as his substitute. Yet Washington himself always had his slaves in camp for menial non-military chores—building fortifications, clearing roads, and serving his officers. If James had any skills or could be taught them quickly, he might be useful in repairing or maintaining weapons, making ammunition, shoeing horses, tending animals, fixing and loading supply wagons, or repairing clothes and tents.

Armistead's certificate stated that he had freed James and was giving his consent for James to join my army. I had not spoken to Armistead directly about this boy, nor could I verify Armistead's handwriting, so I could not vouch for the authenticity of the certificate. Until I learned more about him, I would keep him close to me to observe and evaluate his capabilities.

I realized I had been in a situation similar to James'—solely because I was French. Washington, not initially trusting me, had kept me close. I could not make James my aide nor ask him to copy documents because he could not read or write, so I asked if he would be my valet. He said he had only been a field slave and had no idea what was expected of a valet. I explained that he would be by my side day and night serving my food, setting out my clothes, helping me shave, saddling my horse—whatever I might have need of. I asked my aide to instruct James on his duties and how to perform them and show him his shelter among the camp followers and non-military personnel.

I returned to the impending confrontation with Phillips and Arnold, under the weight of Washington's words on May 1 bemoaning the American situation:

> *In a word—instead of having everything in readiness to take the field, we have nothing; and instead of having the prospect of a glorious offensive campaign before us, we have a bewildered and gloomy defensive one—unless we receive a powerful aid of ships, land troops, and money from our generous allies; and these at present, are too contingent to build upon.*

While I waited impatiently for Wayne to arrive with the promised reinforcements, a scout delivered the news that General Phillips had died suddenly of typhoid fever. I was stunned—and very disappointed. The army of the man who had deprived me of my father was now commanded by Arnold, a man so despicable that I returned his letters unopened. I focused my energies on attacking, capturing, and hanging him. Unfortunately I was not able to act fast enough—on May 20 he marched into Petersburg and assumed command of 8800 well-equipped, well-rested, professional soldiers.

When Cornwallis arrived in Petersburgh as senior officer, he assumed command of all British troops and four days later Arnold was seen leaving Petersburg.

Four days later Arnold was seen leaving Petersburg with 1500 troops towards Portsmouth to board ships to reinforce Clinton against the imminent attack of Washington and Rochambeau on New York. And Cornwallis was sighted leaving Petersburg directly towards me. I had no doubt that he was capable of destroying my army. He was a clever and able general and had never lost a battle against Greene, one of America's most experienced and best generals. Cornwallis was intent on destroying all resistance in Virginia and capturing me to gain control of Virginia and the mouth of Chesapeake Bay. Fortunately we had intercepted one of his couriers carrying a letter from Cornwallis to Clinton in which he referred to me neither by rank nor name nor title, confidently boasting to his superior officer that "the boy cannot escape me." If I wanted to avoid being captured or killed, I had no choice but to stay out of his path. I sent a dispatch to Washington informing him of Cornwallis' boast, jesting that he should not worry because I was "not strong enough even to get beaten."

Washington, still intent on attacking British headquarters in Manhattan which required the assistance of the French fleet in the West Indies, dispatched a ship to Cap-Français (now Cap-Haïtien, Haiti) with a letter to Rear Admiral François Joseph Paul, comte de Grasse outlining his plan of attack. Rochambeau, in a private note to de Grasse sent on the same ship, indicated his preference for an operation in Virginia to prevent the British from seizing control of Chesapeake Bay to assure the safe transport of the army's supplies.

De Grasse replied that to avoid the hurricane season, he could only be available for operations in July or August, and hoped to leave the West Indies and sail north soon, though no destination was indicated.

Washington notified me that "an attempt upon New York with its present Garrison (which by estimation is reduced to 4500 Troops and about 3000 irregulars) was deemed preferable to a Southern operation." Rochambeau, in the spirit of Franco-American cooperation which he, more than anyone else represented, promised his full cooperation.

It was clear that I had to act fast and flee the Richmond area while the British were working their way across several rivers. Our smaller numbers, which was our weakness in battle, was our only advantage in flight, since we carried far less artillery and equipment. We abandoned Malvern Hills, trying to keep between Cornwallis and our lines of communications to the north, the direction from which I thought Wayne would be arriving.

Cornwallis repeatedly sent smaller cavalry units to get around and behind us to force me to fight, but I avoided confrontation using the successful strategy of "Swamp Fox" Francis Marion, who had successfully eluded the cavalry of Banastre Tarleton in South Carolina by using irregular methods and the guerrilla tactics of the Indians. My troops felled trees across roads, destroyed bridges, attacked suddenly and withdrew swiftly. Riflemen harassed the enemy's flanks, and snipers covered our retreat with multidirectional fire from hidden shooters. After a week of trying and failing to entrap my army, Cornwallis unexpectedly stopped pursuing us. And on June 1 he abruptly changed direction and began marching west towards the Rivanna River, a tributary of the James. I stopped retreating and followed him at a safe distance. I sent scouts to track his movements with orders not to engage in even small skirmishes until we knew his plans and had a clear advantage.

When Cornwallis reached the Rivanna he marched upstream towards Monticello and Charlottesville where Jefferson and the state legislators had set up temporary offices. Although his huge army marched slowly, he used two mobile light cavalry units to scout and take swift advanced action as needed. Tarleton led one to Monticello to capture Governor Jefferson—who was warned and fled to Staunton, though seven members of the Virginia legislature and some officers were captured at Charlottesville. The other under Simcoe was ordered to seize the state arsenal at Point of Fork, where the Rivanna and Fluvanna Rivers joined to form the James. Von Steuben, with only 500 militiamen and thinking Cornwallis' full army was coming, abandoned the arsenal. Cornwallis continued upstream towards Staunton and Charlottesville.

There was no way for me to prevent the two cities from being captured, looted, and destroyed, nor prevent Cornwallis from killing

Jefferson and the legislators. But just when I had lost hope, General Wayne rode into camp with 800 Continentals. Though our combined armies were merely a quarter of Cornwallis', we were enough to discourage Cornwallis from attempting to reach Staunton—if I could place my army between his at Elk Hill and Staunton. Unfortunately, to the west the broad Rivanna had neither fords nor boats, and east lay thick forests and impassable ravines.

While my staff and I were discussing our options in the staff tent, the young black boy coughed, politely drawing attention to himself, and respectfully asked permission to speak. We all stared at his insolence. For any slave or any black man in the south to be so forward in the presence of white or older men was imprudent, even perilous. For any color of civilian to interfere in a military discussion was inconceivable.

Nevertheless James stood silent and undaunted. Skeptically I gave James permission to address our war council. He told us that he knew of an overgrown back road that was believed impassable, but he thought it would permit us to move around Cornwallis without detection.

Even though I had not known this boy for very long, and did not fully trust him, I had little choice but to investigate. I sent James out with a small group of light cavalry.

For three days I was increasingly impatient, worried that Cornwallis might resume marching before they could come back to camp. But they had cut their way through some sections of impenetrable road and reached Machunk Creek to the north of Cornwallis in only two days.

The entire staff realized the importance of James' information and treated him with a new respect, some talking to him for the first time and telling him how much they appreciated his assistance. James accepted our collective gratitude quietly, with modesty and wary silence.

Within a few hours we decamped and set out on horseback. Getting around Cornwallis boosted everyone's morale, and shortly after we arrived, we were joined by more reinforcements—600 tough and experienced Virginian militiamen who had successfully defeated the British at King's Mountain and Guilford Courthouse. We now had enough men to inflict serious casualties on Cornwallis if he attempted to proceed north, and, at the very least, to provide sufficient time for Jefferson and the delegates to flee to safer locations.

When informed that we had been able to get around his encampment, Cornwallis decided not to risk engaging us. He was lacking food and supplies that he hoped to obtain in Charlottesville. The entire British army turned south towards Richmond.

I thanked James again, telling him he might have saved the lives of Jefferson and the Virginia legislators, as well as prevented the destruction of Charlottesville, Staunton, and Monticello and a large arsenal of weapons and supplies. Virginia and the Continentals owed him a great debt, and I trusted they would be grateful. James nodded, softly thanking me for my kind words, but seemed less certain about the gratitude of the colony.

Soon after, I received a dispatch that Rochambeau had begun marching his army toward New York.

I continued to monitor Cornwallis. My communications with Washington and Greene were often slow, and sometimes intercepted by the enemy. Washington and Rochambeau were about to launch their attack on New York, though no doubt more British warships with reinforcements were heading north from the West Indies. Washington was concerned that Clinton might order Cornwallis to New York to bolster his troops, so I was assigned to prevent Cornwallis from leaving the area.

Greene was expecting Cornwallis to be sent back to South Carolina with rested and well-supplied troops who could destroy his army. If Cornwallis were successful, it would "lay a train to sap the foundation of all the rest," and the revolution might be lost. Both were urging me to keep Cornwallis in Virginia.

Cornwallis reached Williamsburg and left on July 4. When his army had completely withdrawn, I moved mine in. After camp was set up, I ordered a celebration of the fifth anniversary of the Declaration of

Independence while Wayne followed Cornwallis to reconnoiter his activities.

During the celebration a dispatch from Wayne reported that Cornwallis was marching south towards Portsmouth, which required his army to ford the James River, likely at Green Spring. It would be a great opportunity to attack—for those who had already crossed would be isolated, while those in the water helpless, and rear guard troops easily defeated.

Soon a rider galloped into camp with another dispatch—a local slave had told Wayne that much of the British army had already crossed the river, and a small rear guard had been left to protect those still crossing. I ordered Wayne to take half his men and advance upon the rear guard.

The narrow causeway down to the ferry was surrounded by swampy marshlands. When Wayne saw British troops in the water he attacked the rear guard, a small company of German light infantry and part of Tarleton's Legions who, by retreating, drew Wayne further along the causeway. Wayne's riflemen performed particularly well, shot several British officers. I rode onto a spit of land on the river bank to observe the action. From there I could see the main British forces hiding. I rode toward Wayne to warn him of the trap, but was not able to reach him before the full-scale counterattack. Wayne ordered his 800 bewildered infantrymen to counter-charge with fixed bayonets against a much larger contingent. This maneuver so startled the redcoats that they halted their advance long enough for Wayne to pull back and for me time to arrive with reinforcements to cover his withdrawal.

When Cornwallis' trap failed, he personally led an infantry charge, which forced us to withdraw. With the sun setting, Cornwallis chose not to pursue, and we were able to return to Williamsburg to tend our wounded and regroup. Early the next morning Cornwallis led all of his troops on to Portsmouth.

We were shaken by falling for Cornwallis' trap of sending the slave with false information. It was a humbling lesson. I sent a dispatch to Washington about the incident and assessed the situation:

This devil Cornwallis is much wiser than the other generals with whom I have dealt. He inspires me with a sincere fear, and his name has greatly troubled my sleep. This campaign is a good school for me. God grant that the public does not pay for my lessons.

I was not sure I would be able to stop Cornwallis from taking over the state and preventing supplies from reaching Nathanael Greene.

Cornwallis arrived in Portsmouth on July 20. Our scouts followed two men the next day to a small barren land extension that jutted out near the mouth of Chesapeake Bay, where they tested the soil. Apparently it was unsuitable for fortifications, so on August 1, Cornwallis led his army up the Virginia peninsula to Yorktown, the largest deep-water port between Charlestown and Philadelphia, which had a well-developed waterfront which harbored merchant vessels.

Most of the townspeople fled, leaving Cornwallis to choose as his headquarters the largest house with its outbuildings for kitchens, washhouses, poultry houses, dairy houses, smoke houses, spinning houses, and servants' quarters. To defend his encampment, Cornwallis ordered the erection of fortifications, trenches, and redoubts around the town, and directed Lieutenant Colonels Thomas Dundas and Banastre Tarelton to seize the village of Gloucester Point across the York River.

I set up our camp twelve miles northwest of Yorktown, and sent spies into the port to gather information. There was a great deal of activity outside town with British troops cutting down trees to build fortifications, piers, shelters, corrals, and pens.

I needed someone who could pass unnoticed through the British camp to find out more about what Cornwallis may be planning. I had no idea when Washington and Rochambeau would arrive. I was voicing my ponder aloud as if I were alone, while preparing for a meeting with my officers. But I wasn't—James, as usual, was by my side. If he could be so invisible to me, he would likely not exist at all to the British, making him the perfect spy. He was particularly bright and resourceful, and had shown a great deal of composure, cleverness, and confidence in dealing with unfamiliar white officers.

Armistead was no doubt worried about danger to his own plantation and the tobacco stores for which he was responsible, and would want information to ascertain the precise nature of any threat. Unable to risk being captured by the British himself, he would have undoubtedly sent someone he trusted to try to gather information. Young James did not seem to be the most likely person to accomplish that task, yet Armistead had chosen him. I wondered why Armistead would send this specific slave into my camp. Moreover, as a Frenchman whose information about slavery had come from Raynal and Franklin, I was simply curious about his life, so I questioned James to still my inquisitiveness.

He was born and raised on Armistead's plantation. As an infant, he had been looked after by an unrelated, elderly female slave, too weak to work in the fields, storage sheds, or the master's house. He knew of no relative. When he was four or five, he was removed from the old woman and led to a hut shared by eight female slaves. In the center was a fire pit on the floor beneath a vent hole in the thatched roof. He said that they sat around the pit to eat and talk. The fire served as their sole source of heat, light, cooking, and gathering place. The hole let in cold air, and rain turned the floor to squishy mud. Each person's meager belongings were placed carefully beside their straw bed. Except for the stifling days of summer, at night he placed his bed of straw as close to the fire as possible, covered in whatever he could find.

There was no privacy and everything in the hut was shared, including the meager fatty meat, salted herring, and cornbread the boss provided, and whatever the women could grow in their truck patch from the seeds found in their food—pumpkins, squash, and watermelon. They were not permitted knifes or forks, so they ate with their fingers out of one large squash scooped out for a bowl. Everyone washed in a single wooden bucket. With no privacy, he learned whom to trust, how to share, and behaviors to avoid fights. Every other Sunday the slave owner gave them the day off in order to mend their hut and grow or forage for food. He did not allow them to go to church, nor learn to read—which was unnecessary to their work.

The women taught him where to find food, what weeds, flowers, and berries could safely be eaten, and how to lay traps for possums, squirrels, and raccoons. He learned who would protect him, whom to avoid, how to stay safe, and how to avoid being whipped, dismembered, or killed for violating the boss's rules. When he was about ten and strong enough to work in the tobacco fields, Armistead moved him from the women's hut to a hut of male field slaves. He had to get up at the break of dawn, and without eating breakfast march out to the fields. Being late for work was cause for whipping. The man supervising the field hands served a breakfast of salt herring at 10:00, and nothing else until work ended around 11 at night when he might be given some kind of soup or stew made from black eyed peas flavored with meat. He worked the same long day as the adults, seven days a week, although because of his size and age, he was permitted to perform simple chores like carrying water to the field hands, sweeping yards, churning milk, gathering kindling, chasing birds from the crops, and taking care of children younger than he.

When he was about twelve, the master thought James was ready for actual field work, so he was taught how to do transplanting, weeding, and pinching of tassels on thousands of tobacco plants per acre. In the fall he harvested leaves, cured them, and helped transport them to market. In winter, he had to prepare the fields for planting, mend tools, lay out seedbeds, and plant seeds in a cold frame.

Armistead occasionally took James along to help bring tobacco to the store or ship. In town, when whites humiliated him, he learned to control his temper. Armistead eventually disclosed to the boy that he was his father, yet James was merely a commodity to Armistead, the most valuable type he owned.

In town James came into contact with urban and domestic slaves who worked as tradesmen, gardeners, or coachmen who kept a keen ear to political events that might impact their lives. James had already learned how to spy on the white man.

I asked James if he would be willing to risk his life for a country that had afforded him neither education, career, nor opportunities, he told me that more than anything, he cherished his freedom and would do whatever was necessary to obtain it. Before sending him out on his own, Armistead had promised him his freedom if his service proved beneficial, aware that James could simply run away.

Since the British actively recruited blacks, James would be just one more ignored, unidentified runaway slave. He looked harmless, no different from the thousands of other slaves that the British had permitted to enter their camp. Because of his youth and lack of education he would be routinely ignored by the educated, arrogant upper class British officers. I warned James that his undertaking would be dangerous, for if the British discovered that he was a spy, he would probably be hung, and there would be nothing I could do to save him. I told James about the American spy Nathaniel Hale and the British spy Major John André who had both been caught and hung. I promised him nothing—not financial reward, honors, nor even his freedom. James seemed unfazed by the risk and motivated to help me. Before he left camp, I arranged for him, when possible, to pass on information to others I assigned while James remained in town.

On August 3 James left our camp to walk to Yorktown. He returned about a week later tired and extremely hungry, but came directly to my tent, and reported about his mission:

He could not risk walking on the main paths that led to Yorktown because suspicious whites might harm a black person. And even blacks working for the British were eager to earn a reward. Without shoes through the underbrush, his feet were bleeding by the time he reached the outskirts of Yorktown.

Although he had been there several times with Armistead, he barely recognized its transformation into a military camp. Much of it was unrecognizable and all the trees around town had been felled. What had been a village was populated by thousands of people. Construction was underway everywhere. A guard on the periphery stopped him. He said he was looking for work, that he would do anything for food and a place safe from the cursed Americans. He was directed to an area set aside for blacks and told to go out foraging with them for food for the army. He kept count of cannons, tents, muskets, and whatever might have military significance, including bearskin and leather caps.

Separated from the soldiers were women and children in tents and shelters of limbs and boughs. Tiny hillside caves served the thousands of non-military whites—blacksmiths, cooks, washerwomen, prostitutes, and grooms. There were hundreds of supply wagons, corrals for several hundred horses, enclosures for the cart-oxen, cows, and pigs, and numerous pens filled with chickens.

The living area for blacks was a sprawling village of its own. Every British soldier seemed to have his own personal Negro helper to carry his provisions, and every officer had three or four plus one or two Negresses as cook or maid. The black community had a restricted section for blacks suspected of having smallpox. To avoid questioning, he kept to himself and constructed his shelter, a mud cave. Early next morning, he went out with a large contingent of blacks whom the British, desperate for food, sent to forage, drive livestock from farms, strip fields and storage cellars, and procure horses. Slaves were never sent out unescorted because the British did not trust blacks to bring back the food they found or use weapons to mete out revenge against slave owners.

His party returned with a small herd of cows, hundreds of horses, lots of corn, some wild greens, and berries. Soldiers and others in camp talked openly, dismissive of his presence, about what they thought they might be doing and where they might be going. Even officers talked freely of the construction or actions being planned—a fleet of ships anchored nearby might soon be taking them to either New York or Philadelphia.

After several foraging expeditions, he was taken to Cornwallis' headquarters. A soldier escorted him to a room where the general asked his name and congratulated him on his fine work of foraging. He suspected he had not been brought here simply to be complimented, so he was surprised when he was asked if he would work at headquarters as an attendant, for all the slaves who had served the owner of the house had fled.

This opportunity was unique, being near Cornwallis and his staff as they discussed plans openly about the serious health problems in camp—an outbreak of typhoid fever, and an eruption of smallpox among the loyalist refugees and the blacks. Though isolated, all of the sick had to be tended to and fed. Officers complained that the sick were consuming too much food. They discussed releasing infected slaves into the American camp to weaken their enemy. They also spoke of the urgency of building facilities to accommodate the arrival of British warships.

His information was extremely helpful. We now knew the exact location of Cornwallis' headquarters, their vulnerability to illness and starvation, and the risk of infected slaves coming to our camp. Cornwallis' desperation might make him unwilling to wait to be rescued, perhaps even try to break out of camp.

I was most pleased by James' success. I was about to dismiss him when James informed there was more—Cornwallis had asked him to spy for him, and James had agreed. I was incredulous that in so short a time the wily British commander would ask an unknown black boy to serve him in such an important mission. Perhaps even more surprised that James had the presence of mind to consent. Cornwallis had promised him his freedom when the British won the war, and would provide him some money. James replied that more than anything, he wanted his freedom.

For the first time, James looked directly at me and smiled—Cornwallis had warned him that if the Americans found out he was providing Cornwallis information, they would immediately hang him. There would be nothing Cornwallis could do to help. James commented wryly that this must be dangerous work for two generals to give him the same advice.

I was astonished how easily James had been able to win the confidence and trust of three powerful white men—Armistead, Cornwallis, and myself—a Frenchman, an Englishman, and an American, all experienced in assessing the abilities and character of subordinates. Yet we each trusted an uneducated slave with our very lives. I immediately stationed additional guards to ensure that smallpox did not enter our camp and began an inoculation program like I had witnessed at Valley Forge. Fortunately one of my officers was a physician familiar with the process of variolation, rubbing material from a smallpox pustule from a mild case into a scratch. James' information undoubtedly prevented decimation of our troop strength.

With James spying for both sides, I could return to Cornwallis a lesson he had taught me and Wayne prior to our engagement at Green Springs. By sending a slave to feed false information we could convince him that it was not worth the risk to try to break out of his encampment or attempt to engage me.

I had my staff prepare a fake dispatch from the colonial command in New York to inform me that 7000 veteran soldiers and a large amount of weaponry would be arriving momentarily. I read the fake communication to James to make sure he understood what I wanted. He should try to convince Cornwallis that the note was authentic.

For several days I was anxious for his safety—and much relieved when he returned. Though he was unfamiliar with military dispatches, he assumed a note from New York would have been handled by numerous people, so James crumpled it up and put some dirt on it. He reported to Cornwallis that he had seen lots of men in the American camp in fresh uniform, counted over 2200 unsullied tents, and seen cannons and other artillery that appeared to have just arrived, as well as many fresh horses. He apologized for being delayed, but to avoid the main roadway he was forced by fatigue and hunger to spend one night sleeping beside the trail.

When he awoke at dawn to relieve himself, he spotted in the underbrush a piece of paper that would be useful for cleaning himself. Though he couldn't read it, the paper looked important, so he brought it along. Cornwallis uncrumpled it, scrutinized it carefully, thanked him for his diligence, and rewarded him with food from the officers' mess.

From Cornwallis' subsequent actions it appeared that James had been able to convince him that our army had been significantly reinforced, and his army had lost any chance to retreat up the Virginia peninsula without suffering major casualties.

I sent Washington an urgent plea for support:

Forks of York River, 21 August, 1781.

My Dear General,

From the enemy's preparations I should infer that they are working for the protection of a fleet. In the present state of affairs, my dear General, I hope you will come yourself to Virginia, and that, if the French army moves this way, I shall have, at least, the satisfaction of beholding you myself at the head of the combined armies.

The men we have here would not be equal to the task of a campaign upon so large a scale. Was I any ways equal to the enemy, I would be extremely happy in my present command—But Lord Cornwallis must be attacked with a pretty great apparatus. But when a French fleet takes possession of the Bay and rivers, and we form a land force superior to his, that army must, soon or late, be forced to surrender, as we may get what reinforcements we please.

Adieu, my dear General. I heartily thank you for having ordered me to remain in Virginia; and to your goodness to me I am owing the most beautiful prospect I may ever behold. With the most affectionate respect, I have the honor to be, my dear General,

Your Excellency's most obedient, humble servant,

—Lafayette.

Washington also received the long awaited reply from Admiral de Grasse. Rather than going to New York, he would sail to Chesapeake

Bay—but because of the risk of hurricanes, could only stay until October 14. He had twenty-four warships carrying 3200 soldiers. They should meet in Virginia near Chesapeake Bay to plan a major joint operation against the British. Washington urged me to keep Cornwallis at Yorktown. He and Rochambeau were on their way and I should arrange transport for their forces from Head of Elk by September 8.

Washington was concerned that when the British learned he was heading south, Clinton would send reinforcements to Cornwallis or a naval fleet to rescue him. So while the bulk of the armies were marching to Virginia, Washington ordered a few men to continuously burn hundreds of campfires along the shores of the Hudson to convince the British that their headquarters remained the target of his large military offensive.

When Washington neared Philadelphia, he had a message from de Grasse that the French fleet had already arrived at the mouth of the Chesapeake. Meanwhile the British fleet that had been blockading Admiral de Barras at Newport had sailed for the West Indies to search and destroy de Grasse's fleet in order to deflect the attack on New York. Besides diverting themselves pointlessly, since de Grasse was already with us, this permitted Barras' small fleet to sail out of Newport with armaments and siege equipment, ignoring the French Admiralty's orders to go to Newfoundland. Barras sailed a circular route to avoid engaging British ships trying to destroy his fleet.

It seemed to Washington that a major battle at sea was imminent. There was no point going further until he learned the outcome, given Britain's maritime dominance. He informed me that he would rest his troops and obtain necessary supplies in Chester, Pennsylvania while he went to Mount Vernon for the first time in six years to see Martha, bringing Rochambeau along.

Later I learned that the British Admiralty had sent their preeminent Admiral Sir George Rodney to the West Indies to find, engage, and destroy de Grasse's fleet. Rodney could not find them (even though de Grasse was still there) so he assumed that the French fleet had left for North America. He dispatched Rear Admiral Sir Samuel Hood to find de Grasse who finally left the West Indies on August 5, intentionally zigzagging his ships outside normal shipping lanes to avoid British warships. Hood left five days later, yet he arrived at Chesapeake Bay first, having sailed directly and in copper bottom ships that were faster. Hood searched for signs of the French fleet, but since they had not arrived yet, he jumped to the conclusion that de Grasse had already left for Europe—and he proceeded on to New York, where he learned that Barras' fleet had left Newport. Assuming that he was joining up with de Grasse, Clinton ordered Graves and Hood to join their fleets to find and destroy the French.

Meanwhile de Grasse's fleet of twenty-four ships arrived at the mouth of the Chesapeake, anchored in Lynnhaven Bay, and began disembarking 6500 French soldiers and sailors. Graves arrived September 5 to find the vulnerable French ships helplessly anchored, but assumed this was only the small fleet of Barras. Even though he could observe the French unloading artillery, knew the tide was incoming, and the winds against them—essentially the French were trapped—Graves was indecisive. Instead of swooping in and destroying the entire fleet, he did nothing.

When de Grasse saw enemy sails out at sea, though most of his troops were on land unloading weapons, artillery, food, and other supplies, he had to act immediately and ordered his anchor lines cut. With the out-going tide, his fleet sailed into the open ocean, leaving 90 perplexed officers and 1900 men behind. Seriously shorthanded, the French sailors could not even man all their guns, so de Grasse avoided immediate engagement with the British and sailed well beyond reach of their guns, and rearranged his ships.

After six hours of maneuvering, the British and the French fleets were finally arranged in two parallel lines. De Grasse had lined up his best and fastest ships with Grave's slowest and weakest. *HMS Intrepid* opened fire on the *Marseilles*. The battle lasted four days. De Grasse badly damaged five of the British ships and forced them to scuttle another. Graves returned to New York for repairs.

On September 13 de Grasse returned to the Chesapeake to discover that Barras had already arrived with seven ships. The vastness of the ocean and quirks of the human mind had created circumstances in our favor. By dint of circumstances and ungrounded assumptions the British navy was unable to rescue Cornwallis. Though not a single American participated in the battle, nor did it take place on American soil, the French victory had given us a unique opportunity to completely enclose Cornwallis.

The two French fleets with thirty-one ships sailed into the York River. They sent word to Washington that they now controlled the entrance to Chesapeake Bay and that the British army was completely surrounded. They assigned their smaller vessels to assist in the transport of 18,000 ground forces from Head of Elk to Yorktown. Washington and Rochambeau needed to arrive before Graves returned from New York with enough ships to rescue Cornwallis, whose only hope until then was to escape by land while he still outmanned me.

CHAPTER 13

The Siege at Yorktown

1778

WHILE READING REPORTS AND dispatches in my tent, I looked up to see a dust cloud approaching. Soon horses cantered towards my camp. I recognized Washington and Rochambeau, their aides and staff. I was overjoyed to see my friend with the general who had come because of my efforts at Versailles.

We set about catching up on both personal and military matters. The rest of the two armies were expected to start arriving within days. De Grasse had sent ships to Annapolis to transport most of the troops and lighter supplies and weapons down Chesapeake Bay to the Virginia peninsula. The heavier ox-drawn wagon trains and horse-mounted hussars were coming overland. Washington and Rochambeau had ridden ahead to meet with de Grasse, commander of both French fleets, to plan the siege. There was an intensity of impending resolution that gripped everyone, and animation about the most mundane matters.

We were impatient to proceed and excited that the outcome would impact the course of the war.

Immediately after our morning staff meeting I went out to de Grasse's flagship *Ville de Paris,* an impressive vessel with three decks and over a hundred cannons. I knew the Admiral only by reputation. When I was taken to his cabin, he greeted me with irritation that a Frenchman was wearing the blue and white uniform of an American colonial general instead of the red waistcoat and breeches of a French officer. I neither expressed surprise nor explained myself, but informed him that Washington had just arrived with General Rochambeau, and they wished the Admiral's company in Williamsburg to obtain his experience and wisdom in preparing for the siege against their common enemy.

De Grasse appeared flattered by my honest words, but declined to go to Williamsburg, nor leave his flagship, nor even set foot on American soil. But he would be delighted to meet with Washington and Rochambeau aboard his ship, which he considered French territory.

The next morning when we arrived at the landing, Washington was overjoyed to see so many cannon ports on a friendly ship commanded by an ally and colleague. Neatly dressed French sailors were waiting to row us out. The Admiral was on deck to personally welcome us aboard, dressed in a dark blue coat trimmed in gold lace over which he wore the broad bright red sash of the Order of Saint Louis to indicate his superior rank. He proudly insisted on showing us his vessel.

Washington estimated that all the troops would not arrive in Williamsburg for another ten days. Upon their arrival, he wanted to attack without delay, for there was no way to know when a British fleet might arrive to rescue Cornwallis. We spent the early part of the day reviewing the reports of scouts and spies about the defenses of the British encampment, the terrain, and the general logistics of Yorktown. De Grasse told us of the location and military capability of his fleets, so Washington and Rochambeau would avoid accidentally hitting friendly ships anchored in the harbor when firing upon the enemy.

De Grasse agreed to overstay his planned time in the Chesapeake, given the importance of the undertaking.

Neither Washington nor Rochambeau had been engaged in battle for almost two years. Their troops, after months marching in brutal heat, were also anxious to begin the siege. We met each day from dawn to lunch to review new intelligence and strategy, but afterwards Washington and I went riding together to enjoy our deepening friendship before facing cannon balls, musket shot, and perhaps even death.

On September 2 the first soldiers who had sailed from Annapolis appeared in camp. By September 27 the slowest and last of the armies finally arrived. We were ready to begin our attack. Washington was energized and animated as he took command of all three armies—mine, Rochambeau's, and his own—some eighteen thousand soldiers. He turned to me and grinned: "I tell you my friend—I think we have a fighting chance." He assembled his war council and gave orders for the following morning.

Just after dawn Washington mounted Old Nelson and gestured for the drummer to signal the commencement of the march. With Washington, Rochambeau, and myself at the head, we moved out of Williamsburg in a disciplined formation of two parallel columns, streaming towards the encampment of the British army.

Transporting heavy cannons and other siege equipment over uneven terrain littered with rocks, branches, and mud holes, we did not arrive near Yorktown until nightfall. Scouts sent ahead to reconnoiter the British defenses confirmed prior reports that Cornwallis had constructed a chain of ten small earthen redoubts linked by connecting trenches that encircled the town.

Still out of range of British guns, Washington ordered the armies to halt and find a place to sleep—out in the open on bare ground to avoid wasting time setting up and taking down shelters. With the town surrounded by sodden swamps, he dispatched teams to build bridges over the soft ground and others to hunt wild hogs for the troops' dinner.

Lying together on the damp ground, attacked only by mosquitoes, Washington asked if I was nervous. I indeed was, but welcomed the opportunity that had been presented to us. This was what I had trained for—a soldier like Vercingetorix to use his skill to help people win their freedom against foreign intruders. I wanted to make Adrienne, my children, our family and country proud of me and my family name. This was my chance. I knew we would prevail.

Early the next morning Washington organized the combined armies into four divisions for the siege. For the northwestern sector, Washington placed the French contingent, commanded by Rochambeau. On the southern sector he placed American troops divided into three divisions, of which I commanded the light infantry. As we advanced, the first sounds of musket fire cracked and the air around Yorktown began to fill with smoke. Bullets whined from all directions. I heard their impact. The screams of the wounded were an unrelenting refrain. We were committed.

The British outer defenses prevented us from moving closer. When we were 2500 feet back from them, Washington ordered the digging of a parallel trench. While we were waiting for the trench to be dug, my friend Alexander Hamilton rode into camp as an officer commanding a light infantry battalion from New York—what he had always wanted instead of being an aide-de-camp, however dependent Washington had been on him.

Our troops were still digging our parallel on October 5 when the soldiers manning the British outer defenses inexplicably fell back a half mile to the inner lines of fortifications. Gratified by our good fortune, Washington ordered soldiers to quit digging and move into the abandoned outer defenses and dig a new trench closer to town and the inner defenses—to be done at night so the British would not see what was going on. The soil was sandy, so the digging progressed rapidly. When the siege line just 1200 feet from the center of town was finished, we set the heavy siege artillery in place—close enough to fire directly on the town. Washington announced we would commence the next day, October 8. He appointed me General Officer of the Day, acting directly under him, responsible for camp security and order. It was a great honor.

I thought it appropriate to invite Thomas Nelson, commander in chief of the Virginia Militia, to be present at one of the batteries for the opening fire. He had succeeded Thomas Jefferson as governor, represented Virginia in the Continental Congress, signed the Declaration of Independence, and been born in Yorktown.

"To what particular spot would your Excellency ask that we point the cannon?" I asked.

"There, to that house. It is mine, the best one in town. There you will be almost certain to find Lord Cornwallis and the British headquarters. Fire upon it, my dear marquis, and never spare a particle of my property so long as it affords comfort or shelter to the enemies of my country." And he offered five guineas to the first man to hit his house.

At exactly 5:00 General Washington solemnly walked over to the largest cannon, asked for the igniter, and personally fired it. Immediately 52 other cannons commenced firing, which continued steadily for two days and two nights. Nowhere in town was out of range of our guns. Everyone in camp was forced underground. Some cannon balls even flew over town into the harbor, damaging British merchant ships trapped in the York River.

The next day we moved closer and started building a parallel only 900 feet from British defenses. However we could not complete the parallel and move our cannons into them until we had destroyed two redoubts close to the river on the east side of the town. This would enable us to fire artillery shells into the town from three directions.

Outside each redoubt there was a fifteen-foot impenetrable circle of tree branches with their sharpened tips directed outwards and held together by interlacing wires. Inside, a firing platform gave the men a tremendous advantage over attackers. It would be necessary to take them, but it would not be easy.

Washington honored me by assigning the task of taking the redoubt close to the river to my American light infantry corps. Rochambeau gave the task of taking the redoubt to the left of it to his second-in-command. Both Washington and Rochambeau prohibited their commanding officers from personally leading the attacks. Because there was a new moon, the night would be particularly dark. He decided we would suffer fewer casualties if we were able to surprise those in the redoubts, so he ordered the attacks to begin late at night. To avoid an accidental warning discharge, he ordered that muskets not be loaded.

I selected Alexander Hamilton to lead the attack on the left side of my redoubt, and Washington gave him a temporary promotion to colonel and 400 men—his opportunity to improve his station through glory on the battlefield. Hamilton eagerly took the dangerous task of leading the frontal bayonet attack and asked our friend, aide-de-camp John Laurens, to circle behind the redoubt to prevent those inside from escaping.

The troops were perfectly disciplined and quiet. We caught the British completely by surprise, and took the redoubt in a few minutes, sustaining just a few casualties. The French were equally successful, capturing their redoubt in half an hour. We were now able to complete the connection between the first and second parallels without risk. The cannons were moved into them, and we bombarded the British nonstop.

Rapidly running out of food, ammunition, supplies, and time, the British were desperate to escape. At midnight Cornwallis attempted to cross the river by ferrying his troops to Gloucester Point. The first wave of small, heavily loaded boats made it safely across the river. But a sudden squall made further attempts too risky.

The morning of October 17 at about ten o'clock, after almost three weeks of siege, a young drummer mounted the British battle works and began beating a long roll to announce the enemy's desire to talk. However we could not hear the boy because explosions were still raining down on the town. A lieutenant waving a white flag of surrender joined the drummer, but even the flag was barely visible through all the cannon smoke. Washington immediately ordered the bombardment to cease and sent one of our officers out to the lieutenant, who was blindfolded and led into Washington's tent. He tried his best to pull himself together and look Washington in the eye. "I have been instructed to tell you that Lord Cornwallis is ready to negotiate terms of surrender."

A meeting was arranged for the next day at the Moore House, a neutral and convenient location. Cornwallis sent two officers with the proposed terms of surrender. Washington sent John Laurens to represent the Americans, and my brother-in-law, Louis-Marie, vicomte de Noailles, to represent French interests.

With Laurens' strong support, I urged Washington to insist that Cornwallis agree to the same terms as General Lincoln when Clinton forced him to surrender at Charleston—to remind Cornwallis that Clinton had refused to grant Lincoln the customary honors of war. Washington agreed.

Washington prepared Articles of Capitulation, which Cornwallis had little choice but to sign. Washington, Rochambeau, and Barras signed for the allies. De Grasse had been invited to the signing but still refused to step upon American soil.

All of Cornwallis' officers were released on parole, and his troops were declared prisoners of war. Washington ordered the surrender ceremony set for the next afternoon. Aware of the importance of the French participation in the American success, he pleaded with de Grasse to share in every step of the capitulation process. However, de Grasse had received intelligence that Admiral Graves' fleet was approaching and might threaten the French ships so he declined.

At noon the French army, headed by Rochambeau, lined up on the left side of the road under the white flag of the Bourbon King of France. The American army lined up across from them and parallel, headed by George Washington, with a light blue ribbon across his chest and riding Blueskin, and his officers dressed smartly in blue coats, white garments, and red trim. Behind us the militia men proudly stood in their shabby jackets of coarse brown cloth.

I waited to see my adversary General Cornwallis at precisely two o'clock leading British soldiers and sailors and camp followers march out along the road. "The boy" wanted to remind him that it was the French who had trapped him at Yorktown, and French siege equipment and French troops that had captured him. I never had the chance. Cornwallis did not march out with his troops.

Instead of bravely facing his victors, Cornwallis sent his second-in-command, Brigadier General Charles O'Hara, to lead his troops. When O'Hara reached Washington he informed him that General Cornwallis was ill and could not attend the ceremony of surrender. Then O'Hara slowly walked his horse towards Rochambeau to present the sword. Rochambeau refused this discourteous defiance of practice, and pointed to Washington. O'Hara reluctantly went back to Washington, who stared at him and motioned toward General Benjamin Lincoln.

Led by O'Hara, the captives marched along Hampton Road a mile and a half between our two lines towards the field of surrender, their drums beating a British march, "The World Turned Upside Down." Every step they took toward laying down their arms was a humiliation.

After grounding their arms and divesting themselves of their accessories, the captives were conducted back to Yorktown to be counted and guarded by Hamilton's light infantry and a French regiment. Immediately after the surrender, Washington sent a rider to Philadelphia to report our success to Congress, which incited several days of celebration. He also sent a messenger to the *Ville de Paris* asking to meet with de Grasse on board his ship.

All the British officers—except Tarleton—were invited to a feast commemorating the resolution of the battle. The American officers had resolutely refused to eat with Tarleton, and Cornwallis did not attend, again claiming illness and sending O'Hara in his place. I had hoped that Admiral de Grasse would join us and share in the victory, but he declined. The next morning Rochambeau, Washington, Hamilton, and I went out to the flagship so that Washington could personally thank de Grasse and celebrate the victory with him.

When I returned to camp I wrote to Adrienne to share the victory:

The end of this campaign is truly brilliant for the allied troops. There was a rare coordination in our movements, and I would be finicky indeed if I were not pleased with the end of my campaign in Virginia. You must have been informed of all the toil the superiority and talents of Lord Cornwallis gave me and of the advantage that we then gained in recovering lost ground, until at length we had Lord Cornwallis in the position we needed in order to capture him. It was then that everyone pounced on him.

And to comte de Maurepas:

The play is over, Monsieur le Comte. The fifth act has just ended. I was a bit uneasy during the first acts, but my heart keenly enjoyed the last one.

The days immediately following the surrender were chaotic and exhausting. The battle was won, but the war was not over—the British still had more troops in America than the Continentals. And we had much to do before we could leave Yorktown.

But on Sunday, October 20 there were special services of worship and thanksgiving by the several brigade chaplains. Washington sent a message to me asking me to accompany him into Yorktown to participate in a Freemason ceremony at Masonic Lodge Number 9. I had been a Freemason for just a short time and had not participated in many ceremonies, but even during the war, Washington participated regularly. At least twelve of his generals were Freemasons, and he never willingly gave independent command to officers who were not Freemasons. Its rituals had provided the internal strength and fortitude for us, and he wanted to share a moment in the Masonic Lodge with me.

After we left the Lodge Washington began issuing a series of orders to tie up all the loose ends incurred in our victory. Within the battered garrison, the ill and wounded had died en masse for lack of medicine or food. We were sickened to find the place littered with amputated arms and legs eaten by rats and dogs, and men in every stage of smallpox. We had to march their wounded troops to a Convalescent Hospital in Fredericksburg, imprison their sound troops, and send their officers back to England on parole. Their artillery, muskets, horses, wagons, and transport ships had to be reassigned and transported, and arrangements made for the disposition of loyalists and blacks. Provisions of Article 10 of the Articles of Capitulation granted loyalists immunity, but Washington wanted to punish them—and they feared reprisal from angry colonists. Many attempted to flee by sneaking aboard merchant ships bound for New York, Savannah, or the West Indies, but Washington placed guards along the shore.

Washington also issued orders that any black who had helped the British would be returned to his owner. Those poor souls huddled fearfully in the woods—offering themselves as servants to French and American officers, or representing themselves as free men. No one knew the pre-battle status of the blacks who had served in the American army. Washington had to decide whether to free them, return them to their likely owners, or let them board British merchant ships which had been trapped in the York River by de Grasse's arrival, along with British officers.

I was concerned about James being swept up in the chaos, yet in the turmoil he slipped into the background and disappeared before I had a chance to thank him for his enormous contribution to our success. None of my fellow officers had seen him. At the harbor neither the guards, British officers, nor other blacks recognized James' description. I looked until I was drawn into dealing with the continuing complications of the surrender.

Washington, eager to attack British headquarters in Manhattan and needing naval support for Greene to reclaim Charleston, asked me to go out to the *Ville de Paris* to inquire whether Admiral de Grasse would be willing to remain in American waters to assist, or at least to transport me and American troops and supplies to Wilmington, North Carolina. But before the French fleet could leave, the repaired warships of Admiral Graves arrived back at Chesapeake Bay intending to rescue Cornwallis. Graves was dismayed to learn that Cornwallis' army had surrendered five days earlier. Graves was thwarted, but he could still threaten de Grasse and de Barras and prevent them from leaving the York River. He remained there until most of the British prisoners had been taken to prison camps, then he set sail for New York to inform his commander of the catastrophe.

Washington then released the merchant ships, and the French forces were re-embarked—along with two fine Virginia horses, a gift from Washington—for the West Indies, leaving the colonials without naval support. That same day Washington received word that his twenty-six-year-old step-son John Parke Custis, Martha's last remaining child and one of his civilian aides-de-camp, had died of malaria. Concerned about the impact of Jackie's death on Martha, he dropped everything and rode with his wife up to her sister's house in Eltham where Jackie had died.

Washington had intended to return to New York to prevent the British from crossing the Hudson in search of food and supplies, and to continue preparations for his attack on them. He was hoping that the colossal success at Yorktown would convince the king of France that the colonists might finally drive the British out of North America—and perhaps enable the French to regain Canada, or force the British to negotiate an end of their ongoing war that was draining everyone's treasury. He asked me to return to France and beg the king to send another naval fleet and additional aid.

I was eager to help my wise friend, but our impending separation hung over us like an unpleasant specter, present but unspoken. We parted sorrowfully, promising each other to write frequently, with assurance that we would be together soon. With Washington's encouragement, permission, and blessings I left Yorktown for Philadelphia.

I appeared once again before Congress to ask permission for a leave of absence. Congress treated me like a hero, promptly granting permission and adding their own letter requesting more ships. The speaker told me that even though peace negotiations between America and Britain had been going on since the beginning of the war, after Yorktown the process had been intensified, and the Americans believed they finally had some leverage.

I managed to secure passage on the French warship *Alliance*, which was stopping first in Boston, allowing me time to write:

Alliance, off Boston, 21 December, 1781.

My dear General,

The moment I arrive in France, I will write to you minutely how things stand, and give you the best accounts in my power.

I have received every mark of affection in Boston, and am much attached to this town, to which I owe so many obligations but, from public considerations, I have been impatient to leave it and go on board the frigate, where I receive all possible civilities, but where I had rather be under sail than at anchor.

I beg your pardon, my dear General, for giving you so much trouble in reading my scrawls; but we are going to sail, and my last adieu I must dedicate to my beloved General.

Adieu, my dear General. I know your heart so well, that I am sure that no distance can alter your attachment to me. With the same candor, I assure you that my love, my respect, my gratitude for you, are above expression; that, at the moment of leaving you, I felt more than ever the strength of those friendly ties that forever bind me to you, and that I anticipate the pleasure, the most wished-for pleasure, to be again with you, and, by my zeal and services, to gratify the feelings of my respect and affection. Will you be pleased to present my compliments and respects to Mrs. Washington, and to remember me to General Knox and General Lincoln.

Adieu, my dear General.

Your respectful and tender friend,

—Lafayette.

The *Alliance* sailed out of Boston on Christmas Eve. I was still euphoric over our success at Yorktown, and the role France had played in securing our victory. Without Rochambeau, de Grasse, Barras, and all the thousands of other French soldiers and sailors, it is unlikely that the colonists would have been able to achieve their success. During my voyage I had ample time to plan my strategy for obtaining another navy from the king which, I hoped, would force the British to grant independence to their colony.

America had had a great impact on me and the other French officers and troops who lived there for several years. And it was to have a significant economic and political impact on France.

CHAPTER 14

Return to Paris

1782

THE *Alliance* SAILED INTO L'ORIENT four weeks later. I was impatient to complete the overland part of my journey, looking forward to a fireplace, a heated bath, and the comforts of a cozy warm bed that did not swing throughout the night, but mostly looking forward to seeing Adrienne and our family.

When the servant opened the front door, he informed me that Adrienne was not at home. Along with most of the nobility of Paris she had, at the personal invitation of the queen, gone to the Hôtel de Ville, Paris city hall, to celebrate the birth of the dauphin, heir to the French throne. Under other circumstances, I would have loved to join the celebration, but I was much too tired to travel a step further, to say nothing of being unpresentable, so I dispatched a servant to tell Adrienne that I had arrived home safely.

Adrienne told me later that when the servant arrived, a royal guard insisted on knowing the purpose of his visit and, when informed, took him directly to Marie Antoinette. The queen theatrically stopped the celebration and announced that she had just received news that required her urgent departure. In a stern voice she ordered Adrienne to go immediately to the royal carriage. Adrienne naturally followed the queen into the royal carriage, which drove off at great speed followed by a caravan of curious, festive nobility. She was bewildered that the carriage was stopping in front of her home, and even more mystified when the queen stepped out of the carriage and melodramatically ordered Adrienne to remain seated.

The queen rushed passed our servant and began looking about, impatiently calling for me. She greeted me enthusiastically, congratulating me on bringing glory to France in the defeat at Yorktown, and announcing breathlessly that to honor my heroics she had brought me a priceless gift worthy of my deeds. She motioned me imperiously to follow her. She opened her carriage and exaggerated a super-royal-command to the passenger. Stepping out of the coach and seeing me, Adrienne was so stunned that she fainted. The queen was royally pleased by her own performance and the enchanting result—though I was concerned that Adrienne was ailing. I rushed to hold her, and was rewarded by her quick recovery. Her eyes teared up and she grasped my neck, to the applause of the queen and the partiers. Marie Antoinette motioned for Adrienne and me to enter our home, away from the gaze of hundreds of curious eyes, and we obeyed.

When the front door was shut, still laughing at the queen's mischievousness, we fell into a long hug. That first kiss was worth enduring an ocean crossing. I had missed her more than I realized. We had been apart for five of the seven years of our marriage, and I had probably slept next to George Washington more than my wife. While I was off for the cause of others, my young wife had been consigned to my mental and emotional background.

I wanted to be alone with her, but the king and queen had requested that I join them the following afternoon at Versailles to permit Louis to publicly bestow his beneficent recognition, gratitude, and appreciation upon me in front of his justly grateful noble courtiers.

We appeared before the king with Anastasie and George, dressed for the royal ceremony: I in the uniform of an American general—the blue jacket with scarlet facings and golden yellow buttons, and Adrienne in a lovely blue linen dress. In the Hall of Mirrors, which was filled with the royal family, ministers, noblemen, and hundreds of servants, the king was waiting eagerly to greet me, his dearest brother and colleague; and their royal subjects were waiting to pay tribute to me and to honor my family. The king made an ostentatious display of promoting me to *maréchal de camp*—I had been promoted to major general at age twenty-four and grandly titled the "Conqueror of Cornwallis."

Immediately after the ceremony, the queen invited everyone to a banquet in my honor. I was flattered that the king was using the revenue of the state to honor me, but after four years of austerity, undernourishment, struggle, and sacrifice, I found it profligate.

During the party, I approached the king and asked to speak with him privately. He led me to a quiet room where I thanked him for honoring me and for the magnificent state reception. I told him that I had been sent by the American Congress on a matter of great urgency and asked to personally deliver an important letter to him at the earliest opportunity. Congress was requesting additional naval support.

I learned from him that American, British, French, Spanish, and Dutch diplomats had been negotiating the terms of a peace agreement in the backrooms at Versailles for some time. But news of the defeat at Yorktown broke the political will of Britain to continue fighting. London papers reported that the royalist Prime Minister Lord North exclaimed, "Oh god, it's all over." In late February, the House of Common's no confidence vote led to Lord North's resignation. In April they voted to end the war in America, and peace negotiations with the colonists began. Washington would no longer need French warships. Slowly the ramifications of my participation, particularly at Yorktown, dawned on me, reinforcing my commitment to play my part on the world stage.

I had indeed played a part, but it was not all me of course. Part of the reason for Britain conceding to America was that they were still at war with France and Spain and wanted to use their limited resources in areas that were more valuable to them, especially with French forces capturing small British islands in the West Indies and their Mediterranean base on Minorca. Congress had selected John Adams, Ben Franklin, and John Jay as their peace negotiators, but Adams was in the Dutch Republic securing recognition for the new nation, as well as a much-needed loan. Success was achieved on April 19 when the Dutch became the first country to officially recognize the United States of America, but he was not able to help Franklin negotiate in Paris with the British until early May.

Jay had been appointed Minister to Spain with a parallel mission, but the royal court of Spain refused to receive him, fearing that recognition could spark revolution in Spain's colonies in the Americas. However Jay was able to secure a loan before arriving in Paris on June 23.

Congress had instructed the three delegates to insist only on the independence of the United States, deferring in all other matters to the French. The American delegates met with the British negotiator in private, and the British were able to convince Adams and Jay that Britain was no longer their enemy, but that France was America's main threat, despite their financial and military support during the war for independence.

Since I knew both Adams and Jay, I thought I might be able to help convince them that France was indeed their ally. I agreed to join the peace negotiations as my first attempt at diplomacy, in part to support my friend Franklin.

I quickly learned the extent of my naivety and ignorance, as they led me to believe that I was being taken seriously while the real negotiations were taking place behind closed doors—between the Americans and the British—without France, because its alliance with Spain prevented a peace accord without Spanish agreement and King Carlos refused to consider the matter until Spain had won Gibraltar, a conflict that showed no sign of resolution.

Though still involved in peace negotiations on September 6, I took the day off to be with Adrienne to celebrate my twenty-fifth birthday—

a very special one for us, for I had reached the legal age of majority, enabling me to enter into contracts on my own. Eleven days later, there was another celebration when Adrienne delivered the loveliest present of all, though more harrowing and disconcerting than many a battle: having me present during the delivery of Marie Antoinette Virginie du Motier, named in honor of the queen who had helped me get to America and for the American colony where I procured my celebrity.

With our addition and lack of privacy, within a few months it became apparent that it was time to have our own home. With my public recognition, people were seeking my attention, and as a negotiator I needed to entertain ministers and government officials, officers and soldiers returning from America, and Americans visiting or living in Paris. I had been billeted with Adrienne's family at the Hôtel de Noailles for almost ten years, and though I was treated like a son, I was nonetheless only a guest. I felt intrusive bringing home friends and associates or entertaining large groups.

It took nearly a year for us to find the well-located spacious house at 183, rue de Bourbon near the Luxembourg Gardens, just across the Seine from the Hôtel de Noailles. Although the building needed extensive repairs, we decided to purchase it, and I proudly entered into my first written contract.

Adrienne and I began working closely, exchanging ideas regarding the work that needed to be done to rehabilitate and modernize the building. Her input was practical, constructive, and very creative, which helped me develop an appreciation of Adrienne's resourcefulness and business skills that I had not previously observed. When at last all the work was done, we were very proud.

CHAPTER 15

Diplomatic Mission to Spain

1782

THOUGH **BRITISH AND AMERICANS** had signed only preliminary peace articles, by the end of November there was pressure
to re-establish commercial trade, for both countries were facing economic collapse.

However the talks between Britain and France were not going well,
and Britain did not seem motivated. The king and Vergennes sent
me to Madrid to persuade Louis' cousin Carlos III to participate in
joint attacks on the British on several possible fronts—Charleston,
New York, Canada, the West Indies, Gibraltar, even invading England
itself—hoping to push the British to end the global war.

During the Seven Years War both Bourbon lines had entered a family compact to fight the British. Carlos had supported Louis from the
beginning, secretly participating in the fictitious *Roderique Hortalez
& Co* to fund the revolutionaries and smuggle weapons through their
ports of New Orleans and Havana. Carlos had expected his cousin

to replace the British as colonial rulers. Because Spain's economy depended almost entirely on its colonial empire in the Americas, Carlos did not want to encourage revolt by subjects of another colonial empire—though he sent money directly to Rochambeau to purchase critical supplies for the siege at Yorktown.

I left immediately for Brest to catch a ship bound for Cádiz. I reported to Washington that I had asked Vergennes for more naval support, and updated him on the peace negotiations. Since he was retired at Mount Vernon, I asked him to contact his many friends in the Virginia state legislature and to find out whether James had been freed—and if not, why not. I side-stepped telling him why I was in Spain, but I asked him to join Adrienne and me in a bold venture:

> Now, my dear General, that you are going to enjoy some ease and quiet permit me to propose a plan to you, which might become greatly beneficial to the Black Part of Mankind. Let us unite in purchasing a small estate where we may try the experiment to free the Negroes, and use them only as tenants, such an example as yours might render it a general practice. And if we succeed in America, I will cheerfully devote a part of my time to render the method fashionable in the West Indies. If it be a mad scheme, I had rather be mad that way, than to be thought wise on the other track.

I left Cádiz for Madrid and was escorted into Carlos' presence wearing my American General's uniform and ceremonial sword. The king welcomed me as a conquering hero and representative of the Bourbon royal dynasty. Carlos enthusiastically agreed with my mission. Encouraged by my quick success, I urged the king to recognize American independence and fix formal boundaries between the United States and the Spanish territories in Florida and along the Mississippi. Carlos reluctantly agreed to acknowledge the independence of the British colonies, and would look into fixing the boundaries. But he was adamant that he would not establish diplomatic relations with the rebellious colonials.

On my return to Versailles at the end of May, I found the answer to my letter from Cádiz:

> *The scheme which you propose as a precedent to encourage the emancipation of the black people of this Country from that state of Bondage in which they are held is a striking evidence of the benevolence of your Heart. I shall be happy to join you in so laudable a work; but will defer going into a detail of the business, 'till I have the pleasure of seeing you.*
>
> *I need not add how happy I shall be to see you in America, and more particularly at Mount Vernon; or with what truth and warmth of Affection I am etc.*

With news of my success in Spain, Vergennes and the king began assembling at Cádiz sixty French and Spanish warships and transports that could carry 25,000 troops to invade England. Vergennes named Admiral d'Estaing commander in chief of the armada, and d'Estaing named me as his second in command and commander in chief of all land forces. I was thrilled that my tactical skill was being acknowledged and put to use. I began gathering intelligence and planning strategy to invade in January. D'Estaing told me that he had proposed to King Carlos that, with defeat of the British in the West Indies, I be appointed provisional governor. The king rejected his suggestion, fearful I would "turn the place into a republic." I had to smile at the compliment.

Though the invasion was highly secret, the British became aware of ships assembling in the Channel, and on January 20 they signed preliminary treaties with France and Spain to end hostilities and begin work on a final treaty.

On September 3 a final peace treaty was signed at Versailles between Britain and France. On the same day a final peace treaty was signed in Paris between Britain and America.

The signing of the two treaties and news of world peace were causes of joyous celebrations and festivities around the globe. Louis XVI declared an official French holiday, the Festival of Peace. The aristocracy celebrated by throwing masked balls, extravagant dinners, and gala soirées at the theater, opera, and ballet. The first amazing lighter-than-air balloons were sent soaring over Paris. Louis offered free food and wine in public squares, and massive bonfires were lit at city hall. Dr. Franz Mesmer came from Vienna to take part in the celebration and demonstrate his theory of "animal magnetism" to cure the sick with trance states. I took this unique opportunity to have him cure my persistent seasickness. Marie Antoinette invited Dr. Mesmer to Versailles frequently to perform for her, but the king had his doubts and appointed a commission of renown Parisian scientists to investigate, including chemist Antoine Lavoisier, the doctor Joseph-Ignace Guillotin (who had recently invented a more humane form of execution), astronomer Jean Sylvain Bailly, and the eclectic Benjamin Franklin.

On November 25 the last British troops evacuated New York, taking with them more than 29,000 loyalist refugees and former slaves they had liberated. In one last act of defiance they left British flags flying from tall flag poles, greased the poles, and cut the ropes. One of the departing British ships passing Staten Island fired a last cannon at the jeering crowd.

Before the British fleet had sailed out of sight, American ingenuity had replaced that flag with the Stars and Stripes. And on the seventh anniversary of his retreat from Manhattan, Washington marched his army down Broadway to the Battery. I wished I could have ridden beside him.

A week later General Washington formally said farewell to his officers at Fraunces Tavern and left the city for Annapolis, where he addressed the Continental Congress on December 23 to resign his commission as commander in chief, saying:

> Having now finished the work assigned me, I retire from the great theatre of Action—and bidding an Affectionate farewell to this August body under whose orders I have so long acted,

I here offer my Commission, and take my leave of all the employments of public life.

When I heard the news of his resignation, I was mystified—as it was extraordinary. Soldiers aspired to the honor of leading men for the glory of their country. My ambition had always been to command an army and win the respect and regard of leadership. His voluntary resignation as head of the new country's army caused his former foe George III to describe him as "the greatest character of his age."

Washington and the colonists' struggle against the enemy of France had been epic and inspiring. French officers and soldiers returning from years in America told stories of equality and liberty to their wives, family, and friends—commoners owned their own farms; were permitted to have guns and allowed to shoot deer (and their British oppressors); all men (except blacks and Indians) were treated equally, with no deference paid to aristocracy; commoners even had a say in deciding on their own taxes and laws. Their American experience began to filter through French society, and American-style *égalité* and *liberté* became fashionable.

Parisians were suddenly enamored with everything American, wearing simpler, less formal American dress. American businessmen, expatriates, and tourists descended upon Paris. The Hôtel de Lafayette became a destination for people looking for work, information, or simply to meet the Frenchman who was a hero of the American Revolution. Our new house quickly became a gathering place for my American friends in Paris—Ben Franklin, Mr. and Mrs. John Jay, Mr. and Mrs. John Adams, Gouverneur Morris—as well as our French friends and members of the liberal nobility. Frenchmen who had previously read the Declaration of Independence with amusement now looked at it again—the successful liberation from the yoke of a king was an empowering concept, filling people throughout the world with hope. Paris was abuzz, and papers and salons spread the dream.

Adrienne established our own Monday night salon. It was she who determined the guests invited to these dinners, what would be served, and what topics would be discussed. She moderated the flow of the conversation and tempered disputes that grew intense. Those invited to our salon were knowledgeable and articulate people. I was pleasantly surprised that my wife could hold her own on almost any topic—more so than I, for I had rarely been able to read a book during the war, and was not as current on events in France. Adrienne knew more about economics and business, of which I had little interest before I saw the relationship between soldiering and commerce. Both America and France had to pay for the costs of war, and the new country's insolvency particularly impacted France which had lent the colonists a great deal of money and sold them most of their weapons and supplies on credit. France was nearly bankrupted between two lengthy wars and the cost of maintaining an aristocracy.

Many of the people attending our salons were bilingual, and we switched between French and English with the needs of our guests. Adrienne's English, non-existent before I left for America, improved with each salon, and each new topic expanded her vocabulary. The salons made me realize that I did not know the depths of my wife.

Though now independent, America continued operating as thirteen separate colonies functioning under the antiquated Articles of Confederation—with no elected leader, nor judiciary, nor authority to collect taxes. Congress was insolvent and inflation was skyrocketing. The new country was vulnerable to being dominated by ambitious, more powerful countries.

The British Navy had destroyed most American merchant ships, which had crippled the flow of trade. The British restricted American exports to both Britain and their sugar colonies in the Caribbean. Unpaid soldiers were threatening to march on Congress. Washington informed me that they discussed physically forcing Congress to pay what had been promised—and even overthrowing Congress. Aware that an insurrection might stop democracy before it started, Washington showed up at a gathering of dissident senior officers in Newburgh, New York unexpectedly and asked the most senior, Major General Horatio Gates, for permission to speak. Gates respectfully relinquished the floor to his commander in chief, but other officers were angry and disrespectful. Washington took out a letter from a member of Congress explaining the financial difficulties of the government.

After reading a few paragraphs of small writing, he reached into his coat pocket and said, "Gentlemen, you will permit me to put on my spectacles, for I have not only grown gray but almost blind in the service of my country."

In that moment of utter vulnerability, Washington's men were moved to tears, seeing the man who had led them through so much with sympathy and affection. Washington left the room and his officers voted unanimously to agree to civilian rule. Washington had effectively prevented a coup d'état.

With other threats to the institutions of national government, Congress decided to create a federal district, distinct from the states, where Congress could provide for its own security.

Shortly after the new year, I received a letter from Mount Vernon:

At length my Dear Marquis:

I am become a private citizen on the banks of the Potomac, and under the shadow of my own Vine and my own Fig-tree, free from the bustle of a camp and the busy scenes of public life, I am solacing myself with those tranquil enjoyments, of which the Soldier who is ever in pursuit of fame, the Statesman whose watchful days and sleepless nights are spent in devising schemes to promote the welfare of his own, perhaps the ruin of other countries, as if this globe was insufficient for us all, and the Courtier who is always watching the countenance of his Prince, in hopes of catching a gracious smile, can have very little conception.

I am not only retired from all public employments, but I am retiring within myself; and shall be able to view the solitary walk, and tread the paths of private life with heartfelt satisfaction. Envious of none, I am determined to be pleased with all; and this my dear friend, being the order for my march, I will move gently down the stream of life, until I sleep with my Fathers.

I thank you most sincerely My Dear Marqs. for your kind invitation to your house, if I should come to Paris. At present I see but little prospect of such a voyage, the deranged situation of my private concerns, occasioned by an absence of almost nine years, and an entire disregard of all private business during that period, will not only suspend, but may put it for ever out of my power to gratify this wish. This not being the case with you, come with Madame la Fayette and view me in my domestic walks. I have often told you, and repeat it again, that no man could receive you in them with more friendship and affection than I should do; in which I am sure Mrs. Washington would cordially join me. We unite in respectful compliments to your Lady, and best wishes for your little flock. With every sentiment of esteem, Admiration and Love, I am etc.

I was honored to receive his invitation for Adrienne and me to visit him at Mount Vernon. I was hoping that Adrienne would join me, as I thought that she would enjoy meeting Martha and George, vacationing at the plantation at Mount Vernon, taste the vitality of America's breadbasket, visit people and places that had been part of my life. But she was worried about the dangers of a sea crossing on the health and safety of our children. However, she encouraged me to go and enjoy my reunion. I accepted Washington's invitation.

While I was busy making arrangements, Adrienne embroidered a Masonic apron for Washington. I was amazed by her creative skills and the craftsmanship of the apron—another aspect of my wife that I had not previously been aware of.

CHAPTER 16

Mount Vernon

1784

I SPENT THE ENTIRE MONTH of July on the royal frigate *La Nymphe* from L'Orient, excited to arrive in New York, the former British stronghold. I was welcomed by a large celebration, and received by the State Assembly.

In Philadelphia the First Troop Philadelphia City Cavalry, which had fought with me at Brandywine, escorted me triumphantly into the city where I was greeted by cheering crowds. 'Mad' Anthony Wayne and others who served with me during the Yorktown campaign held a reunion banquet that evening.

More honors in Baltimore, then I took a small ship down the Atlantic coast and up the Potomac River to Alexandria where I hired a carriage for the eight miles to Mount Vernon.

The two and a half story white wood house was first visible as a red roof with an octagonal cupola and weather vane topped by a gilded dove bearing an olive branch. The carriage entered a circular road surrounding a large bowling green. George and Martha greeted me enthusiastically along with Martha's four doted-upon grandchildren that had been left in their custody after the death of Martha's son John Parke Custis. The general looked healthy and serene, and I was thrilled to see him with an uncommon smile lighting his familiar stoic face. I had never seen him dressed so informally—appropriate for the humid tidewater summer. At fifty his hair had thinned and turned gray, and his face was etched handsomely.

We sat on the front porch and watched the Potomac River flow by. A domestic slave brought cold apple cider and the children ran around on the lawn. We had never experienced such tranquility in our four years together fighting the British. I took from my valise the present that Adrienne had made for him—the French silk apron decorated with Masonic symbols. He was touched by the gift and admired her talent.

The next morning we walked to the outer buildings—the smoke house, blacksmith shop, distillery, grist mill, dung depository, and the houses for slave families where they wove and worked. Then we rode across his 500 acres of gardens, orchards, greenhouses, and croplands. Farming was his passion and his main source of income. He had greatly reduced the acreage of tobacco to adopt a seven-year rotation focusing on wheat as the principal cash crop, corn for domestic use, and legumes to rejuvenate the soil. He took great interest in improving fertilizers and breeding better wheat, corn, oats, and rye, as well as horses, mules, sheep, cows, and pigs.

I was enjoying our ride immensely until we rode through the fields with bent over slaves, bare backs glistening with sweat in the harsh sun. The sight of this inhumanity made me uneasy and I was glad when we stopped for lunch at a scenic spot overlooking the Potomac. It was good to catch up on those who served with us and the unfolding political drama of the young nation, and its inspiration for Europeans.

The next morning George was called to some unanticipated business matters on the other side of the mountains near the Ohio River, so we rode up to Alexandria where Washington turned west and I continuing north to Baltimore. At a reception I happened to meet James Madison, Jr. He was going to New York and suggested that we ride up there together. I learned that he was the son of a slaveholding Virginian tobacco farmer, had served in the Virginia state legislature, and was a close friend of Governor Jefferson.

In New York I received more honors, was proclaimed a citizen of their state, and asked to travel upstate to help commissioners who were negotiating a treaty with the Six Nations of Native Americans. They thought that a friendly Frenchmen might be of some help to the commissioners since many Indians remembered the French fondly, especially those who had served with me at Barren Hill. Madison volunteered to go with me to meet with the commissioners. I thought my appearance among the Six Nations might be appreciated more if I brought several casks of brandy and some French coins to create an advantageous climate for the negotiations. Indeed, the Indians agreed to sign the treaty, and the commissioners were very happy. One of the tribesmen asked me to take Peter Otisquette, a boy who was half French, back with me, and he accompanied me for the rest of my stay in America.

Madison and I traveled on toward Boston. When we neared Watertown, about seven miles outside the city, we were met by officers of the Continental Army with drums and fifes, a full military band, and citizens in carriages who escorted me to my hotel where I was greeted with a thirteen gun salute and a salvo from a French fleet anchored in the harbor. Besides parades, dinners, and dances, I was granted the honorary Doctor of Laws from Harvard University.

The governor and president of the state senate, speaker of the house, and members of the two houses held a joint meeting on October 19, the anniversary of the capture of Cornwallis, followed by a party for 500 with dinner and thirteen patriotic toasts, including one to "The firm Asserters of Liberty in every part of the Globe," of which I believe I was one. At the dinner, they showed me a large oil painting of George Washington encircled with laurel branches and flags of America and France. I shouted "Long live Washington," and the entire room responded enthusiastically.

Madison and I parted company and I boarded *La Nymphe* for Yorktown, then proceeded by horseback to Williamsburg and Richmond, where I had arranged to meet Washington. While waiting for him, I was asked to address the Virginia House of Delegates and took the opportunity to find information about James. From Washington's inquiries I learned that the delegates had not freed James. He was still a slave.

I was angry that the delegates were compelling James to grovel for his freedom. Either they had no idea what this man had done for his country or they did not care—solely because he was black. All the influential politicians in Virginia were slaveholders, so when the delegates permitted me to address them, I fought to control my anger and speak diplomatically, urging them to pass legislation emancipating all their slaves and live up to the beautiful words in Jefferson's Declaration of Independence. I was neither hopeful nor successful. I wrote a letter to the delegates, most of whom appreciated my efforts in protecting their colony, hoping to motivate them to free the one man I knew who had risked his life for their freedom:

> *This is to certify that the bearer by the name of James has done essential services for me while I had the honor to command in this state. His intelligence from the enemy's camp were industriously collected and faithfully delivered. He perfectly acquitted himself with some important commissions I gave him and appears to me entitled to every reward his situation can admit of.*
>
> *Done under my hand, Richmond, November 21st, 1784*
>
> *—Lafayette*

While waiting for Washington I went to see Thomas Jefferson's children who he had left with his sister-in-law at a nearby plantation.

I learned that Jefferson's youngest child had died and they gave me a letter to deliver to him when I returned to Paris.

Washington finally arrived in Richmond and we returned to Mount Vernon together. An officer came to Mount Vernon with John Edward Caldwell, the fourteen-year-old orphaned son of a Continental Army chaplain who had been killed during the war, and asked me to take him back to France to complete his education.

When it came time for me to return to France, Washington insisted on traveling with me as far as Marlboro, Maryland where on December 1 we bid our farewells. George gave me a packet of letters to take back to France, including one to Adrienne. We were extremely emotional, knowing that it was unlikely we would see one another again.

From Annapolis I caught a ship to Trenton, where Congress was sitting. I had been asked to appear before them so that Secretary of War Henry Knox could present me with one of the standards surrendered by Cornwallis at Yorktown. In my address to Congress I said, "May this immense temple of freedom ever stand a lesson to oppressors, an example to the oppressed, a sanctuary for the rights of mankind."

La Nymphe arrived in New York harbor on December 20, two weeks before the city would become the capital of the United States and new home of Congress. Amidst the celebration of this historic event, my arrival was greeted with fanfare. New York Governor George Clinton (no relation to Henry Clinton) organized a grand farewell attended by numerous of my friends and comrades.

I had last seen Nathanael Greene just before Washington sent him to the Carolinas, where he fought until the British withdrew in August 1783. The states of North Carolina, South Carolina, and Georgia had each voted him large grants of land for his service, but he was forced to sell much of it to pay off debts he incurred during the war. He asked me to take his eldest son, George Washington Greene, back to France to pursue his education. I was bringing home a fine entourage of young American men, and was proud to be given responsibility for seeing them grow into responsible worldly men.

Alexander Hamilton had promptly left the surrender ceremonies at Yorktown to rejoin his wife in Albany for the birth of their first child. In May he had begun studying law in Albany, and before winter completed the three year curriculum and was admitted to the New York bar. He had written to me:

I have been employed for the last ten months in rocking the cradle and studying the art of fleecing my neighbors. I am now a Grave Counselor at law, and shall soon be a grand member of Congress. The Legislature at their last session took it into their heads to name me pretty unanimously one of their delegates.

He was presently defending loyalists and British subjects, whom the Americans had agreed not to prosecute for their support of the British. He also believed that New York's anti-loyalist laws were a flagrant violation of the Treaty of Paris, and continuing enforcement might precipitate a reaction by England. He said:

> The world has its eye upon America. The noble struggle we have made in the cause of liberty, has occasioned a kind of revolution in human sentiment. The influence of our example has penetrated the gloomy regions of despotism. If the consequences prove that we really have asserted the cause of human happiness, what may not be expected from so illustrious an example? In a greater or less degree, the world will bless and imitate!

I left for France curious what impact our struggle in America might have in Europe and the rest of the world.

My friends escorted me out to *La Nymphe* on a specially decorated barge. As I boarded, Hamilton handed me a letter that the general had written on December 8, upon his return to Mount Vernon:

> *My Dr. Marqs:*
>
> *The peregrination of the day in which I parted with you, ended at Marlbro': the next day, bad as it was, I got home*

before dinner. In the moment of our separation upon the road as I travelled, and every hour since, I felt all that love, respect and attachment for you, with which length of years, close connexion and your merits have inspired me. I often asked myself, as our carriages distended, whether that was the last sight I ever should have of you? And tho' I wished to say no, my fears answered yes. I called to mind the days of my youth, and found they had long since fled to return no more; that I was now descending the hill, I had been 52 years climbing, and that tho' I was blessed with a good constitution, I was of a short lived family, and might soon expect to be entombed in the dreary mansions of my fathers. These things darkened the shades and gave a gloom to the picture, consequently to my prospects of seeing you again: but I will not repine, I have had my day. It is unnecessary, I persuade myself to repeat to you my Dr. Marqs. the sincerity of my regards and friendship, nor have I words which could express my affection for you, were I to attempt it. My fervent prayers are offered for your safe and pleasant passage, happy meeting with Madame la Fayette and family, and the completion of every wish of your heart, in all which Mrs. Washington joins me. With every sentiment which is propitious and endearing, I am, etc.

The next day *La Nymphe* put out to sea, but ran aground. During our brief delay, I had an opportunity to respond immediately to Washington's letter and send it from New York harbor:

21 December, 1784

My dear General,

I have received your affectionate letter of the 8th and from the known sentiments of my heart to you, you will easily guess what my feelings have been in perusing the tender expressions of your friendship. No, my beloved General, our late parting was not by any means a last interview. My whole soul revolts at the idea; and could I harbor it an instant, indeed, my dear

General, it would make me miserable. I well see you never will go to France. The inexpressible pleasure of embracing you in my own house, of welcoming you in a family where your name is adored, I do not much expect to experience; but to you I shall return, and, within the walls of Mount Vernon, we shall yet often speak of old times. My firm plan is to visit now and then my friend on this side of the Atlantic; and the most beloved of all friends I ever had, or ever shall have anywhere, is too strong an inducement for me to return to him, not to think that whenever it is possible I shall renew my so pleasing visits to Mount Vernon. Adieu, adieu, my dear General. It is with inexpressible pain that I feel I am going to be severed from you by the Atlantic. Everything that admiration, respect, gratitude, friendship, and filial love can inspire is combined in my affectionate heart to devote me most tenderly to you. In your friendship I find a delight which words cannot express. Adieu, my dear General. It is not without emotion that I write this word, although I know I shall soon visit you again. Be attentive to your health. Let me hear from you every month. Adieu, adieu.

—Lafayette.

La Nymphe sailed for France on December 23, and once again I was separated from my friends and the country I had grown to love.

PART III

France

1785

CHAPTER 17

A Rash of Problems

1785

I ARRIVED IN BREST IN the new year bringing John Edward Caldwell, George Washington Greene, Peter Otisquette, and a sorrowful letter I had been asked to personally deliver to Thomas Jefferson who had left for Paris while I was on my way to America, as minister plenipotentiary to France, succeeding Franklin. As I was unable to host him in Paris, I had written to offer the hospitality of my home:

> *My House, Dear Sir, my family, and anything that is mine are entirely at your disposal and I beg you will come and see Mde. de Lafayette as you would act by your brother's wife. Her knowledge of the country may be of some use to Miss Jefferson whom she will be happy to attend in everything that may be agreeable to her. Indeed, my dear Sir, I would be very angry*

with you, if either you or she, did not consider my house as a second home.

Jefferson had arrived in Paris with his personal secretary, William Short, and James Hemings, his nineteen-year-old slave, to be instructed in the art of French cuisine. Because I was not there, he found a villa complete with stables and an extensive garden close to the Hôtel de Lafayette. Because the Catholic Church ran all schools, he was forced to place his daughter Patsy in a convent school, the Abbaye Panthemont, the most select school for girls in Paris. Jefferson was concerned that the nuns would attempt to convert her, but the Abbess assured him, saying there were a number of Protestant girls from England among the fifty students. However he regularly stayed in touch with his daughter to make sure there were no problems.

After seeing my family, I delivered the letter entrusted to my care. I had not met him during the war, although we had communicated by military dispatch about raising the state's militia. He made little effort even for a defensive force, as he was opposed to standing armies. Despite his lack of support, with 1200 militiamen from New England and New Jersey and the help of James, I had protected him and the colony from Arnold, Phillips, and Cornwallis' attempts to capture him and destroy Monticello. He welcomed me enthusiastically.

Our first meeting went well, and we continued seeing one another frequently. He knew very few people in Paris and needed access to Versailles, as his primary responsibility was to manage the United States' massive international debt. We were both concerned for the dire circumstances of our countries, but neither had much experience in trade and economics. I introduced him to men who might be of assistance, including ministers and influential noblemen, and Adrienne invited Jefferson to our Monday salons.

Vergennes, now the minister in charge of foreign trade and controller-general, invited us and heads of several prominent business houses to serve on a committee investigating the tobacco monopolies the king had given to certain farmers for importing American tobacco.

The Americans insisted on being paid in cash rather than French exports, which created an unfavorable trade balance. The fees and port regulations discouraged American vessels from entering French ports, so Americans preferred to market their tobacco in London or Amsterdam.

Initially Jefferson disliked the extravagance and pomposity of Versailles, was scandalized by the lack of domestic morality among the aristocrats, and disdainful of the off-handed manner his associates treated their liaisons. At that moment a rumor circulated that the queen's reported lover was a mulatto from Guadeloupe, Joseph Bologne, Chevalier Saint-George. He was the finest swordsman in Europe, a concert violinist, renowned composer, and conductor of the largest orchestra in Paris—perhaps the most accomplished man in Europe. France's first black Freemason was referred to admiringly as the Black Mozart, the Black Don Juan, and even the Black Voltaire. The queen had personally requested Saint-George and his orchestra to conduct at Versailles the premières of Haydn's "Paris" symphonies, which Saint-George had commissioned. That he and the queen mysteriously vanished at the same time infuriated the racist aristocrats at the Court, upset the king, and discomforted Jefferson.

Still an officer by profession and eager to improve my skills, I obtained permission to observe maneuvers in Silesia by the master of military strategy, Frederick the Great, King of Prussia. Frederick held a dinner for all his guests and mischievously placed me between two influential British lords: the Duke of York, George III's brother, and Lord Charles Cornwallis. I had not been in the vicinity of the general since Yorktown, and had been looking forward to teasing him about "the boy not being able to escape me," but he was clearly not even amused by Frederick's humor of seating us together. He ignored me the entire evening.

I traveled on to Vienna to promote trade with America and met with Adrienne's uncle, the marquis de Noailles, who was then French ambassador to Austria. He presented me to Marie Antoinette's brother, the newly crowned Joseph II.

I returned to Paris in October for the heartbreaking news that Nathanael Greene had died of sunstroke. He was only 43. I wished I had had a chance to say goodbye to my friend. A pacifist Quaker, his zeal for liberty had led to his expulsion from the community, and the local militia had refused his service because of a pronounced limp. He had begun the war with the lowest rank possible, militia private, yet rose to be Washington's second-in-command. His death was a terrible waste of an amazing man, a fine person, and a great general. I continued to look after his son for the three years he remained in Paris.

Since my return from Yorktown I had been in great demand socially. Young admirers no longer saw me as the gawky provincial red-headed boy who could not dance, but now as the conquering hero who had helped defeat the enemy of France. I was twenty-six years old and neither unappreciative nor unreceptive to feminine allures.

One woman in particular stood out, comtesse Diane-Adelaide de Simiane. She was four years younger, statuesque, strikingly beautiful, voluptuous, and married to a homosexual courtier. According to gossip, she had been often courted, but no one could claim to be her lover. When she approached me, I was surprised, nervous, and full of hope.

She said she respected the great service I had done for France. One of her brothers had been among the officers who had gone to America with me, and her husband had also served there. I could not take my eyes off her, and probably rambled on inanely. The crucial communication was with our eyes, and it was clear from my uncommon nervousness that there was an intense animal attraction between us. Her fragrance and body heat made me feel like an adolescent. She softly whispered an invitation to join her later in her apartment in the palace for tea.

I was on time for tea and more nervous with anticipation than I had felt risking my life going into battle. She, rather than a servant, opened the door. Her hair was down and she was wearing a thin white evening robe. When she handed me the teacup our hands touched, sending a shockwave coursing through me.

That two married persons were to have an affair was certainly not unusual in the court of Louis XVI, though it was unique for both Diane and myself. I found her irresistible, and she was apparently attracted. For many years after our first encounter we enjoyed a passionate physical relationship, deep respect, and tender affection. She was enchanting, witty, and smart.

Adrienne soon learned about my affair. But if Adrienne was jealous or resentful, she did not communicate it in any way, ever. She never reacted by asking to be pitied or placated. She acted remarkably, demonstrating her extraordinary qualities. Adrienne warmly welcomed Diane, cultivated a close friendship with her which they maintained for the rest of their lives. Though I knew both women well, the nature and depth of their connection astonished me.

Of her own accord, Adrienne invited Diane to family gatherings, encouraged our children to call Diane "aunt," and when Adrienne was otherwise occupied, she suggested I go on separate vacations with Diane. Adrienne maintained a regular private correspondence with Diane, often informing her of news about me.

Meanwhile, Jefferson and I were able to get the government to give America most favored nation status, obtain a waiver of the duty on whale oil imports that fired the lamps of Paris, obtain from the naval minister an order for American oak and cedar, open up the French market for New England fisheries, and convince the French government to postpone the first payments of the American debt. Yet we knew that trade was hampered without a new government that had the power to collect taxes and regulate trade. The Congress of the Confederation, also acutely aware of the urgency, had called for a convention of state delegates at Philadelphia to revise the Articles of Confederation and develop a new plan of government.

Presided over by George Washington, the Convention began meeting in Philadelphia in May 1787 to draft a new constitution. James Madison sketched out his initial draft, which became known as the Virginia Plan. After some debate, Congress unanimously decided to submit the Constitution to the states for ratification. It made no recommendation for or against adoption. Madison, Hamilton and John Jay had written commentaries now known as *The Federalist Papers* under the name of "Publius," and Madison sent a copy to Jefferson in November.

Jefferson favored an unwritten constitution like Britain's, with laws passed by the legislature as supreme and final, though Madison and others eventually convinced him of the need for a stronger government. He supported the ratification, but was troubled that there was no bill of rights. Our unsuccessful efforts to secure religious rights for the minors entrusted to our care convinced both Jefferson and me that each of our countries desperately needed such protections.

Jefferson's younger daughter Mary (Polly) arrived in Paris, accompanied by a beautiful, light-skinned fourteen-year-old slave, Sally Hemings, half-sister of Jefferson's dead wife. Jefferson enrolled Polly in the same convent school as her sister, but soon received a letter from Patsy that she wanted to convert to Catholicism and take vows as a nun. Jefferson ran out of the house, drove a carriage directly to the school, and instantly removed both girls and arranged for a suitable tutor at home.

I had also had a problem with the schools for my young Protestant charge from Virginia, John Edward Caldwell. I had enrolled him in the Pension Lemoyne, a Benedictine boarding school. The priests insisted that he attend daily Catholic services and made no apology for their efforts to proselytize him. Each weekend when the young man came home to me, he bore new tales of efforts to convert him. I did not feel I could jeopardize his medical education by withdrawing him, but I was motivated to do what I could to try to protect his religious rights as well as those of my American friends in France.

Jefferson told me of a similar problem in Virginia where the Church of England attempted a state-established church. An act of 1705 stated that if a person is brought up in the Christian religion and denies the existence of God or the Trinity, asserts that Christianity is not the true religion, or that the scriptures are not from a divine authority, that person can be barred from any employment and jailed for three years without bail. In addition, anyone accused of acts of heresy against the

Church of England could be burned at the stake, and the state could take children from their parents. Jefferson considered this "religious slavery." It was not until 1786 that the Virginia legislature passed his Ordinance of Religious Freedom, guaranteeing that no man may be forced to attend or support any church or be discriminated against because of his religious preference.

Franklin had also asked me to help an American widow present her claims to the estate of her French husband who had served in America where they met and were married. The courts found their marriage invalid because a Protestant minister had performed it, and granted the widow nothing. I was embarrassed by the injustice, and knew that something must be done to establish religious freedom in France.

I agreed with Jefferson that men's minds must be free, and that "religion was a private matter." To guarantee this liberty, clearly church and state must be separated. Jefferson also saw that many rights available in America were not in France. We both felt the need for a French bill of rights and even a constitution to protect our liberty. I began to draft a declaration of rights for Frenchmen that I hoped someday to present to the king.

For me, freedom was the most fundamental of all the issues vehemently discussed at our salons. Most of our liberal French friends wanted to end the disgraceful practice of slavery, but some of our distinguished American guests like Jefferson were concerned about the economic and political impact. Having had almost daily contact with the black slaves of General Washington, camp laborers, people in the countryside, and his slaves at Mount Vernon, I had ample opportunity to see the impact of slavery on people. I could not understand how most of the signers of the Declaration of Independence could be slaveholders. I had constantly badgered Washington, Madison, and Monroe to free their slaves. They, too, told me that they could not for economic reasons—the same immoral position used by the king of France to justify slavery in Haiti. Jefferson had also resisted attempts to free his, or any of America's, slaves.

Even as I badgered my friends from America, I was aware that France turned four times as many Africans into slaves as the Americans did, and the king's ancestors had pioneered the triangle of slave trade between Africa, the New World, and Europe. By the mid-seventeenth century they had established sugar economies in their West Indian colonies which depended on cheap labor. In 1685 the Catholic Church actively participated in the drafting of sixty articles of the *Code Noir*, the Black Code, which forbade the practice of any religion in France other than Roman Catholicism and gave plantation owners extreme disciplinary power over their slaves, claiming authority from the Bible which sanctioned the use of slavery in both the old and new testaments. The Church thus justified allowing slave masters to "chain and beat slaves," brand and cut off the ears of slaves "absent for a month," and allowed the master to kill a slave if the slave "struck his or her master, his wife, mistress or children." Critics opposing these barbaric practices were met with the full power of the Church.

In late February 1786 I wrote to the new American Ambassador to Great Britain, John Adams:

> *In the cause of my black brethren I feel myself warmly interested, and most decidedly side, so far as respects them, against the white part of mankind. Whatever be the complexion of the enslaved, it does not, in my opinion, alter the complexion of the crime which the enslaver commits—a crime much blacker than any African face. It is to me a matter of great anxiety and concern to find that this trade is sometimes perpetrated under the flag of liberty, our dear and noble stripes, to which virtue and glory have been constant standard-bearers.*

Accomplishing little toward abolishing slavery by haranguing our acquaintances, Adrienne and I increasing lent our names and prestige to abolitionist groups around the world, and gave them considerable money. In 1785 we had decided to start a new business venture together, hoping to demonstrate the economic benefit of an alternative to slavery—showing that the slave trade and slavery were economically unnecessary, as well as un-Christian and inherently evil.

Washington had declined to join us in this endeavor, so Adrienne and I drew from our separate estates to purchase two large clove and cinnamon plantations in the French colony of Cayenne (French Guiana) which we named La Belle Gabrielle. We hired a man to manage our estate and sent him with instructions to select seventy slaves between the ages of one and fifty-nine to be tenant farmers paid to grow sugar. None of the tenants could be sold, and they and their children would be educated. Adrienne personally arranged for seminarians in Cayenne who had trained at the Séminaire du Saint-Esprit in Paris to teach our new tenants.

When our manager died in 1786, Adrienne took over the accounting for the plantation, and when I became involved in pressing matters in Paris, Adrienne took over managing the entire plantation, playing a very active roll. Again I was impressed with her business skills and acumen.

As trade between our countries continued to bring us together, Jefferson wrote to Washington:

> The Marquis de Lafayette is a most valuable auxiliary to me. His zeal is unbounded and his weight with those in power is great. . . . He has a great deal of sound genius, is well remarked by the King, and rising in popularity: He has nothing against him but the suspicion of republican principles. I think he will one day be of the ministry.

It seemed unlikely that I would ever serve in the king's government. We were friendly, but not friends, as Louis thought me much too liberal. Yet he invited me to spend three days with him in Cherbourg to inaugurate a huge engineering project to expand the port, riding with him on the royal barge and in his royal coach. At Versailles he regularly invited me to play cards or billiards, hunt with him, and occasionally join him for dinner. I might have been even closer if I had not attempted whenever I could to broach issues of social reform, religious intolerance, and emancipating slaves. These sensitive issues made the king uncomfortable—he preferred pleasant and enlightening conversations.

I had been working hard in Paris, so I decided to take my family to see my boyhood home in the quiet and beauty of the Auvergne for our first real vacation together. I had not been back since I was eleven. After eight days in the carriage, when I saw the old castle looming in the distance I grew excited. But a small group of impoverished people stood outside the château gates, and I recognized some of my boyhood acquaintances begging for food. There had not been such poverty and desperation in Chavaniac when I was young—that harvest had been unusually poor. We immediately arranged to deliver food, but we remained concerned for their general well-being.

We learned that much had changed during the eighteen years I had been away. My grandmother Catherine, one of my two aunts, and my beloved cousin Louise had died. The surviving aunt was doing her best, but the building had deteriorated badly, since the dire condition of the peasants had impacted her income.

They needed something more than temporary handouts of stored grain. Adrienne observed that despite a bad crop, they still had an abundance of sheep, whose wool would have more value spun and woven into cloth. She wrote to the comptroller-general asking for a subsidy to open a weaving school for the peasants and for funds for frames, wheels, and instructors, and when the funds were received the peasants benefited greatly.

When we returned to Paris I was eager to go out to Versailles, distressed by our experience in Chavaniac. The war in America had cost France a huge sum, borrowed at high interest rates, yet the Church and nobility were exempt from taxation, while commoners paid a tenth of their income or crop yields to the Church (*tithe*), a land tax to the state (the *taille*), a 5% property tax (*vingtième*), a tax for each family member (*capitation*), as well as obligations to their landlords for rent in cash (the *cens*), a payment on annual production (the *champart*), and fees to use the mills, wine-presses, and bakeries (*banalités*) owned by the nobility. Even the king realized that the peasants were taxed to the maximum, and he knew of dissatisfaction with the monarchy of sympathizers from the liberal aristocracy and thousands of Frenchmen who had served in America.

Books, pamphlets, and gossip spread the fact that commoners in America owned land and had a say in their taxes. Despite the pretense that France had an absolute monarch, the royal government could not successfully implement changes, including taxing the nobility, without the consent of the nobility.

Concerned that the national treasury was empty and the royal finances insolvent, Louis scheduled an Assembly of Notables at Versailles for his closest advisors to discuss the crisis. Since I had worked on trade and economy committees, and had important contacts in America, he had chosen me to be one of only twenty Notables to be housed in the royal palace. I was, at twenty-nine, by far the youngest delegate invited. I was excited, and thought naively it might be an opportunity to discuss ways to develop trade, revamp the tax structure, improve the French economy, and perhaps be of economic benefit to America.

From the start the intransigence of the nobles and clergy led to public clashes—they were simply interested in preserving their opulent lifestyle, and even devising ways to enhance their fortunes. The nobles opposed any changes to their vested interests, and no one was willing to suggest that the nobility or clergy—the largest landowners—pay their fair share of the tax burden. There was a prompt impasse, and after three months the Assembly of Notables had to be dissolved.

The inability of the Assembly of Notables to deal with the critical financial problem opened the eyes of people to the defects of government leaders who, unlike the leaders of the American revolution, were neither used to nor trained in self-governance. Most of the nobility were royalists obeying the dictates of their monarch. I wrote Washington that the "notables" were surely "not ables." I was no longer optimistic that a solution could be reached.

The financial crisis did not go away. In June the king appointed a new finance minister, Etienne Brienne, who promptly sent edicts for tax reform legislation to the Parlement of Paris, the king's regional legislative and judicial body. The Parlement had ancient and customary rights of consultation and deliberation, and a duty to register all royal edicts. They overwhelmingly rejected the royal legislation aimed at raising revenue.

The next month, a royal order required a formal session of the Parlement under the presidency of the king for the compulsory registration of the royal edict. But after the session the Parlement declared the registration illegal. Unable to raise revenues, repayments on government loans were stopped. The French government effectively declared bankruptcy. In August, after learning that the state was unable to meet its loan repayments, Etienne Brienne scheduled an Estates General for May of the following year to restore confidence with his creditors. But a week later he resigned as Minister of Finance and was replaced by Jacques Necker, a Swiss banker favored by the commoners.

Before the Estates General convened, Louis met again with his ministers and me to discuss in private possible solutions to his formidable problems. I pointed out that it was essential to include commoners in any discussion of a truly "national" assembly—a single body representing all three classes or "Estates" of French feudal society—clergy, nobility, and commoners—with one person, one vote similar to the American Congress, for neither noblemen nor clergy would ever vote against their self-interests. I reminded him that George III had tried to solve his economic problems in England by imposing additional taxes on his colonists—with unintended consequences. I had just spent five years risking my life and taken a musket ball in the leg in pursuit of taxpayer representation in government.

The king, however, was not persuaded by the example of the American colonists. He had supported them to undermine his enemy in the hope that France might regain Canada and even step into the colonial leadership vacancy. Instead he had not benefited at all, and the economy of France had been devastated. Moreover, the successful revolt against a monarch had undoubtedly set a bad precedent, making him fearful of any vote by commoners. He disregarded my proposal and sought another opinion from Minister Necker.

Necker, however, was also sympathetic to the commoners, and his suggestion was similar to mine, though in a different format—an Estates General with three chambers, one-person-one-vote, but doubling the representation of the Third Estate. Louis' advisors, however, suggested one vote per estate—which would pit nobles and clergy (appointed from nobility) against commoners. The king accepted their recommendation.

Appointed one of twenty-five delegates to the new provincial assembly in the Auvergne, I took my family to Chavaniac to appraise the economic situation from a new perspective. When I returned to Paris, I joined a club of nobility who embraced American ideas of individual liberties, republicanism, popular sovereignty, and a constitution for France. We called ourselves the Society of the Thirty.

That spring enormous hailstones destroyed orchards, vineyards, and fields of grain, followed by drought and scorching sun that shriveled the harvest. With food shortages and rising prices for other necessities, there was unrest. The next winter, one of the coldest in memory, was followed by flooding. The price of bread rose sharply, and restrictions had to be put on its sale. Food and firewood prices soared. Laborers and artisans were without work. Though the entire economy was devastated, peasants were still required to pay feudal dues to the lord of the manor and tithes to the Church. If they could not, their leases were placed in default. Displaced peasants from the ravaged countryside and unemployed workers from towns poured into Paris calling for the abolition of serfdom and feudal obligations. There was a breakdown of civic order, with desperate protestors arming themselves, and pillaging and looting in mobs.

More people began forming groups to propose solutions. When the Estates General met on May 5, the attention of the entire country was focused on this event. Yet at the suggestion of the archaic Parlement of Paris, Louis agreed to maintain all the ceremonial rites traditional since 1614, even though the opulent blaze of medieval pageantry was inappropriate to the dire economic circumstances. Each delegate was instructed by the king's coordinator to dress in cloths of gold with a plumed hat in the style of a seventeenth century courtier. The procession was led by the profligately dressed king and queen, lavishly clad royal pages and falconers, followed by the clergy, and nobles dressed in their most garish finery. Lastly, dressed solemnly in plain black were the commoners, alienated from the start. I was embarrassed and uncomfortable.

The king opened the meeting the next day with the verification of powers. The Third Estate discovered that voting would be by the tradition of the collective vote of each estate weighing equally—the commoners would have no real voice in the process of taxation. The king, aware of their displeasure, tried to avoid the issue of representation by focusing solely on taxes. The Estates General reached an impasse, the three estates discussing separately the organization of the legislature. Some 500 commoners met on their own on June 17 and were soon joined by sympathetic nobles and clergy. They declared themselves a National Assembly, based on one person, one vote. I supported this group wholeheartedly, but felt I could not join them during the Estates General without breaking the oath I had taken to represent the nobility.

When the king learned of this inconsequential act of insolence, he was defiant. He was not used to sharing his God-given royal prerogatives, much less with people not of noble birth. Instead of merely ignoring this modest gathering, he ordered his fully armed Swiss Guard to lock them out of their meeting hall.

The delegation refused to be stifled, so the next day they met on the king's indoor tennis court. To preside over their meeting they chose not a politician or radical, but the astronomer Jean Sylvain Bailly. Concerned by the king's unwarranted hostile actions, they took an oath not to separate until they could write a new constitution for the people that limited the powers of the monarchy and created a government by the people. The next day they were locked out of the tennis court.

Undaunted, the commoners moved to the nearby church of Saint Louis. When the Estates General officially ended on June 27, I believed I was no longer bound by my oath and joined the new National Assembly along with a few dozen other nobles. This increased the size of the new Assembly—604 commoners, 279 nobles, and 295 clergy, all asserting independence from the king.

This modest act of defiance was akin to the little skirmish at Concord—but without the bloodshed. And I was hoping that—unlike in America—violence could be avoided in convincing the king to accept reasonable limits on his authority set out in a constitution.

The army regiment specifically created to protect the king—the *Gardes Françaises,* the French Guard—were responsible for both guarding the exterior of the Palace of Versailles and maintaining public order in Paris. However, Louis sent for additional troops, including foreign mercenaries, to re-establish his authority.

As a Frenchman, I felt threatened by the presence of foreign troops on French soil, and I remember fondly that my first speech before the Assembly was to demand that the king remove these troops. The king refused our request. The *Gardes Françaises* had, through marriage and off-duty employment, local ties in Paris, and were resentful of the harsh Prussian style discipline imposed by their officers from the nobility. Many, having served with Rochambeau in America, were sympathetic. By July 14 most had deserted.

I had been drafting a *Declaration of the Rights of Man and of the Citizen* over many months, and reflecting on it with Jefferson. It enumerated seventeen natural rights based on liberal principles, such as presumption of innocence; freedom of speech, press, and religion; and the right to property. I hoped to establish as the law of France that "men are born free, and remain free and equal in rights," and end the aristocratic privilege of exemption from taxation. It would restrict monarchy, and permit all citizens to take part in the legislative process.

On July 11 I read the draft of my Declaration to the delegates and made a motion to enact it in connection with any constitution that was enacted by the Assembly. The Assembly was considering my motion when we received word that the king, upset that his finance minister had tried to give the commoners more voice in their own taxation by restructuring the ministry, had dismissed Jacques Necker and expelled him from France. The news sparked rumors that the king was going to send Broglie, my old commander at Metz, to arrest the deputies. He had 30,000 armed troops waiting between Versailles and Paris.

A young journalist and Freemason, Camille Desmoulins, who like Robespierre had attended the Collège du Plessis at the same time I was there, was sitting in a café in the gardens of the Royal Palace when he heard of Necker's dismissal. He was so upset that he jumped on a chair with a sword in one hand and a pistol in the other calling on the people of Paris to take up arms, shouting, "There is not a moment to lose!" His reaction spread rapidly through the city, and that night hundreds of hungry and desperate people responded to Desmoulins's summons and began searching for weapons to protect themselves from the foreign troops. They plundered the grandiose homes of Parisian aristocrats for whatever weapons might be stored inside, and looting, protests, rioting, and destruction escalated throughout Paris.

The king sent Swiss, Hussars, Dragoons, and French infantry to quiet the crowd, but an angry throng surrounded them. Most of the foreign troops were mercenaries, paid not to maintain public order, only to protect the king. The Gardes Françaises opened fire on the Royal German regiment, and the Swiss Guard refused to fire on the crowd. The crowd pressed in, broke through their ranks, and forced the foreign regiments to retire to the Champs de Mars where they did nothing to try to stop the chaos.

The newly constituted Assembly of commoners and their sympathizers were still meeting in Versailles. We agreed to ask the king again to withdraw foreign troops and reappoint the exiled finance minister. Concerned that our requests would anger the king even more, we decided that our personal safety lay in remaining together, and agreed that all one thousand delegates would work through that night of crisis.

To establish order within the Assembly, we elected Jean Sylvain Bailly, as president. In the unlikely event that he became fatigued, ill, or some condition forced him to leave the Assembly, the Assembly chose a vice-president. It was a great honor for me to be elected the first vice-president of the first National Assembly of France. I was just 32, and this was my first reluctant foray into public office.

The city council passed a resolution authorizing the establishment of a local Parisian militia, made up of all middle-class male citizens, to serve their fellow citizens without pay, be given arms as needed, and be identified by a blue and red cockade representing the city.

On the morning of July 14, the Assembly was still working at Versailles when the comte de Noailles came running into the Assembly hall to bring us word of events in Paris. A crowd of about 900 people had seized 30,000 muskets from the *Hôtel des Invalides*, but had not been able to find gunpowder or ammunition. Led by Camille Desmoulins and a well-known Parisian attorney, Georges Danton, they had begun marching toward the quantities of arms and ammunition known to be stored in the small Bastille prison, a dreaded landmark and primary symbol of arbitrary despotism in Paris—where for hundreds of years the kings of France had housed political and religious dissidents there, including Voltaire and the marquis de Sade. The old fortress was easily identified by its eight foreboding black towers and irregular triangular shape.

Some of the Gardes Françaises had the foresight to bring a few cannons to the scene. Two representatives of the crowd were invited into the fortress to negotiate for the surrender of the prison, the removal of the guns, and the release of the arms and gunpowder. But the throng outside grew impatient, and angry guardsmen used the cannons to destroy the main gate. The crowd surged inside, captured the administrator, removed the prisoners, and beheaded the chief jailer.

Stunned Parisians expected a counterattack. They armed themselves, built barricades of paving stones, and dug trenches. The Gardes Françaises had almost all mutinied, while the foreign troops, camped in the Champs de Mars, were not being paid to maintain order in Paris. When the delegates to the National Assembly heard the news, we understood that to retain any semblance of order, we had to immediately assert our authority. The new city government in Paris that had been formed by delegates from the various districts—the Paris Commune and the Permanent Committee—organized a municipal militia to uphold the peace.

The day after the Bastille was seized, the National Assembly called on my military training and experience to command both the Paris municipal guard and a people's National Guard, independent of the king's. They hoped that my reputation and stature would enable me to command the respect of the mutinous guardsmen and convince them to join our cause and work with the diverse men who would be asked to serve as militiamen.

When the king was informed that an armed mob had seized the Bastille and that the troops he had relied on to quell the disorder and protect him were deserting, he realized that his throne was in jeopardy. He walked down to the Assembly flanked only by his two brothers, and deferentially asked our help in restoring calm in Paris. To show his good faith, he agreed to order the withdrawal of all his troops from Paris and Versailles, and asked the Assembly to meet as soon as possible with the government of Paris to re-establish stability. The Assembly asked me to inform Mayor Bailly of the king's actions.

The next morning I left Versailles for Paris leading a caravan of eighty deputies in forty carriages. When we arrived at the Hôtel de Ville, delegates from the local districts met us and escorted me inside. The Assembly of Electors convened and elected me commander in chief of the Militia of Paris, in charge of all military and police matters in Paris and the Ile-de-France.

A week later the king formally disbanded the Gardes Françaises because of their role in the storming of the Bastille and their mass desertions. I hoped they would now be interested in becoming the professional core of a new National Guard, a military organization made from the diverse group of men available—40,000 unpaid volunteer amateurs from sixty districts, each of which was often treated as a fiefdom protected by those who lived there. These men were not happy about the change in structure.

To insure my personal safety, I selected officers from among the men who had served with me in America plus a handful from the Gardes Françaises to surround and protect me. I created a united esprit de corps to unify the local militiamen into an integrated military force, and supported it by replacing the white symbol of Bourbon monarchs with a new flag of red, white, and blue to represent the Masonic virtues of *liberté, egalité, and fraternité*, the slogan I adopted for our new republican government. I designed new uniforms and cockades with the three colors, and encouraged the men of each battalion to design their own flag, in order to generate a feeling of brotherhood. Each flag was blessed in a church in the battalion's district, and I tried to attend each ceremony to show my appreciation and support, often bringing Adrienne.

The problems of integrating the various districts were exemplified one morning when a local guardsman from the Cordeliers district, Georges-Jacques Danton, who had led the assault on the Bastille, challenged my authority as I was approaching the Hôtel de Ville. Danton was leading a large angry crowd outside the building, intent on hanging an old man they suspected of being an agent of the king. I stopped them, confirming that I had been appointed commander of the National Guard by the Assembly and was authorized to maintain order. Because of the many groups and bodies competing for authority, Danton at first refused to release the old man. I insisted that the man had been appointed by the Assembly to safeguard the prison until it could be demolished, and persuaded the crowd to let me take him inside. Danton was upset by his authority being questioned and his mistake pointed out to his followers. He thought I had intentionally humiliated him. He never forgave me.

Despite this incident, I soon had a reliable organization in place to maintain order. For the most part the people of Paris appreciated my efforts, for they were suffering as victims of the disorder and criminality. My role was to enforce those things essential to the survival of municipal government, such as the collection of excise taxes and prevention of crime, looting, and violence. Having to deal with thousands of hungry, angry, unemployed people who were desperate and threatening, we were not always popular. This made the Guards' job risky, and the risk often appeared pointless because no criminal justice system had replaced royal procedures.

When I impressed on my men the necessity of protecting their own homes and shops from pillaging, most seemed willing to serve and to respect my attempts to bring order to their lives. The Guards of one district even gave a special dinner for Adrienne and me, praising Adrienne for her work with the poor and calling her the "universal mother." They celebrated us in songs and poems. The guardsmen from another district honored our family by naming ten-year-old George a second lieutenant in the Guard and holding a party in his honor.

Slowly we were creating a new government independent from the king. To preserve his throne and demonstrate his good will, Louis asked the Assembly to arrange for him to meet with the new government in Paris. He rode into Paris between thousands of civilians lining the road in an unadorned black carriage, escorted only by a small detachment of bodyguards and a hundred deputies appointed by the Assembly. To protect him I had lined his route from Versailles to Paris with 10,000 National Guard. As the king passed, people defiantly shouted *"Vive la France"* rather than *"Vive le roi,"* but there was no violence.

At the outskirts of the city—atop my white horse and holding my ceremonial sword in hand—I officially greeted the king and escorted him through the walls of the city to the Hôtel de Ville. Beneath a large banner praising Louis as "Father of the French/The King of a Free People," he was received by Mayor Bailly who made an elaborate show of presenting the king with the keys to the city and gave him a revolutionary cockade. Louis accepted it with a smile, but pinned it beside his white Bourbon rosette.

The king entered the Hôtel de Ville, then appeared on the balcony to address the crowd assembled in the plaza below. He commended the selection of Bailly as mayor and me as the Commander of the Paris militia. The crowd seemed pleased by his show of good will. When the king returned to Versailles later that evening, the crowd lining the way greeted him shouting "*Vive le roi.*"

In the background of the political pageantry, the business class was hampered by unjust laws; the nobility were still idle, corrupt, and grossly extravagant; and reports of peasant revolts were pouring into Paris. The Assembly, which took up a proposal to abolish feudalism, continued through the night of August 5, and voted for it. This legislation laid the foundation for significant changes in the social, political, and economic structure of France. Besides ending serfdom, it allowed commoners to hold any civil or military office, and ended the tax exemption, privileges, and many rights of the nobility, and the tithes of the clergy. The class of nobility was effectively abolished, unnerving many of the nobles and royalists in the Assembly, who took flight to more hospitable lands and favorable regimes.

On August 4 I had submitted my *Declaration of the Rights of Man and the Citizen* to the National Assembly, which debated each of the seventeen provisions. The declaration had been circulated and discussed throughout France, and articles began appearing regularly in favor of a republic. Some of delegates to the Assembly from Brittany began meeting on their own in a Jacobin church to discuss other changes. They were soon joined by middle-class lawyers, doctors, teachers, merchants, writers, and artists, most of whom were monarchists, and included the king's brother Louis Philippe.

I also joined this Jacobin Club, a broad organization for political debate, with the goal of creating a constitution respecting legally constituted authority and the Rights of Man. As the organization grew, various factions developed which formed other clubs. Danton's Cordeliers—the Society of the Friends of the Rights of Man and of the Citizen—wanted a direct democracy and the active repression of counter-revolutionary activities. Thomas Paine joined the Girondists who opposed any monarchy and wanted a republic like ancient Rome prior to the empire. Mayor Bailley, Dr. Guillotin, and I joined the Feuillants to support a constitutional monarchy.

After several weeks the Assembly adopted a revised version of my Declaration of the Rights of Man and published it. The Assembly's version, unfortunately, only applied to male property owners—excluding women, slaves, children, and foreigners. But it did assert social equality among male citizens and the principles of popular sovereignty in contrast to the divine right of the kings.

The effect was immediate and profound. Street corner orators in Paris began shouting the provisions of my Declaration of Rights to illiterates whom priests had cowed into believing God had created them inferior to king, noblemen, and priests. Pamphleteers added to the frenzy. Commoners suddenly had a sense of empowerment and new hopes for the future.

As a gesture of good will, the Assembly voted to demolish the dreaded Bastille, symbol of royal repression. As commander of the National Guard, I was ordered to supervise the demolition. I kept the key to the main gate as a memento, which I asked my friend Patrick Henry to bring to George Washington, acknowledging the leading role he played in breaking the chains that had prevented autonomy.

With the fall of the Bastille, the ending of feudalism, and the publication of my Declaration of the Rights of Man, the king was concerned about the safety of his family. His minister of war doubled the palace Swiss Guards and summoned the ultra-royalist Flanders Regiment to Versailles. Louis ordered both of his brothers to leave for Coblenz, Austria and the safety of their uncle, the archbishop-elector of that ecclesiastical principality. Marie-Antoinette was kept secluded behind the palace walls.

Jefferson, too, was concerned about the safety of his family. His term as minister ended in September, so he decided to take his children back to Monticello. He sailed to Norfolk, Virginia with Patsy and Polly, James Hemings, the pregnant Sally Hemings, as well as a vast amount of luggage, including portraits he had commissioned of his heroes— Francis Bacon, John Locke, and Isaac Newton, "the three greatest men that ever lived, without any exception"—plus Italian portraits of

Columbus, Amerigo Vespucci, Cortez, and Magellan; as well as heavy marble busts of Franklin, Washington, Voltaire, and me.

Shortly after docking in Norfolk he received a message that George Washington, who had just been sworn into office as the first president of the United States, had named him secretary of state and Hamilton secretary of the treasury.

Foreign troops began arriving in Paris to protect the king. While awaiting orders, they camped at the Champ de Mars. When Parisian newspapers reported the presence of foreign troops, rumors proliferated that the king was about to use them to arrest and imprison the delegates and dissolve the Assembly. Meanwhile, to thank the troops for their prompt arrival, following customary military protocol, the king invited the officers of the Flanders Regiment to a welcoming banquet in the lavish Royal Opera House at the north end of Versailles. The king, queen, and dauphin arrived to rapturous applause, and the dinner turned into a display of drunken royalist enthusiasm, with the soldiers standing on tables singing patriotic songs and chanting "*Vive le roi!*"

Newspapers characterized the banquet as a "gluttonous orgy" and a grievous affront to those hungry Parisians suffering in a time of severe austerity. The papers vividly described the Austrian queen's bodyguards removing their tricolor cockades—the symbol of French republicanism—stomping them underfoot, and replacing them with the black cockades of the Austrian monarchy. Whether this was true was irrelevant, for the people of Paris felt insulted. When they learned that the king had defiantly declared that he did not intend to be limited in any way by a constitution, the idea quickly spread of a march out to Versailles to protest the insult.

CHAPTER 18

The Women's March on Versailles

1789

O N October 5 a group of market women in the eastern section of Paris were upset at the chronic shortage and high price of bread, and offended by the gluttonous orgy. They went to the Hôtel de Ville to demand both bread and arms. To attract supporters, the women shouted in the streets and beat drums. They forced the priest at a nearby church to toll the bells. Thousands of people were drawn to city hall.

Mayor Bailly and the Paris Commune, concerned about possible violence, instructed me to protect city hall and stay with the demonstrators to maintain order. I assembled thousands of Parisian guardsmen on the south side of the Hôtel de Ville and waited in the downpour for the crowd to get tired or bored or disperse. After milling around complaining about their problems and venting their anger with the authorities, a handful entered the building, broke doors, and ransacked offices. They even attempted to burn down the building and hang a man trying to protect it.

Stanislaus Maillard, a popular National Guardsman who had led the storming of the Bastille, suggested that everyone march to Versailles to bring their grievances to the king. As they moved slowly out of Paris, the women leading the procession demanded that all men march behind them. They put drummers at the front of the procession to attract other demonstrators, and knocked at the door of every house they passed to force the inhabitants to join the march. Along the way they armed themselves with broomsticks, pitchforks, swords, pistols, muskets, branches, stones, shovels, knives, and scythes—anything that could be used as a weapon.

I was concerned that once the marchers reached Versailles they might storm the palace, or that the king's soldiers would open fire on them. I sent a horseman ahead to warn the Assembly and the court, and ordered my men to surround the demonstrators to contain any violence. The crowd swelled to 8000 and entreated sympathetic guardsmen to join their march. Their repeated cajoling provoked some of my guardsmen to declare their solidarity. To show his zeal, one guardsman even threatened me if I tried to stop the march and another to desert unless I continued leading them out to Versailles. I was facing a possible mutiny.

Six hours in the rain without food put most of the marchers in a foul temper, which was exacerbated when they first saw the foreign uniforms of the Swiss and Austrian troops. The crowd shouted insults at the soldiers, demanding foreigners be expelled. They called their Austrian-born queen *bitch* and *whore*, shouting for her death and for the royal guards to be replaced with the more trustworthy National Guard.

The president of the Assembly, Jean Joseph Mounier, and Assemblyman Maximillien Robespierre came out of the palace to greet the mob and calm things down. They welcomed the marchers warmly with words expressing support and sympathy for their issues. Mounier offered to accompany a deputation of six market women nominated by the crowd into the palace to personally present their grievances to the king. This proposal immediately calmed the crowd.

Mounier escorted the chosen women directly to the king's chamber. None of them had ever seen a building of such grandeur and luxury. They were further awed and intimidated when they came into the presence of their monarch, and remained respectful and courteous. The king was gracious and attentive.

The women meekly asked only for the opportunity to buy a four-pound loaf of bread for eight *sous*. The king responded sympathetically, saying that he would do his best to comply with their reasonable request. To show his good faith, he immediately arranged to dispense food directly from the royal stores to the crowd, promising the women seventy wagons of flour right away and more to follow.

The delegation, convinced that their audience had gone well, reported back to those waiting impatiently in the autumn downpour. Their optimistic report satisfied some, and the multitude began leaving. But a large contingent was unwilling to accept mere promises, so they decided to stay at Versailles until they received the promised flour.

I entered the building and asked to speak with the king. He would only see me if I entered unaccompanied by my guardsmen. I was surprised to find my father-in-law staring hostilely at me. He said nothing, but led the king's bodyguards to Louis's chambers, where he agreed to most of my suggestions. I reported this to both the Assembly and my men. The king withdrew to meet with his advisors to work out a solution to the mob's demands, and everyone retired for the night.

The crowd slept outside in the pouring rain, joined by tired guardsmen. During the night someone, perhaps seeking cover from the rain, discovered an unguarded entry into the palace. At six the next morning, hundreds of people began pouring into the palace—some to get warm, some curious to see the luxurious interior. They wandered aimlessly about the palace, awed by the gold, crystal, and marble, the copious paintings, sculptures, and chandeliers—with no idea who or what they were looking for. A few people innocently wandered into the bedchamber of the queen, causing her edgy royal guards to panic and open fire. Hearing gunshots, people began running towards the blast. Frightened and incensed when they heard that a woman had been killed, they began looking for weapons to defend themselves and to retaliate.

Two of the royal guards were attacked, their heads cut off and appallingly placed atop long pikes. In reaction to this brutality, the guards were ready to retaliate, but I rushed in to prevent the violence from escalating. I assembled guardsmen who had formerly worked in the Gardes Françaises and asked them to meet with the Royal Guardsmen, hoping that with a history of cooperation their mutual respect would stabilize the situation. Fighting ceased and the guardsmen jointly helped clear the palace of intruders.

However the crowd outside the palace refused to leave until the king personally assured them he would provide cheaper bread. I delivered their demands to the king and we discussed the situation. I suggested that to avert further fatalities and maintain peace, he should address the crowd. I offered to escort him onto a balcony and stay with him while he addressed them.

Louis appeared on the balcony and promised to provide bread soon. He movingly assured them that he had their best interests at heart. To relieve the tension, I playfully stuck a tricolor cockade onto the hat of the king's nearest bodyguard. The crowd began cheering "*Vive le roi.*" The much-relieved king left the balcony thinking that his brief address had ended the matter. But the crowd was not satisfied.

Many blamed the bread shortage on the foreign queen and believed she would force the king to break his promise. They began chanting for the queen to also make an appearance. I conferred with Marie Antoinette, still in her bedclothes after her frightening episode, doing my best to calm and comfort her. I suggested that she also accede to the demands of the crowd, and I assured her that I would accompany her onto the balcony. She nervously acquiesced, but refused to be separated from her children, concerned about their well-being. Holding her hand I led her, her young son, and daughter out onto the balcony, and stayed close to her.

The crowd pointed weapons at her, calling her nasty names and demanding that the children be taken away. The queen responded to their blatant hostility by showing great courage, impressing the crowd with her strength and calmness. To show my support and affection for the queen, I knelt beside her and kissed her hand. The demonstrators responded with restrained respect, then shouted "*Vive la reine.*" With this sign of approval, I led the shaken queen and her children back inside the palace.

The king and queen, troubled by these events, realized that I had been able to minimize the violence and avoid what could have been a bloodbath, and appreciated what I had done for them. In turn, they had cooperated with me and tried to comply with all reasonable demands of the demonstrators. Unfortunately, this did not end the demonstration. The crowd began chanting new demands—insisting that the king return with them to Paris. The demonstrators felt that spare food might be more readily available and fulfillment of their demands would be easier if the king, his court, and the Assembly resided in Paris where they would be more accessible.

We discussed this latest demand during the night. To calm the escalating possibility of violence, and with little alternative except to forcibly remove thousands of demonstrators and their sympathetic guardsmen, the king agreed to go to Paris. I assured the king and queen that I would escort them and do everything I could to protect them from the mob.

Early in the afternoon of October 6, with the royal family, most of their ministers, and a hundred deputies tucked into royal carriages, I led a caravan of wagons, coaches, and thousands of commoners on foot back to the capital. Some of the marching women hoisted loaves of bread on bayonets, some sang, some fired celebratory gunshots in the air, and two carried pikes crowned with the ghastly heads. It took over nine hours to arrive at the city gate. Mayor Bailly welcomed us, and Louis entered city hall, went upstairs and out onto the balcony to address the crowd. Placated, they returned to their homes. I escorted the royal family to their new home in the nearby Tuileries Palace that been the home of French monarchs for centuries before Louis XIV moved the court to Versailles. I shepherded the royal family and an assortment of ministers and functionaries into the building, stationed guardsmen to keep demonstrators out, and remained with them inside.

The Mothers of the Nation, as the women were proclaimed, were celebrated upon their return. These humble commoners had forced one of the most powerful monarchs in the world to bend to their will. The women's march on Versailles gave Parisians a sense of empowerment. Within a few weeks, the royal family was joined in the refurbished Tuileries by the Assembly, ministers, government functionaries, nobles, and courtiers to establish the legislature near the king. Parisians viewed the king's move to Paris as a peaceful transition of power.

The size and outcome of the women's march demonstrated to the Assembly that economic and political changes were desperately needed. Robespierre's part in the women's march made him a heroic patron of the poor. However, sixty of the Assembly's royalist deputies, fearing for their own personal safety, fled the country. Their loss created even more turmoil, as authority to govern was claimed by various committees, the mayor, the Assembly, and the individual districts—each claiming independence from the others.

As commander of the strongest armed force in the region, and with the virtual confinement of the royal family in the Tuileries, I was the most powerful man in France. I considered myself the defender of constituted authority, with the respect, confidence, gratitude, and support of the people of Paris. For the moment.

But I soon discovered that many of the people who marched on Versailles thought that even my brief appearance on the balcony had shown I was too closely tied to the royal family. The Jacobin journalist Jean Paul Marat charged that my speech at Versailles was intended to trap and confuse the French public and accused me of being a "vile flatterer" of the king. Danton, opposed to any type of monarchy, disparaged me for protecting the royal family and making the National

Guard into the satellite of a corrupt legislature that merely wanted to limit the monarchy with a constitution, instead of ending it forever.

The royalist right painted me as the instigator of the revolution, a traitor to my class, and the jailer of their king. They blamed me for placing the royal family under house arrest and criticized my Declaration of Rights for violating royal prerogatives.

The king remained the head of government, but it was clear that change was underway—and propaganda wars broke out over the type of change. It would be debated in the Assembly and by the public for some time, not just in France but throughout Europe and America. I had been arguing these issues with Jefferson, Hamilton, Paine, and others at our salons, and I was certain that the revolution in France was going to follow the path of the revolution in America. However my friend Hamilton thought differently:

> *I have seen, with a mixture of pleasure and apprehension, the progress of events which have lately taken place in your country. As a friend to mankind and to liberty, I rejoice in all the efforts which you are making to establish it, while I fear much for the final success of the attempts, and for the danger, in case of success, of innovations greater than will consist with the real felicity of your nation.*

> *You will ask why this foreboding of ill when all the appearances have been so much in your favor. I will tell you: I dread disagreements among those who are now united about the nature of your constitution. I dread the vehement character of your people, whom I fear you may find it easier to bring out than to keep within proper bounds after you have put them in motion. I dread the interested refractoriness of your nobles, who cannot be gratified and who may be unwilling to submit to the requisite sacrifices.*

> *—Alexander Hamilton*

There was much truth to Hamilton's comments, especially considering the unresponsiveness of the clergy, whom he had failed to mention. The Assembly had taken steps to abolish the nobility, but had been unsuccessful in restraining the clergy. Unlike America, where most people owned their own land, in France the nobility owned about a third of all the land, and the Catholic Church owned a fifth, with whole villages set upon church land.

In October the Assembly, to relieve the tax burden on the commoners, had abolished all internal customs duties and indirect taxes—leaving unresolved the problem of how to finance its activities. When the Assembly heard that two women in a nearby convent were being forced into the religious life, they decided to solve their financial problem by confiscating and selling the estates belonging to the Church, and they even halted the taking of solemn vows. The Church did not oppose this measure, for the clergy were to be maintained by the state as civil servants. Soon after, however, the new Assembly increased its power and tax base by nationalizing all Church property. The new French state had not only taken control of the Church's revenue and property, but through such radical intervention seemed to be redrawing the boundaries between the Church and the state. Despite thousands of letters of protest, in February the Assembly decreed that all monasteries would be closed, their inhabitants removed, and the buildings and their contents sold in order to stabilize the nation's finances.

Acknowledging the Assembly's increased power, the king asked to address the delegates. On February 4, dressed in a simple black suit, he stood before the Assembly and read a lengthy conciliatory speech promising to accept the constitution and maintain constitutional liberty. The delegates were relieved. They accepted his assurances and were filled with hope.

Jefferson wrote that it might be better to persuade Louis himself to issue a charter defining rights and privileges like the Magna Carta. At the time I was not concerned, because the action by the Assembly in abolishing the nobility and taxing both them and the clergy had established its authority, causing everyone to believe that a constitutional monarchy had been established with a concomitant feeling of unity— not only in Paris, but throughout France and Europe. The president of the Paris Commune encapsulated the national feeling saying, "French, we are free! French, we are brothers!"

Acknowledging its assumption of sovereignty, the National Assembly approved a suggestion by the Commune of Paris that a celebration be held to show national reconciliation. They organized individual feasts throughout France. In Paris, the mammoth official feast, the *Fête de la Fédération*, was scheduled for the anniversary of the fall of the Bastille, July 14, 1790.

In accordance with the Assembly's meticulous plans, I was at the site where the Bastille once had stood at eight o'clock that morning. Riding on my white horse I had the honor of leading 14,000 guardsmen from all over France through the streets of Paris, across the Seine, and out to the Champ de Mars. Thousands of volunteers had been turning the huge field into an amphitheater with earthen bleachers. We entered to the acclaim of 400,000 people.

There were National Guard units from all 544 French departments, and deputies from many other nations. There was a delegation from the United States of America bearing the American flag, flying for the first over foreign soil, led by Thomas Paine and John Paul Jones, founder of their navy, to show support for their "sister republic."

Mass was celebrated with 300 supportive priests wearing tricolor waistbands over their priestly vestments officiating at the Altar of the Nation to call down God's blessings on the revolution.

After the clergy, I stepped forward representing the former nobility—no longer the marquis de Lafayette, but simply Commander Gilbert Motier of the National Guard of Paris. I took my oath to obey the Constitution.

Following me, Louis pledged his allegiance and swore to accept and maintain the Constitution as "King of the French" rather than as "King of France," linking the monarch to the people rather than the territory. Marie Antoinette also pledged her allegiance and that of her son, the dauphin.

The acceptance by the royal family, clergy, and former nobility of constitutional limits was seen as a grand conclusion to the unrest that had engulfed France. It seemed that the country was fairly united. I was happy that my unrelenting efforts to give the people a voice in their government were seeing fruition. Both British Prime Minister William Pitt and his opposition, the liberal Charles James Fox, agreed that the revolution which had successfully limited the monarchy with minimal bloodshed, was welcomed in Britain. Before Parliament, Fox said, "Never before was made such a great step toward freeing Humanity."

Having seen the successful end of two revolutions, I was enormously gratified. I had been privileged to be the Assembly's vice-president and head of the government's military, and I thought I had peacefully achieved my goals for a government of the people of France. At the high point of my career, I indeed felt like the hero of two worlds. I was well-respected, my reputation unblemished. I was happy for France, for my family, and for myself.

CHAPTER 19

The Civil Constitution
of the Clergy

1790

W HILE I WAS BUSY commanding the National Guard, preparing for the Fête, dealing with members of the Assembly,
spending time with my family, and fulfilling the responsibilities of a political figure, the Assembly had discreetly passed a new
law entitled the *Civil Constitution of the Clergy*, but intentionally did
not disclose that information prior to the Fête. This new law forced
clergymen to swear an oath of loyalty to the nation, the law, and the
king—rather than to the Church.

There had been no strong objections to secularizing the Church
because it controlled not only the religious life, but secular life as
well—primary and secondary education, hospitals and health care,
and all official documents: births, deaths, burials, and marriages.

However, Frenchmen did not want the government affecting dogma and worship, as would this new law which forced clergymen to swear an oath of loyalty to "the nation, the law, and the king," rather than to the Church. This produced an insurmountable chasm between those willing to take an oath of loyalty to the state and those who refused. Three-quarters of the priests and almost all the high clergy refused to sign, supported by the king who was unwilling to accept the will of the Assembly—who represented the people of France—to say nothing of the Pope who condemned the new law, the Assembly, all provisions of the Constitution, as well as all clergy who complied with the oath. Religious peasants also opposed the law.

A month after it was passed, opposition mounted in southeastern France. Over 25,000 aristocrats, émigrés, and disillusioned guardsman gathered in a plain near the Château de Jales and formed a counterrevolutionary leadership to oppose the Civil Constitution of the Clergy, the Assembly, and the revolution.

When the king delayed implementing the law, at the urging of the pope, he confirmed clearly that he was unwilling to accept the will of the representatives of the people of France. Rather than compromise or try to close the widening chasm, the republican majority in the Assembly fought back. On February 5 they banned priests who did not take the oath from preaching in public. This escalated the violence against both the non-juring priests and the sworn priests who took their place. To force compliance, the Assembly began arresting priests who refused to take the oath and put them on prison-ships, but this brutal punishment shocked and angered many of the Assembly's supporters, including Adrienne and me. Everyone was caught up in this national schism.

Adrienne, a devote Catholic, normally attended services regularly. However she refused to attend services conducted by priests who had signed the oath, believing that the Church ministry could only come from the pope, not a civil government. I was not devout, supported the nationalization of the Church, and believed that all Frenchmen, including priests, should swear loyalty to the Constitution—but I supported the rights of the faithful to worship where, when, and how they saw fit.

The Assembly also passed a law creating an army of 20,000. The king, using his power under the Constitution, vetoed both laws to display his disregard of the will of the Assembly. His action cast doubt on the feasibility of the Constitution. The people of Paris were outraged that their representatives had been ignored and began rioting in protest. And my duty to maintain order put me at odds with the people protesting.

The unrest in Paris made the king's supporters increasingly concerned for his safety. On February 28 a large group of royalist noblemen entered the Tuileries to help the royal family escape and protect them from the wrath of the Parisians. I was four miles away trying to stop an angry mob from destroying the prison near Vincennes and massacring the prisoners. When I was informed that there was trouble at the Tuileries, I went directly to the palace and had the National Guard disarm the royalists and arrest them. This minor incident, which the press sensationalized as "The Day of the Daggers," further alienated me from the king and his supporters, confirming their suspicions that I was a traitor to my class, as well as one of the instigators of the revolution, and the person who had forced their king to live in Paris.

Thousands of noblemen had already sought asylum in foreign lands where they conspired to crush the revolution and warned monarchies throughout Europe of impending danger. They spread fear that the political ideals of the revolution might spread rebellion beyond French borders. Particularly active in supporting the émigrés was Marie Antoinette's brother, Emperor Leopold II, who was plotting to rescue her and the king. He hoped that, safely in Austria, they could help him, other émigrés, and foreign allies lead a counterrevolution against the republican government of France.

In the middle of the night of June 20 I was awakened by pounding on our front door. The king had disappeared from the Tuileries Palace. I dressed and woke my house guest Thomas Paine to warn him that I had to leave to search for the king. I summoned additional guardsmen and issued an order for the king's arrest, the first in the history of France.

Within twenty-four hours the royal family had been found 150 miles east of Paris, a mere thirty miles from the Austrian border. Their disguised royal coaches had been spotted by an observant local postmaster, Jean-Baptiste Drouet, of the village of Saint-Menehould. Drouet had seen just the side of a man's head inside one of the carriages and had recognized the profile on several French coins. The townspeople detained the carriage until they received instructions from the Assembly.

The Assembly directed me to take the king and his party into custody and return them without delay to Paris. I sent 6000 armed Guardsmen to force the humiliated king and queen to return to house arrest, which also was unprecedented. The king's treasonous conduct undermined support for a constitutional monarchy. Tens of thousands of royalist noblemen fled France to seek safety elsewhere in Europe. Adrienne's father went to Switzerland, Diane fled to London.

Republicanism became the dominant philosophy of the radicalized French revolution. I saw no reason to flee, for I supported the revolution, was one of its leaders, and had issued the orders that led to the arrest of the royal family.

PART IV

My World Turns Upside Down

1791

CHAPTER 20

Disorder and Confusion

1791

OUIS, AWARE OF THE treasonous nature of his escape and its impact on this subjects, pledged to support and abide by a new stricter Constitution. Despite this escape attempt, most of the delegates to the Assembly voted to permit him to remain king in order to salvage a limited monarchy. However, everyone understood that the limitations on the king's authority would be tightened without reservations—in effect making France a republic.

The people of Paris, however, no longer trusted the king, which made the decision of the Assembly exceedingly unpopular. Danton, Robespierre, and the radical republican clubs rallied against the decision. The anti-royalist press needed a scapegoat in order to end the constitutional monarchy. Even though I had known nothing of the king's escape, had promptly ordered his arrest, and quickly returned the king and royal family to custody at the Tuileries, the radicals blamed me for letting them escape. They set about undermining my authority as commander of the National Guard and destroying my reputation. They created a petition demanding that the Assembly remove the king from any executive power, unless the majority expressed a desire to maintain the present constitution. Signing the petition would happen at the Champ de Mars. Expecting a large turnout, the Assembly and mayor ordered me to take sufficient numbers of guardsmen to the field to ensure public safety and order.

The crowd began calmly assembling on the morning of July 17. Petitions were signed without incident until the late afternoon when Danton and his journalist friend Camille Desmoulins came to the Champ de Mars leading a raucous mob that shouted slogans, threw rocks at the guardsmen, and stabbed and beat people suspected of being royalists. Two accused royalist spies were left hanging under the Altar of the Fatherland. When I saw the red flag of martial law hoisted by Mayor Bailly, I ordered my men to peacefully disperse the crowd, which had grown to 50,000. Most left, but a small number refused, cursing at us and exhorting those remaining to kill me and my guardsmen. I ordered the firing of warning shots into the air, but one of the guardsmen, who had been injured, retaliated by firing directly into the crowd. When other guardsmen heard the shot, their firing became indiscriminate. The crowd panicked, with general chaos and more injuries. Fortunately nightfall ended the demonstration.

The Assembly promptly began hearing witnesses to determine what had happened and to assess blame. They determined that I had not ordered the shooting and that my actions were merely to protect my men and the crowd. They concluded that Danton and Desmoulins were primarily responsible for the mayhem, and issued warrants for their arrest. Unfortunately, Danton was informed of the warrants and fled the city before he could be served, and Desmoulins went into hiding.

The people of Paris were justifiably appalled—for the first time revolutionaries had fired upon fellow revolutionaries. With passions extreme, the Assembly ordered martial law to remain in force for three weeks. They suppressed several democratic newspapers, seized presses, arrested journalists and several hundred political militants. To represent the interests of the general will, the Assembly began revising the Constitution to redefine the organization of government, citizenship, and the limits of power. A wave of revulsion against popular movements swept France, rekindling efforts to preserve powers for the crown.

The republican press was relentless in attacking me and Mayor Bailly. I was held to blame me for the tragedy at the Champ de Mar in every issue of every paper. There was no chance for the people to weigh the truth of all of the allegations. To Danton and his associates, I was no longer the people's general, but an enemy of the public. They did everything to falsely defame me—even as an unscrupulous libertine—and went so far as attacking Adrienne with accusations of infidelity. The slander destroyed Parisians' trust in their government. They wanted to be rid of me, all royalty, all nobility, all clergy, and start from scratch without laws, structure, or fetters of any kind. It was a blow to whatever respect and affection I enjoyed among the Jacobins and their urban radical working-class supporters. My credibility as a leader ceased to exist, and it was becoming impossible to command the National Guards.

In retrospect, my precipitous collapse as a leader in the revolution came of embracing the values of law and order. Unlike educated American farmers, our revolution was not one that utilized law and order in the pursuit of liberty. Having thrown off the remnants of feudalism, the revolutionary government had not yet established a judicial system. The popular violence was a natural reaction against ancient tyranny, combined with the simple want for bread. Born into the nobility and appreciative of the orderliness of American society, I was unwilling to support extreme attempts by republicans to accomplish liberty.

The chaotic situation worsened when the people of Paris learned that the kings of Austria and Prussia had met in Pillnitz Castle near Dresden in Saxony, and published a joint statement on August 27 appealing to all European powers to intervene in the affairs of France if either Marie Antoinette or Louis XVI were threatened or harmed. The declaration was interpreted as proof that the queen was in league with her brother. Parisians considered the declaration made by the rulers of two powerful countries to be so serious a threat, that an attack was imminent.

Louis came before the Assembly again on September 13 to swear to accept the new constitution's limit to his authority and its separation of powers. The Assembly decreed that if the king retracted his oath or formed an army to make war upon the nation—or permitted anyone to do so in his name—it would be considered, de facto, his abdication. The Assembly agreed to hold elections for a new legislative body to empower the people. France still had a chance of becoming a stable constitutional monarchy.

The Assembly dissolved itself on September 30 and, upon Robespierre's motion, decreed that none of its members should be permitted to sit in the new Legislative Assembly. Mayor Bailly resigned his position, and I mine as head of the National Guard and armed forces.

Though I decided to retire from the frenzy of Paris to my old home in Chavaniac, some of my friends asked me to run for mayor of Paris. With my name in tatters I did not think that was a good idea, but I agreed to their entreaties. Unfortunately my candidacy focused the ire of the Cordeliers and Jacobins who launched another war against me. By constant character assassination they persuaded the people to hold me responsible for the king's flight and the tragedy at the Champ de Mars. I lost by an embarrassingly wide margin—which freed me to gather my family and leave Paris. I was tired and felt unappreciated, and was hopeful that without me the election would give us a new government and some stability.

According to the new Constitution, active citizens voted for electors, men of substantial wealth, who ultimately elected the 745 new deputies. When the new delegates met on the first of October, most were opposed to monarchy. This republican majority had three perceived enemies—the royal family, the émigrés, and the non-juring clergy—and one real enemy, the powerful emperors of Austria and Prussia. In November they ordered all émigrés to return to France under threat of death and decreed that every non-juring clergyman must take the oath of allegiance to civil authority within eight days or be subject to arrest. These new laws were vetoed by the king.

To preempt an actual invasion, on April 20 the Assembly impulsively declared war on Austria. However, France was not prepared militarily or economically to embark on a war against anyone, especially since most of the officers were from the nobility, many of whom had fled. Those who remained were not trusted, troops lacked discipline, fortresses were in bad condition, and there was a shortage of supplies. With no money to pay them, soldiers began deserting en masse.

In fact, war might not have been necessary, since Emperor Leopold had died two months earlier and no one knew the intentions of his inexperienced brother Francis. Nevertheless, just a week after declaring war, the first French armies boldly marched into the Austrian Netherlands. With the onset of war, the influence of Danton, Robespierre, and the Paris Commune increased greatly. It is a phenomenon of the frail human mind that in times of chaos or personal distress, people are drawn to war for a sense of empowerment and communal coherence.

With the urgent need for experienced officers, and with my time in America giving me more experience than most officers, the Assembly sent an urgent letter to Chavaniac appealing to my patriotism to serve as commander of one of the three armies on the eastern front.

Despite the Jacobins' attempt to defame me and despite my own feeling of being maligned, I could not refuse to defend my country—I hoped this might be an opportunity to rehabilitate my reputation. Risking my life was easier and safer than dealing with defaming pamphleteers and the tumultuous crowds. I reluctantly left Adrienne and the children, and traveled hastily up to Paris to appear before the Assembly. I was assigned command of the Army of the Center and ordered me to Metz immediately.

I sent a letter to Adrienne asking her to bring the children and join me in Metz as soon as she could. As the commander of an army, I thought I might be better able to protect my family in a war zone than I could in the chaotic and dangerous battlefields of Paris, where the increasing hostility towards the nobility had already caused so many to flee.

Her reply was waiting when I arrived in Metz. After careful consideration she had decided to remain in Chavaniac, feeling that she and the children might hinder my movements, and that proximity to the battlefield would jeopardize the children. Chavaniac seemed sufficiently far from the chaos in Paris, and less risky for women and children. They would stay with my aunt in the relative safety of the Auvergne.

My Army of the Center had been ordered to invade the small city of Namur. But before we left Metz, both the Army of the North under Rochambeau and the Army of the Rhine under Marshal Nicolas Luchner were quickly routed by the Austrians, because the hastily-trained revolutionary forces were insubordinate and lacked discipline—on one occasion, troops murdered their general to avoid a battle, on another troops insisted on putting their commander's orders to a vote.

The revolutionary forces retreated in disarray. Radicals in Paris, particularly Danton and Robespierre, blamed the defeats not on inexperienced troops but on traitorous aristocratic officers, claiming that the royalist generals had purposely conspired to lose—giving concern to even some republican officers about their own safety. Rochambeau resigned and was replaced by Luchner. Other generals simply fled.

I wrote to the Assembly my concern that radicals were rejoicing in our disorder, preaching insubordination to the army, and sowing distrust that was detrimental to the effectiveness of the commanders. Apparently the Assembly reacted favorably to my letter, because when the Jacobins met in August, Danton accused the whole Assembly of being "accomplices of Lafayette." He persuaded the Jacobins to appeal neither to law nor legislature, but to take up arms. When they named him their minister of justice, even more officers resigned in protest or fled. Unpaid troops, unlike those in America, would not tolerate hunger, lack of clothing, nor lack of compensation—they deserted in large numbers. These simultaneous losses undermined our ability to protect France.

In addition, I was receiving numerous letters, newspapers, and magazines from Paris that confirmed that France was being ripped apart by extremists—both royalist and republican. Juror priests were against non-jurist clergy, émigrés and royalist noblemen were helping Austria, and Jacobins—anti-monarchy and anti-Church—were denouncing one another. Worried that the divisiveness would further damage our military capabilities, I wrote a letter to the National Assembly on June 16 denouncing the Cordeliers, Jacobins, and other radical groups for hurting the war effort.

I received no response and the Assembly took no action, so for the defense of the nation, I left Metz and returned to Paris, appearing before them on June 28 to protest the growing verbal abuse of officers at the front. As I entered the room, I received a few friendly cheers. In retrospect, these may have caused me to be overly optimistic. I confidently addressed the delegates, earnestly demanding an end to the chaos and disruption by asking the Assembly to close all the radical clubs, including the powerful Jacobins, because they were undermining the war effort and jeopardizing the country. The Jacobins brought a motion to censure me for leaving my troops without permission. Their motion lost, but it was clear that the Jacobins were solidly in control of the Assembly. I returned to Metz and the command of my army to await some action by the Assembly.

On July 26 the duke of Brunswick, commander of the allied Austrian-Prussian army, issued another declaration threatening to harm French civilians if the royal family were harmed. The manifesto was interpreted by the Jacobins as proof that Louis XVI had been collaborating with the foreign coalition, a traitor who had been giving them information detrimental to France. The same day that Paris learned of the manifesto, the Duke led his armies into France and captured the first French city. Three days later at a meeting of the Jacobin Club, Robespierre called for the removal of the king. Forty-seven of the forty-eight sections of Paris subsequently petitioned the Assembly to end the king's powers, swearing that if the Assembly refused to remove the king, they would themselves by August 10.

On August 8, solely because I had been born a nobleman and must, therefore, be sympathetic to the king, the Jacobins moved that the Assembly impeach me. Two-thirds of the delegates voted against it, but they were hissed and subsequently harassed, their homes invaded, and some even received death threats. Most delegates still believed that they needed my military experience, but to appease the more radical Jacobins they decided to relieve me of my command and consolidate three armies into two. I was ordered to serve in the north under General Charles Dumouriez, and report to his headquarters in Sedan.

On the night of August 9 the revolutionary commune, led by the Jacobins under the leadership of Robespierre, took possession of city hall and the government of Paris. They declared themselves the insurrectionary Paris Commune, and claimed exclusive sovereignty. The next morning, they forced the arsenal at city hall and armed themselves. The new commander in chief of the National Guard, Antoine Jean Galiot Mandat, marched with 30,000 people to the Tuileries.

When the Swiss Guard protecting the king saw the crowd approaching, they opened fire, killing about 200. To avoid further bloodshed, the king ordered the badly outnumbered Swiss Guard to cease firing and retire to their barracks—except for a small squad who would escort the royal family from the Tuileries to the Assembly Hall and place them in a ten-foot square room for their own protection. All the Swiss Guardsmen who stayed in the Tuileries were surrounded, hunted down, and killed. The Assembly consigned the royal family to the Luxembourg Palace, but the insurrectionary Paris Commune demanded they have custody of the royal family and transferred them to the Temple Tower, a virtual prison.

For six weeks the Commune, with more power than the Assembly, established an ad hoc executive council to assert its imperious authority. The Legislative Assembly declared the suspension of the king, officially ending the monarchy. Upon the arrival at the Assembly of the victorious insurgents carrying banners of "Liberté, Egalité, Fraternité," the Assembly implored the people to respect justice, their magistrates, the rights of man, liberty, and equality. But the mob and their leaders had all the power in their hands—and were determined to use it.

The Paris Commune called on the Assembly to establish a revolutionary tribunal, so the National Convention was formed with 749 members. Although it was a legislative assembly, it entrusted executive power to its own members, with Danton responsible for maintaining the legal system and public order.

The radical Convention immediately set out to remove all traces of king, Church, and anti-republican enemies. They authorized the prompt and permanent elimination of the king, adopted a non-Christian Revolutionary Calendar, prohibited all royalist newspapers, set about removing all religious or royal names from street signs, abolished all remnants of noble privilege, sold the properties of émigrés, armed the civilian population, assumed the power of arrest, and killed 1400 people in prisons. Every section of Paris supported a committee of vigilance. They began closing monasteries and arresting non-juring priests, 4000 of whom were exiled. A list of "opponents of the Revolution" were drawn up, and the gates to the city were sealed.

The Convention sent delegates to Sedan to offer me an executive role in the new government. I refused, for I abhorred the senseless slaughter of the Swiss Guard at the Tuileries as much as I had Tarleton's brutal slaughter of the surrendering militia at the Battle of Waxhaw. I was appalled by the arbitrary ruthlessness. Instead, I ordered their arrest. When the Commune learned of this, they sent agents to relieve me of my command, but I refused to see them. I assembled my troops and asked them to renew their oath of loyalty to the constitution, the nation, the law, and the king, and to go with me to Paris to reestablish order. They refused, shouting, "Liberty, Fraternity, the National Convention." I was powerless.

When Danton and Robespierre were informed that I had refused to see their agents, they called me a traitor and demanded my arrest for treason. Warned that the Commune had set a price upon my head and had sent commissioners to Sedan to arrest me, I had no choice but to flee, though I was worried about the impact on my family—

fearing they would be at risk from vindictive revolutionaries, perhaps even killed. I was also concerned about the financial hardship, for all my properties, estates, businesses, and assets including the Hôtel de Lafayette, La Belle Gabrielle, and Chavaniac would be forfeited to the government. If I wanted to avoid the guillotine or imprisonment, I would have to leave Sedan immediately.

I wrote Adrienne that I intended to go to the safety of America by way of the neutral Dutch Republic and London, and asked her to join me in London as soon as she could, apologizing for any unhappiness my actions might cause her. I fled with twelve similarly endangered staff officers and managed to escape France before the Commune could arrest me.

My companions and I crossed the frontier on our way to Brussels. Austrian and Prussian troops held the northern border of France and the outpost towns of the Austrian Netherlands, but we rode toward the technically neutral bishopric of Liège. In the village of Rochefort we stumbled onto a unit of Flemish troops under Austrian command. The officer in charge gave assurances to me of free passage, and beckoned us to ride up the main street to accommodations in the Auberge du Pélican. Soon, however, he reversed himself and announced our arrest. I protested that my friends and I were non-combatants and on neutral territory in Belgium. Nevertheless we were arrested, taken to the citadel of Antwerp, and imprisoned.

I was separated from the others, and a message handed to me. I was told that I could have my freedom if I would forswear my republican principles and reveal military secrets such as troop locations and strengths as well as the locations of supply depots. When I refused to be disloyal to my country or buy my liberty, a cavalry escort was summoned to take all of us to a prison in Namur. We were confined there briefly and transferred to Nivelles. Most of my staff of officers were separated from me. The four former Assembly deputies were detained and taken to Luxembourg to a tribunal of coalition representatives. They informed us that we were all ideological threats, and particularly that, "Monsieur de Lafayette is not only the promoter of the French

Revolution but of world-wide liberty. The existence of Monsieur de Lafayette is inconsistent with the safety of the government of Europe." They ordered that we be held as "prisoners of state" for our leading roles in the revolution until the old royal regime could return to power in France and its king render final judgment. We were turned over to a military escort for imprisonment in the Prussian fortress of Wesel.

During the 160 mile journey I was repeatedly questioned about the French army I had commanded. At one town, an officer of the duke of Saxe Teschen demanded that I turn over the treasure chest of my army, which he assumed I had taken with me. I thought the request a joke, but when the demand was repeated I turned on the officer and said, "I am to infer, then, that if the duke of Saxe Teschen had been in my place, he would have stolen the military chest of the army?" The officer backed out of the room in confusion.

I was put in solitary confinement under constant guard, prohibited from talking to anyone, forbidden books or mail, and deprived of exercise and sunlight. With a wooden board for a bed and rats scurrying about my damp cell, I was unable to sleep. The food was slop, and my health began quickly deteriorating. I grew weak, had trouble breathing, and thought I was about to die. To every protest the answer was that I would receive better treatment if I would reveal the military plans of the army of France, for the duke of Brunswick, augmented by large complements of Hessians and the émigré royalist Army of Condé formed by Louis' brother, the comte d'Artois, had been advancing deep into France intent on ending the revolution and restoring the monarchy. Though the Jacobins had declared me a traitor to the government of the Commune, I never repaid them with treason.

Even deep in the Prussian prison, I heard that the duke had seized Verdun and was advancing on Paris. The Prussians were one of the most effective armies in Europe, trained by the famous military technician Frederick the Great, the king of Prussia who had attracted me years earlier to witness his advanced techniques. Rallying to the invasion of their country, thousands of volunteers from all over France had joined the armies of Dumouriez and François Kellerman to face the well-armed professional coalition. Near the little town of Valmy, 36,000 untrained working-class Frenchmen stopped the career soldiers—a major emotional victory for the republic. The next day the monarchy was abolished, and on September 22 the First French Republic was declared.

All Europe was shocked. Francis II, the Austrian and Holy Roman Emperor, blamed me for creating launching republicanism in Europe. Feeling true danger to his reign and authority, as well as to other European monarchies, Francis issued directives transferring me as far as possible from the anti-royalist revolution. Because of my reputation I doubted that he would publicly assassinate me, for he would not want to alienate the Americans. However, I was concerned that Francis might try to have me poisoned or make my conditions so deplorable that disease would take me. He made it known that he personally held me responsible for the imprisonment and downfall of his aunt, the queen, and dubbed me "the most dangerous revolutionary in Europe." He was intent on insuring I would henceforth be unable to conspire with those who might seek to end his reign. He transferred me further east, first to a prison at Magdeburg, then to Neisse in the province of Silesia near the border of the emperor's Bohemian and Moravian territories.

Prussian King Wilhelm grew tired of paying the costs of holding state prisoners for the Austrians, so he arranged for a Prussian military escort to hand us back to them at the Moravian border town of Zuckmantel. The Austrians transported us even further east to their military prison in the fortress city of Olmutz, which their Czech subjects called Olomouc. On May 17, 1794 at midnight we arrived in a walled complex adjoining an army hospital. All my possessions were taken and I was escorted down a long hallway and locked behind door #2.

My cell was on the ground floor in the rear wing of the former monastery. Its two large wooden doors were reinforced horizontally with broad iron strapping for greater security. My cell had the luxury of two connecting rooms. In one was a worm-eaten wooden bench, some straw, and a foul-smelling chamber pot. High in the exterior walls were two windows protected by a double iron grate which enabled me to look down on a narrow terrace along the edge of which was a stone gutter that carried latrine waste to a nearby stream. The wind filled my cell with the odor. To the right I could see the rear of the military hospital, and to the left the back of some cathedral cannons. In the distance, past two guard towers and other fortifications, lay wheat fields, and beyond, the Oder Mountains. Paris was 800 miles away.

The guards were ordered, upon threat of flogging, to neither address nor refer to me by name. I was referred to only as "State Prisoner #2." All correspondence and reading material were denied me. I was shut off from the outside world and permitted no contact with anyone. In the twenty months of successive incarcerations, I had not been permitted to write or receive letters. I was plagued by guilt at having placed my family in danger, afraid that the Commune would arrest them.

In the first six months my health deteriorated rapidly. My hair began falling out and I lost considerable weight. I suspected that I was being slowly poisoned, even though I had been treated for months by a kindly prison doctor, Karl Haberlein.

One day in November the good doctor came into my cell and handed me a book. I was both surprised and grateful. Lacking diversions of any kind, I was excited to have anything to read, though my eyesight had deteriorated. At night, I sometimes had a bit of moonlight to augment the single candle that I held the book close to. I was surprised when the heat from the flame brought out a hidden message written on the flyleaf. It informed me that people were in Olmutz plotting my escape. The message was terse and lacking in details.

Later that week, when the guards took me out for my weekly exercise to the usual nearby field, two men rode up trailing an additional horse, and directing me in English to mount it. But I was so weak that the guard was able to grab me. In the struggle, he bit my finger almost to the bone and my horse ran away. The two men overpowered the guard, and managed to get me on one of the horses. A purse of money was pushed into my hands and I was told to "Get to Hoff." As I rode away from the prison, they both were shouting frantically for me to "Get to

Hoff." I had no idea who or what "Hoff" was, and in the confusion I thought they were shouting "Get Off."

I was so feeble and disoriented from my time in prison that I had no idea where I was, nor what I was supposed to do now. I was quickly recaptured in the unfamiliar territory by townspeople unused to seeing an emaciated, bedraggled person riding aimlessly around. They summoned the police who suspected from my tattered clothes and disheveled appearance that I was an escaped prisoner, and immediately brought me back.

For trying to escape I was punished by being chained to the wall. The superintendent of the prison ordered that I be permitted to talk to no one, not even the guards, and certainly not other prisoners. I tried to fill the lengthy days by remembering better times, and by organizing my thoughts so that if I were ever released, I could include them in my journal.

CHAPTER 21

Olmutz Surprise

1795

I HAD BEEN A PRISONER in solitary confinement for three years, and a year past my farcical escape attempt, when on October 15, 1795. I was sitting on one of my rickety chairs when I heard the outer door to my cell being opened. I was riveted to see who would enter my cell, and to know why. I listened intently as a guard turned the key in the inner door and watched as it swung slowly open, letting in a narrow stream of light from the torches of the guards in the hallway.

Instead of the usual gruff prison guard, three-well dressed women walked tentatively into my disgusting cell. I had not been permitted the slightest amenity for a year, and certainly no visitors. I feared that ill health, malnutrition, and weight loss might be producing hallucinations. I stared at the intruders and my stares were returned. The women wore bonnets and their hair partially obscured their faces. What possible reason might such angelic creatures have for visiting me? Why were the authorities suddenly permitting these people to come into my cell?

The three women scrutinized me in silence. I could not have been more astonished nor fearful. The shortest one, hesitant to approach me, cautiously took a step, staring unwaveringly at my face. When she was within reach, she took my hands, drew me closer, and put her arms around me gently, as if she were afraid to break my bones. Only when I saw tears flooding out of her eyes did I realize I was touching Adrienne, so the others must be Anastastie and Virginie. I was so weak that if Adrienne had not been holding me I would have collapsed. It was the most extraordinary moment of my life. I could not guess how they could have found me in this remote corner of the world—nor how, nor why—they gained admission to my cell. How could three unescorted women have traveled hundreds of miles through hostile countries by themselves?

I was engulfed by a tidal wave of shame and humiliation. Four years ago I had left them, the hero of two worlds. Now I was filthy and bedraggled, no different than a common criminal. My bones stood out aggressively, my breath was labored and foul. My hair had turned gray and thinned to a few long, scraggly strands. My beard was long, unkempt, and tangled. My tattered clothing and the ragged wrappings I used for shoes were moldy and worn through.

I stared at the two girls with tears running down their smiling faces. They were more beautiful than I remembered, and no longer children. Adrienne was so affected by my condition that I thought she might faint. I guided her to one of the straight-back wooden chairs and knelt beside her, held her hand, desperately wanting to hold and comfort her, but mortified to move closer, much less touch her. I felt like a leper. I wanted to ask a million questions, but being with her was far more powerful than words. I was awed as by a miracle, and relieved of guilt to know that all in my family were safe.

That night, after the guards removed Adrienne and the children to escort them to their own cell, I lay awake tearful and hard of breath on my warped plank, my mind a scherzo of free-floating thoughts. A poem drifted into it like a wind-blown leaf into an open window:

When, in disgrace with fortune and men's eyes,

I all alone beweep my outcast state

And trouble deaf heaven with my bootless cries

And look upon myself and curse my fate,

Wishing me like to one more rich in hope,

Featured like him, like him with friends possess'd,

Desiring this man's art and that man's scope,

With what I most enjoy contented least;

Yet in these thoughts myself almost despising,

Haply I think on thee, and then my state,

Like to the lark at break of day arising

From sullen earth, sings hymns at heaven's gate;

For thy sweet love remember'd such wealth brings

That then I scorn to change my state with kings.

A perceptive poet from the past had pierced my soul. Most assuredly I cursed my fate, yet happily did I think on Adrienne, glad in the wealth she brought me. By impartial standards she was a truly extraordinary woman. Her presence had rescued me and bestowed the will to keep me living, but I was resolved to spare her and the girls further suffering. I vowed to be firm, accept no excuses, and be resolute.

When Adrienne and the girls returned to my cell the next day, I summoned my energy and demanded Adrienne take the girls and leave Olmutz immediately. My daughters were only 18 and 13, and I insisted that Adrienne not subject them to these inhumane conditions. I told her that I could not bear subjecting my family to another day in this hole of hell. It was enough that they had shown me they were alive, safe and, for the moment at least, sound. They had bolstered my spirits by their humane visit, but their continued presence would distress me considerably, making me feel responsible for living in these deplorable conditions and watching their health fail.

The women were patient with my rant, nodded their heads in agreement with every word I uttered, but they all adamantly refused to leave me. Adrienne told me that in Vienna she had attempted to leave the girls with friends, but they would not abandon their mother. They were prepared to do whatever was necessary to keep the family together, even if it meant suffering for their voluntary confinement.

The prison authorities knew Adrienne and the girls were imprisoned by personal order of the emperor and could leave anytime they chose. Even the toughest guard did not relish the idea of treating innocent young girls to these appalling conditions. They were shocked that anyone would voluntarily incarcerate herself, and they were impressed that this frail woman and her two young daughters would willingly be confined out of love for a prisoner, however renown. They were in awe of these dainty foreigners and respectful, according them better and more attentive treatment.

Though sequestered in the cell next to mine, the guards gave them access to certain amenities such as better food (meaning only that it did not have hair and rodent feces intentionally added), eating utensils, sturdier furniture, books and blankets, as well as allowing them to regularly see visitors. They could exercise more frequently, and were provided basins of clean water twice a week for bathing. But by order of the emperor, they were not permitted to send or receive letters. The guards confined the women to their cell until the evening meal, after which they were permitted to join me for a few hours in my cell until bedtime.

During the day, Adrienne instructed the girls in French, literature, history, and math. After lessons the women stayed busy mending my clothes or making new ones for me. Anastasie constructed a pair of soft, warm quilted shoes out of material she salvaged from one of my dilapidated coats and pieces of her mother's corset. Virginie used fabric from her full skirt to sew me a shirt.

The writing pens Adrienne had brought to Olmutz had been confiscated, so she utilized toothpicks for pens, and made use of the ashes from her stove, which she mixed with urine and water to improvise India ink. Her only paper was what she could find on the margins and fly leaves of the battered books that were provided to her. With these pathetic writing provisions, she began writing a biography of her beloved mother, to remind Frenchmen and the world of the horrible atrocities that had been committed.

The women definitely improved my life, and even the guards began to treat me differently. Bit by bit, Adrienne and the girls filled in the details of what had taken place during my absence from the march of history.

I had last seen my family in Chavaniac. News of my flight and the political turmoil in Paris, as well as the war, quickly found its way down to the Auvergne. Aware of the danger she and the children faced because of the Jacobin denunciation of me, and especially by my fleeing, Adrienne had taken immediate steps to protect George and the two girls. Since our thirteen-year-old son was known throughout France as the son of the infamous traitor Lafayette, she sent him into hiding in an isolated mountain village. The girls were not as well known nor as vulnerable, so she arranged for them to stay out of sight with some American friends who rented a large farmhouse we owned nearby.

Her measures were timely because less than a month after I fled France, local commissioners and a party of soldiers from the revolutionary government in Paris came to the château with a directive to arrest her. They transported her to the nearby village of Le Puy to appear before the town councilors. Since the councilors knew, liked, and trusted Adrienne—a woman whose only crime was being married to me—they permitted her to return to Chavaniac on condition that she place herself under house arrest.

On October 3, 1792 Adrienne was relieved to learn that I had been transferred to the prison in Magdeburg. At least I was still alive. She had not heard from me, and she knew the Jacobins were massacring thousands of aristocrats, priests, and prisoners; the Austrians were invading France; and émigrés were also intent on killing French anti-royalists.

With the children safely in hiding, Adrienne wrote to the minister of the interior asking permission to leave her house arrest to look for me in Magdeburg. The minister summarily denied her request. She sent numerous letters to me at the Magdeburg prison—which the prison authorities confiscated. She waited in vain for a reply.

In desperation, she wrote George Washington (now president of the United States), the duke of Brunswick, the king of Prussia, as well as his sister the princess of Orange asking them to help affect my release. Not even Washington responded.

On January 21, 1793 the world received the appalling news that could not be kept secret even from me—the gruesome guillotining of the thirty-eight-year-old Louis XVI. The brutality of the murder frightened Adrienne. His death was cruel, a disgrace on the depraved perpetrators. And it was unnecessary—he had actively supported the North American colonists, signed the Edict of Tolerance ending religious persecution in France, had tried to reform the economic system, and was not a ruthless man. His murder unleashed a torrent of needless bloodshed. The Constitution was suspended and by September the Revolutionary Tribunal decreed that suspected traitors—all nobles, relatives of émigrés, and any likely enemies of the revolution—were subject to arrest and guillotine without trial. As victims of anger, jealousy, and revenge, the heads of royalty, nobility, and clergy began to roll. Marie Antoinette was falsely charged with sexually abusing her son. A sham trial before the Revolutionary Tribunal was held to humiliate her. Two days later she was guillotined. So much for laws and constitutions—they protected no one. The madness intensified, with the Committee of Public Safety—which included Robespierre—purging thousands of fellow revolutionaries including Danton and Desmoulins.

There were so many arrests that the Committee found it necessary to create new holding facilities out of many mansions of noblemen to house over 10,000 prisoners awaiting execution. Robespierre had guillotines set up at three convenient locations—the Place de la Revolution, Place de la Bastille, and Place de Throne—each capable of lopping off at least twenty heads a day. Not even the most distinguished men of France were spared, including the great poet André Chenier, the famous chemist Antoine Lavoisier, the eminent Admiral d'Estaing, and the king's seventy-two-year-old defense attorney and prominent abolitionist, Lamoignon de Malesherbes.

In October Jean Sylvain Bailly was arrested and charged with conspiring in the king's flight to Varennes, a ludicrous charge. He was imprisoned in La Force prison, denied time to prepare for the trial, the right to counsel, or to call witnesses, and quickly found guilty. Robespierre, to make an example of Bailly, chose to execute him not at one of the usual locations in Paris, but at the Champ de Mars as a symbol of Bailly's "great betrayal" of the democratic movement. The elderly mayor and leader of the revolution was humiliated, and forced to endure freezing rain and the insults of a howling mob before he was guillotined.

Knowing that her husband had also participated in the tragic occurrence at the Champs de Mars, Adrienne feared that she would soon follow. In May 1794 she saw a band of policemen approaching Chavaniac with great fanfare. She was terrified. With apparent pleasure they placed her under arrest, forced her into a secured police carriage, and transported her all the way to Paris where she was deposited in the dreaded La Force prison.

The jailers responsible for registering all arriving prisoners had been informed that they would be receiving the once renown "Universal Mother." When they recognized the wife of the marquis de Lafayette, their hostile reception increased her anxiety. The callous jailers amused themselves by trying to embarrass and humiliate incoming prisoners, especially nobility. To have fun at Adrienne's expense, they tried to shame her into giving a false name to avoid the guillotine. She, however, would not allow ill-mannered men to intimidate her, and proudly and loudly announce her true name. The thwarted jailers notified her that she had already been tried, found guilty of treason, and sentenced to death, and would be seeing the guillotine shortly.

They led her to the door of a cell and rudely shoved her into a dimly lit room. Frayed by her arrest, Adrienne was unprepared when she saw her beloved mother Henriette, her sister Louise, and her elderly grandmother Catherine inside her small cell. She did not want to believe that her fellow Frenchmen would kill these three women, innocent of no crime but being born into the nobility, but it did not seem coincidental that four members of the same family had been rounded up together.

The shock of seeing her family was exacerbated by the filthy conditions of their room. She tried to suppress her tears, feeling guilty that she might be upsetting her family. They were nearly starved and unable to sleep night after night, not knowing their fate. Their fear was tangible. Adrienne was scared, not so much for herself, but mainly for her children who would be left with neither mother nor father.

On the evening of July 21 a young revolutionary guard opened the door to their cell, entered, and matter-of-factly informed them that they would all be executed in the morning. They knelt together in prayer, and then sat to wait for the door of their cell to open.

Shortly after the first light of dawn, a guard banged open their cell door and guards forcibly removed Henriette, Louise, and Catherine then bolted the door, leaving Adrienne alone with the insects and rodents. She could hear their steps as they were led down the hall to the courtyard outside her window. She could not actually see the cutting blocks, steel guillotine blade, nor black-hooded executioner. Nor could she see her mother forced to climb the scaffold steps, kneel down, and place her head on the chopping block. But she did hear the fall of the axe as each of the three were guillotined. God had turned his back on these pious and pure Catholics, kind and harmless people without sin who had done their best to help the hungry and destitute, and supported republican principles of the revolution that had given the French people a say in their governance.

Adrienne waited fearfully, straining to hear the guards returning and the sounds of keys. Every minute of every day Adrienne expected to be led to the guillotine. But no one came for her. After several tormenting days and sleepless nights, she was taken from her cell without explanation, put in an open cart, and transferred across the Seine to the Collège du Plessis prison—in the school I was attending when I first heard that our marriage was being arranged.

Conditions were even worse than at La Force, and discipline the most severe in Paris. The jailers took pleasure in starving, abusing, and harassing their prisoners, constantly reminding them of their impending fate. Female prisoners were kept separate from the men, but prostitutes and nuns, pickpockets and duchesses shared the same rooms. The food brought in from the neighborhood kitchens was often stolen by the guards. What food they received was placed on a common table with unwashed bowls and wooden spoons. Every day sixty prisoners were taken for execution and their beds quickly filled.

Shortly after arriving at Le Plessis, Adrienne was informed that she had visitors. Almost all of her family and friends had fled or been guillotined, so she was curious. Into her crowded cell walked the United States Minister to France, James Monroe, his wife Elizabeth, and the Minister Plenipotentiary to France, Gouverneur Morris. Adrienne knew them from Monday salons at the Hôtel de Lafayette. They had brought food and a sweater, and assurance that things were being done behind the scenes to affect her release. They gave her a letter from Washington who remembered her gift and was doing everything in his power to locate her husband. He told her how proud he was to wear the Masonic apron when he laid the cornerstone of the United States Capitol in the new federal city that had been named in his honor.

Washington had asked Monroe and Morris to help secure the release of Americans held in French prisons without jeopardizing American neutrality—as the official representative of the American government, one of the few allies France still had. They hoped to make Robespierre and the Committee of Public Safety aware that a friendly trading partner wanted to protect one of their prisoners.

Monroe had repeatedly gone to Robespierre demanding the release of Adrienne, Rochambeau, and Thomas Paine, warning that their execution would turn Americans against France. After that Elizabeth Monroe came regularly to the prison, arriving in the most conspicuous official American carriage to draw notice to her as emissary of President Washington.

On July 27 Robespierre accused his Jacobin club of plotting against him, and demanded the immediate arrest and execution of the entire Convention. Even the Jacobins had had enough. Fearful of their own deaths, the members of the Convention ordered his arrest. They guillotined him without trial and promptly abolished the Commune of Paris. The grip of terror was over.

Soon prisoners, including Rochambeau and Paine, were released. Adrienne was not, but was transferred to a house on the rue des Amandiers, and in November she was sent along to the Desnos house on rue Notre-Dame des Champs. Adrienne no longer had reason to fear being executed, but she had no idea why she was still being detained. She wrote to her daughters that her main concern was getting nearer to them:

> Take all courage, and judge all the tender sentiments of my heart which are known to you. Take the best care of each other, of my aunt, of she who is taking the place of mother. I wait for the response of your brother at any moment with keen emotion. Farewell, my dear children, I embrace you with the maternal tenderness that is the concern and consolation of my life. Those who second it can judge my feelings.
>
> —N. Lafayette
> At the Desnos house, rue Notre Dame Desch

Adrienne remained in Desnos House for two months, having no idea of her future and constantly concerned that she might be harmed in prison. Then on January 22, 1795 a guard courteously asked her to follow him and led her down the hallway. The authorities returned the clothing she had been wearing when she had arrived at La Force prison, and she was summarily released without notice or explanation.

The winter in Paris was one of the coldest in history—even the Seine was frozen over. Her clothing was not adequate for the bitter conditions, and she felt intensely cold. All her property had been confiscated by the revolution. Most of her family and friends had either been killed or fled. Her husband was somewhere in prison, her father in Switzerland, and her children hidden in the distant Auvergne. After more than two years of hell, she was grateful to be alive, and happy to be free. However she was desperate, without money or clothes, home or transportation.

There was only one place she could think of going for help—the American Embassy. She trudged her way there through the vacant streets of Paris until she arrived shivering and blue. The Embassy fireplaces were working to capacity, and the warmth they gave off slowly restored her circulation. Promptly the ambassador appeared at her side. Pleased to see her, Monroe immediately took her to his residential quarters where Elizabeth hugged her and arranged food and a thick blanket.

The Monroes understood and sympathized with her need to be reunited with her children, but insisted that Adrienne stay with them until she could rest, be nourished, and organize the difficult journey to Chavaniac in severe weather. Steps had been taken to ascertain my exact location, but they only knew I was in a prison somewhere in the Austrian Empire. They assured her that they would help her find her children and me.

Gouverneur Morris, who had just finished his official term, was still in Paris and a wealthy man. Given Adrienne's circumstances, the Monroes arranged for him to lend Adrienne a substantial amount of money to purchase suitable clothing and obtain a carriage, horses, and supplies to take her to Chavaniac. Adrienne hurriedly left Paris traveling in disguise to avoid arrest where police might be looking to enhance their reputation. The dirt roads were lumpy with ice, and slippery. It seemed to take forever to get to Chavaniac, but she was relieved to learn that the girls were safe with friends and well. Reassured, she did not go to them immediately, but set out to find George.

He was no longer a child, but a fifteen-year-old man—tall and muscular, fit and healthy, with a fine red beard. She was overjoyed. The weight of parental responsibility, such a stressful burden in prison, was lifted from her shoulders.

They stayed as guests on the farm of the friend who had cared for Anastasie and Virginie while Adrienne organized her search for me. To make sure George continued safely out of harms way, she decided to send him to America. She wrote to President Washington to thank him for his efforts in obtaining her release and letting him know that her children were safe. She implored his assistance in locating her husband, and if he was still in prison to obtain his release. And, while she was searching for her husband, would he be willing to care for his godson?

While she was waiting for a reply, she risked traveling back to Paris with the three children to obtain passports, sufficient money, and accommodations for George's transit to America and for his habitation while there.

The government had specifically forbidden George from leaving France. If his vessel were stopped and George seized, both he and the vessel's owners could face serious consequences. Moreover, the United States could not accept the son of a person whom the French government had branded a traitor, as America could not risk turning a powerful ally into an enemy.

Washington arranged for his godson to be sent incognito to the safety of America, under his indirect protection. Monroe issued an American passport for George under the name of George Motier, and arranged for an American businessman in Paris, James Russell, to escort George and his tutor Félix Fastral to Le Havre and then on to Boston where Russell would turn George over to Cabot Lodge, a close friend of Washington, who would enroll the young man in Harvard University. When not in residence at school, George would stay with Lodge in Boston or in New York City with Alexander Hamilton who would be able to send George to Philadelphia to stay with Washington in the presidential mansion. Washington's friends, agents, and aides would oversee and fund everything.

With our son safe and in good hands, and an American passport for "Mrs. Motier of Hartford, Connecticut" and similar documents for Anastasie and Virginie, on September 1 Adrienne and the girls left Paris for Calais, crossed the channel, and rode up to London. When Washington's direct contact with the Austrian emperor could not secure my release, he had invoked help from Hamilton's British brother-in-law, a member of Parliament. With the participation of influential friends who pooled their resources, they contracted to find me with Justus Erich Bollman, a multilingual physician from Hanover who had smuggled many aristocrats out of France.

Doctor Bollman readily accepted the challenge, as well as the generous payment. His random search of the prisons in Europe eventually led him to the small village of Olmutz. He checked into a country inn, the Golden Swan, for the night. By good fortune, at a nearby table was another physician dining alone. During their collegial chat, Bollman learned that the Dr. Karl Haberlein was staff surgeon at the nearby military prison hospital, and was eager to brag that he was treating a well-known patient whose name the good doctor had been forbidden to disclose.

Bollman did not press the issue, but assumed the patient might be me. He asked Dr. Haberlein to be his guest for dinner the following evening. They were enjoying a glass of wine after dinner when Bollman suggested that the doctor might like to develop his relationship with his celebrated patient by thoughtfully giving him some interesting reading matter to pass his lengthy days of confinement. Desirous of impressing his patient, the doctor agreed. The books were inspected for weapons and messages, but when none were found, the prison doctor was permitted to bring the books to his patient. Using invisible ink made of lemon juice, Bollman had placed a message on the flyleaf of one of the books, tersely informing me of his presence and intention to effect my escape.

Bollman proceeded to Vienna, about 150 miles south of Olmutz, to purchase a carriage and secretly remodel it to contain a coffin-like box hidden under the seat. He happened to meet a young American medical student on holiday from studies in London and looking for adventure. When Bollman asked him if he would be interested in helping rescue the famous marquis de Lafayette, Francis Huger jumped at the chance because he was the son of Major Benjamin Huger who had sheltered me when I first stepped on American soil in South Carolina.

The two men returned to Olmutz and checked in to the Inn, dined with Dr. Haberlein, and asked him to give his prisoner books they had purchased in Vienna. Bollman managed to sneak another brief message to me, inadequate of detail except that my rescue would take place soon.

When Bollman and Huger returned to London they provided indisputable knowledge of my exact location. Adrienne began making plans. She could not go directly to Olmutz and risk being turned away or told that I was no longer there. There was only one person with the power and authority to give official authorization—the man in charge of all the prisons, and everything else, in the Holy Roman Empire—Francis II, the Emperor who feared and despised me.

Adrienne, Anastasie, and Virginie would need travel documents, a carriage and bilingual driver willing to transport three unescorted women safely through a hostile country where they knew no one. They went first to Hamburg—the neutral Danish controlled independent city—where American Consul John Parish assisted in obtaining the items Adrienne needed.

As it was unlikely that the emperor would permit a meeting with the wife of his worst enemy, Adrienne contacted her uncle who, as French Ambassador to Austria, was friendly with Francis' Grand Chamberlain, the minister responsible for granting audiences with Emperors Joseph, Leopold, and Francis. Her uncle wrote a letter introducing her as "Mrs. Motier of Hartford, Connecticut."

Arriving in Vienna in mid-October, Adrienne went promptly to the chambers of the Grand Chamberlain and showed her uncle's letter and her passport. Uncomfortable deceiving him, she took the risk of revealing her true identity and purpose of her mission. He admired her honesty and courage, was sympathetic, and told her that he would try to secure her an audience without other ministers knowing.

Anastasie, Virginie, and Adrienne were driven by carriage out to the grand Hofburg Palace where they were led into a room in the inner apartment. They had barely sat down when the young Emperor walked casually into the room unannounced and sat down near Adrienne. He politely asked the purpose of her visit. She immediately informed the emperor that although she was accurately known as Adrienne Motier, she was the wife of Gilbert Motier, better known as the marquis de Lafayette. The emperor looked surprised at the bold admission, smiled, and asked again only for the purpose of her audience.

Adrienne told him that since her husband had been forced to flee France, they had had no communications. Recently she had learned that he was now in the Olmutz prison. She was concerned about him, wanted to see him, and knew that he would be in despair with concern about his family. Her mere presence might give him emotional strength, and she wanted to render any physical care she might be able to provide. She was clear that she was asking for authorization for her and her two daughters to join her husband in the Olmutz prison.

The emperor seemed surprised by this tiny woman's audacity and unique request. He had doubts about allowing women to be put in prison, even voluntarily. Though her husband might be a potential threat, these women, especially the adolescent girls, were definitely not, and it did not seem right to the youthful emperor.

Despite his reservations, Francis rose quickly and announced she had his permission. However, although he would permit her and her children to leave the prison anytime, once they did, they would not be permitted to return. He made it very clear that even he, the emperor, could not disrupt prison routine by allowing her to come and go whenever she chose.

Overjoyed with the emperor's compassion, she thanked him and returned to their inn, adamant that she would not allow her daughters to be incarcerated even briefly. She would send them back to London to stay with friends. The normally cooperative girls refused to leave their mother, insisting on accompanying her wherever she went and demanding to see their father. Adrienne argued with them repeatedly, trying to make them aware, from her experience, of appalling prison conditions, but they remained obstinate.

I listened with rapture to Adrienne and the girls recount even the dreadful events of nearly three and a half years of our separation. Denied the pleasure of words written and spoken, I simply floated in their presence and delighted in the sound of their voices despite the content of their tales of fear and hardship. I was horrified to learn of the deaths of Henriette and Adrienne's sister and grandmother, as well as of the terror Adrienne sustained afterwards. Each day I expressed my deep pleasure of having them with me, but pleaded with them to leave the abusive conditions of the prison. Seeing signs that their health, especially Adrienne's, was deteriorating, I begged her to spare the children, and asked the children to spare their mother. Respectfully unheeded, I could only watch as conditions exacted toll on them as they had on me.

Adrienne declined rapidly. Within two months she had severe headaches and a high fever. Her arms swelled, sores erupted on her legs, her gums bled and her teeth loosened. She lost weight and her skin dried severely, so that even the guards expressed concern. But Adrienne refused to leave, insisting in her soft but firm way that she would not leave without me, for her happiness was with me.

I insisted that the guards summon the prison doctor. He examined Adrienne but was baffled by her symptoms, proclaiming that she must be suffering some disorder of the blood for which he had no treatment to suggest. He urged her to go immediately to Vienna to consult specialists. She refused. When her symptoms became so painful that she was forced to ask permission of the emperor to visit Vienna, the prison authorities allowed her to write him a letter.

His reply arrived in April expressing his concern for her health, and humanely granting her request. However, he reminded her, once she left the prison, under no circumstances would he permit her to return. Adrienne again thanked him for his kindness in granting her permission to leave. However, she could not take advantage of his offer, explaining that for over half of the twenty years of our marriage she had been separated from her husband. She had often been unable to obtain any news about him, or even learn if he were alive. She was unwilling to expose herself again to such distress, even to the detriment of her well-being.

One day after the doctor had left their cell, the girls found beneath their mattress a bundle of mail from "Feldman" in Hamburg. None of us knew anyone by that name, nor anyone in Hamburg save John Parish.

Thanks to the cooperative (and well-compensated) prison doctor, the women were then able to smuggle letters out to "Feldman," who forwarded them on for delivery. Anastasie and Virginie immediately began communicating with the outside world, especially to their brother George in America, informing him of their mother's deteriorating health, the abominable conditions of our imprisonment, and begging their brother to ask Washington for his immediate help.

My wife was dying. I felt responsible and was hardly consoled when Virginie told me that despite her mother's suffering and constant pain, she was only fearful of never seeing her husband again. It gladdened Adrienne that her presence benefited my health and comfort—she claimed she was happier than she had ever been. These words filled me with even greater despair. I felt remorseful and helpless as my beloved Adrienne deteriorated. I was capable of offering her no balm but my own tears.

CHAPTER 22

Return to the Living

1797

E ARLY IN THE MORNING of September 19, sixty-one months after I was arrested and almost two years after Adrienne and the girls imprisoned themselves at Olmutz, we were abruptly removed from our cells, taken to private rooms in which had been placed large basins of water and a small piece of cloth, and ordered to bathe. I was given a haircut, permitted to shave, given new clothes, and made to look as presentable as circumstances permitted. No explanation was given for these unusual activities. We were respectfully directed out of the prison into a large Austrian government carriage. We were advised of a long journey and told we were officially in their custody until the carriage reached Hamburg. A small caravan of official Austrian carriages would be escorting us, in one of which was "Feldman." During a rest stop, while the horses were being watered and fed, "Feldman" revealed his true identity—a German-speaking French army officer who had been paid by Mr. Parish to pose as a businessman, take mail to Olmutz, and bribe the prison doctor generously to deliver it to us.

Each day toward sunset, the carriages stopped at the nearest village for accommodations and food. As we approached each town, people lined the roads to wave at our carriages. Adrienne's extraordinary boldness was already legendary, and by virtue of her incarceration she had become the heroine of liberty. People threw flowers and sang songs in her honor. I was surprised that townspeople knew we would be coming, and touched that so many thought of us with such fondness.

Two weeks on the road was grueling, the jarring ride further injuring our precarious health, despite the bracing autumn air and accommodations in heated rooms with clean beds, and fresh food.

As our caravan approached Hamburg, large crowds lined the route, shouting approval and waving. In the harbor I saw ships flying American and decorative flags in our honor. The carriages stopped in front of the small building housing the offices of the American consul. Adrienne recognized John Parish, who greeted our Austrian officials politely. While we sat in our carriage, he exchanged and signed papers, and was given the official Austrian satchels containing the belongings that had been confiscated from us and the correspondence kept from me during my isolation. We were then permitted to step down from our coach, free.

Mr. Parish welcomed us warmly and assisted us into the building, away from the Austrian authorities and the noisy crowds. A generous buffet had been laid out for us in a big reception room. We appreciated his generosity, but we ate very little, for our bodies were no longer acclimated to quantities and varieties of food. While we talked with our kind host I enjoyed a small glass of light white wine, the first I had tasted in over five years.

Our host satisfied our curiosity about our release. When Washington found out where we were, he contacted Parish with instructions to get in touch with me. The consul arranged the "Feldman" scheme and helped smuggle out the letters from Adrienne, Anastasie, and Virginie detailing our captivity. They were addressed to various people in America to invoke sympathy for our plight. Word spread through churches, town meetings, newspapers and pamphlets, and people pressured Congress to obtain our release, until they sent Gouverneur Morris to Vienna to negotiate covertly with Francis II. Unfortunately, his negotiations, such as they were, were ineffectual, as reflected in his letter to Adrienne:

Madam,

If this letter ever reaches you, I shall be obliged for the favor to his Excellency, the Baron de Thugut, and I shall expect from his kindness to have your answer forwarded to me. The Marchioness de Montagu informed me, by a letter dated November twenty-seventh, that you had been forbidden to leave the prison, unless you would entirely abandon the intention of returning thither, and that, under this alternative, preferring the duty of a tender and faithful wife to the care of your own safety, you have given that decision, which those who knew the purity of your mind would naturally expect from you. Madame de Montagu adds, that you are not permitted to come here for the purpose of consulting a physician, although the state of your health imperiously requires it.

It is certainly unnecessary for me, Madam, to express here the interest, which I take in your fate, and in that of your unfortunate friend, and to tell you how happy I should be, could I procure for him his liberty. Reasons, which I do not know, and which I nevertheless feel bound to respect, prevent this. But we are far from believing here, that his prison has any other disagreeable things about it, than those which are unavoidably connected with confinement. I am assured, on the contrary, that he is very well lodged, and in want of nothing; that the vigilant exactness, with which he is guarded, arises only from the necessity of using all means to prevent his escape; that, far from entertaining the barbarous idea of depriving you of the assistance of art, the physician of your choice will be sent to you; and that, if you are forbidden to come to Vienna, and then return to Olmutz, it is because circumstances require, that the rules of an exact prudence should be followed.

You must not despair, Madam; time will give liberty to Monsieur De Lafayette; but, in the mean time, if he has been ill treated, as Madame de Montagu has been induced to believe, it is important that it may be known, in order that means may be taken to prevent it; and in case he experiences, in accordance with the benevolent intentions of his Majesty, gentle and humane treatment, it seems to me equally proper to ascertain it, in order to put a stop to odious reports, which cannot but exasperate, and which consequently might postpone the moment of his liberation. To this effect, have the goodness, Madam, I entreat you, to send me your answer open, under cover to his Excellency, the Baron de Thugut. I am still uncertain whether I shall be able to receive it at Vienna, as it is my intention to depart in a few days. But I flatter myself, that we shall meet again in America; and I pray you to believe, that I shall always and everywhere preserve the sincere attachment, with which I have the honor to be, &c.

—*Gouverneur Morris*

The letter enraged the normally composed Adrienne. Morris was a wealthy, sometimes arrogant aristocrat sympathetic to Marie Antoinette and her brother the emperor, and critical of the French Revolution. But his attempt to justify the unacceptable incarceration and prison conditions of her husband made her furious. Adrienne did not appreciate his comments suggestion that the "disagreeable" conditions of the prison were "unavoidable," and the "he is very well lodged, and in want of nothing." It was untrue and irrational. She refrained from letting him know of her anger because Morris was a friend of Washington and members of Congress. Moreover, he had lent her money for which she was indebted to him financially and personally.

Parish told us that despite American efforts being unproductive, our release had been secured by a young artillery captain who supported the revolutionary Jacobin faction. Because of his success in suppressing a counter-revolutionary revolt at a key French naval arsenal, he had been promoted to brigadier general. Within three years, Napoleon was in command of the French army in Italy where he was successful against the armies of Francis II, and was rapidly approaching Vienna when the Austrian government sent emissaries asking for peace negotiations.

During the five months of negotiations, Congress asked Consul Parish to contact representatives of both Napoleon and Francis requesting my release and promising that I would go quietly into exile in America. However neither Napoleon nor Francis were interested in having me released, as both saw me as a threat, as did Francis' powerful British ally, Prime Minister William Pitt, who despised me as a major factor in the loss of their American colony.

Bonaparte, who had political ambitions, believed me his main rival, for I was better known to Frenchmen and had been martyred in prison for five years for my revolutionary sentiments. However he needed the support and skills of well-educated émigrés. Parish convinced his supporters that if Napoleon brought peace to Europe and arranged for my release, he would garner support of the many educated nobles who had fled. These liberal émigrés would return and support Bonaparte's quest for influence. Moreover, with the release of Adrienne Lafayette, he would be seen as the liberator of the forsaken, and earn a reputation for compassion. With her remarkable bravery and sacrifice already becoming legendary throughout Europe, he would be admired by the public.

Napoleon, persuaded, demanded that Francis order my release from prison as a condition of obtaining peace. Francis was not pleased by the upstart's demand, but was forced to agree—though only on condition that I promise to go immediately into exile in America and never set foot within the Holy Roman Empire. A month before the official signing of the peace treaty at Campo Formio, Francis issued orders releasing us to American authorities. President John Adams provided several American ships that were waiting in the harbor to take the Motier family into exile in America. Though all of us were eager to go, it was clearly impossible. I was too weak to survive another lengthy crossing and certainly could not subject Adrienne to such a voyage—the carriage from Olmutz had wreaked havoc on her kidneys, circulation, and added to the swelling in her arms and legs. Rough seas, unhealthy food, stale water, and the prevalence of typhoid, typhus, and dysentery might well kill her.

The consul was concerned that if we did not go into exile as promised, we would be violating the terms of the treaty and subject to re-arrest. We assured him that we were neither able nor interested in being a threat to anyone, and would willingly comply with the intent of the treaty by going into retirement in some neutral territory outside both Austria and France. He could see our pathetic condition, and asked us to stay with him for a few weeks while he arranged for a physician and worked out an alternate plan.

Though we would have preferred to thank each of them in person, during our recuperation we wrote to Bollman, Huger, Washington, Monroe, Napoleon, and even Francis II to let them know that we were truly appreciative of their support of our release.

After we found a temporary place to stay in Holstein, I wrote Napoleon:

> The love of liberty and country would suffice for your arrival to fill me with joy and hope. To this desire for public happiness is joined a lively and profound sentiment for my liberator. Your greetings to the prisoners of Olmutz have been sent to me by her whose life I owe to you. I rejoice in all my obligations to you, citizen-general, and in the happy conviction that to cherish your glory and to wish your success is an act of civism as much as of attachment and gratitude.

I knew little about the young Corsican but wanted to believe that he was an idealistic republican, for he had defeated the royalist insurrections in Toulon, an armed anti-republican uprising in the fiercely

Catholic Vendée region of western France, and extinguished another royalist outbreak in Paris in October that had threatened the Convention. He had liberated my family, and I looked forward to his efforts as a champion of liberty.

We were optimistic in thinking we could convince him that we supported him and were neither rivals nor threat, so he would let us return to France. But until we could obtain passports our best option was to live in the neutral Duchy of Holstein, where Adrienne's sister and aunt had been forced to flee. Anne Paule Dominique de Noailles, marquise de Montague, had settled in the little town of Lemkuhlen, about sixty miles from Hamburg. Their aunt, Adrienne Catherine de Noailles, comtesse de Tesse, had fled early in the revolution with most of her fortune, and lived in a nice estate in the nearby town of Witmold. With a loan from Consul Parish, my friend César de la Tour-Maubourg and I leased a large country house near Lemkuhlen for our two families—five in mine and eight in his.

Immediately upon settling, Adrienne and I wrote letters to both our son and Washington conveying our desire for George to join us as soon as possible. Our letters, of course, would take weeks to reach them, more weeks for our son to arrange passage back to Europe, and even more for him to cross the Atlantic to some European port.

Consul Parish had informed us that Washington's second term as President of the United States had ended in March 1797, and that most of Europe was shocked by his refusal of a third term—shocked that anyone would voluntarily give up the power of his office. John Adams had succeeded him, and my friend Jefferson was his vice-president. When they learned of our release, Adams had sent the ships we had seen in the Hamburg harbor to bring us to America to comply with the conditions of my release.

George, hearing of our release from other sources, had already prepared to sail back to Hamburg on board a British ship. Unfortunately he had not received our letter with our new location, so he went to Paris to look for us, only to learn from Josephine Bonaparte that we were not permitted to return to France. The American ambassador in

Paris told him we were safely in Lemkuhlen, where he arrived in February. I had not seen my son for five years. He was tall, university educated, and world traveled. I was overjoyed to see him safe and healthy, though disappointed to have missed raising him. With our family all together, I was relieved that the children had passed unscathed and sound through the violence of political and cultural upheaval.

Not long after George returned, Tour-Maubourg's younger brother Juste-Charles, who had served in Sedan and been captured with me at Rochefort, moved in with us—an exile whose prospects had been destroyed by the breakdown in France. He and Anastasie, in daily contact under the same roof, fell in love. Charles asked me for Anastasie's hand, and despite Madame Tesse's objections that the marriage was not proper, Adrienne and I were happy to consent even though we had no dowry to give them—the revolution had changed many archaic customs, including arranged marriages. We scheduled the wedding in spring at Witmold.

Shortly after George returned, we received a letter from Diane de Simiane. She had also learned of our release and looked forward to seeing us soon. Gaunt, bald, and still in ill health, I was too self-conscious to see Diane, but my extraordinary wife thoughtfully arranged to have our friend stay with her aunt. Diane expected to find a colony of melancholy exiles in a remote corner of the countryside. Instead, she heard a cheerful family talking of nothing but marriage plans and baptismal arrangements.

Anastasie and Charles were married on May 9 in the chapel of the de Tesse home, Adrienne's aunt providing a splendid trousseau. The wedding was ideal, only dampened by the fact that abscesses on Adrienne's legs required she be carried to the ceremony in an armchair with George on one side and Charles on the other.

Ten days after the wedding, unable to attack England directly without a strong navy, Napoleon took his army to Alexandria to cut off Britain's Mediterranean access to the Red Sea and their colonies in the far east and India. His intention was to cripple the British economy in retaliation for the money, ships, troops, weapons, and food Britain was giving the kings and royalists throughout Europe to overthrow Napoleon and the republican government of France.

He was initially victorious on land, but at the beginning of August Rear-Admiral Sir Horatio Nelson set fire to Bonaparte's fleet, preventing Napoleon from receiving reinforcements and supplies. Then bubonic plague and Ottoman uprisings throughout Egypt weakened his army. With the Austrian monarch advancing on France by way of the Black Forest and the Po Valley, Napoleon abandoned his army. By November he had effected a coup to overthrow the Directory, which had succeeded the Committee of Public Safety, and was elected its first consul. He declared amnesty for most émigrés to encourage them to return to France, and decreed that nobles would be entitled to their confiscated properties if they had not already been sold by the state.

All our property had been seized by the Convention but had not yet been sold, except for La Belle Gabrielle plantation. We were living on money borrowed from relatives and friends, and none of us had work, property, or income. I had begun writing my memoirs, hoping to generate some income, but they had not yet.

When Adrienne learned of Napoleon's decree, she returned to Paris on her American passport. Concerned about her health, I wanted to go with her, but had no passport and she had already shown that she was much better at business matters than I—which added to my pride in her. Because she was still weak, we all went with her as far as Hamburg, and Virginie accompanied her from there.

With Adrienne gone, I had time to read some of the correspondence that had not been delivered to me in Olmutz. She had written from Hamburg:

> So I am free dear heart, since I am here on the road that is bringing me to you. You will know the reasons for all my conduct, for my actions, why I decided to take this route, and it is I myself, my dear heart, who will explain all that to you. I am persuaded that you have not always been just to me, but I have the hope of convincing you that in all that I have done,

there is not a single detail of my conduct that you would not have approved of, as if you had dictated it yourself.

I felt great remorse—she had been arrested, imprisoned, and almost guillotined. Also because of my deeds, her family had been murdered. She had incarcerated herself to be with me, endured great hardships, and suffered intense pain and illness hoping to justify herself to me. I felt responsible for causing her so much distress—from leaving her to go to America when she was pregnant with our first child, to my long affair with Diane. There were other things I thought she might be referring to, but I knew in my heart that her list far exceeded mine, and I could never undo all the injustices I perpetrated upon her. I determined to do everything I could to make amends.

I cherish that letter, now yellowed with age and stained with my tears, which I keep with me at all times in my purse.

Adrienne and Virginie, traveling on American passports, stopped first to obtain French passports for themselves, George, and me. She wrote that she had seen notice of a one-act play with the curious title *The Prisoner of Olmutz, or Conjugal Devotion,* but they were too busy to see it, because they had to go down to Chavaniac to obtain a property left to Adrienne by her murdered mother. While they were dealing with officials in the Auvergne, they received a letter from Anastasie that she was pregnant with our first grandchild. This news took priority over financial considerations, so Adrienne and Virginie returned immediately to Vianen to help Charles and Anastasie during her labor.

George and I, warned that Austrian troops advancing on France were approaching, abandoned the house in Lemkuhlen and travelled to Vianen to join the rest of the family, including Adrienne's sisters Pauline and Rosalie, who had come to assist. Anastasie gave birth to twin girls, but one died after two weeks. The survivor was named Célestine Louise Henriette de la Tour-Maubourg in memory of Anastasie's grandmother and aunt, exceptional women who had died at La Force.

Adrienne, now famous throughout France and Europe for her audacious imprisonment at Olmutz through poems, books, plays, and several operas—eventually including Beethoven's *Fidelio*—hoping Napoleon no longer saw me as a threat, asked him for two French passports, one for herself and another for "Gilbert Motier," now that he had consolidated his political power and satisfied his political ambitions. To encourage other liberal supporters, Napoleon acquiesced.

While in Paris, Adrienne dealt with the estate of her mother which had not yet been settled. Committed to giving her mother, sister, and grandmother a decent Christian burial, she searched for where their bodies might have been disposed of, asking residents around the Place de Throne. She eventually met a lace maker who had witnessed the bodies of her own father and brother that same day thrown with other bodies into a wagon, which she followed to a field near the ruins of the Monastery of Picpus. The bodies had been dumped into a large pit on top of other corpses and covered with a thin layer of dirt.

Adrienne and Pauline wrote to the owner of the deserted field, a German princess, to purchase and consecrate the grounds, but the owner refused to sell. Undeterred, they were able to persuade a local priest to buy the ruins and rebuild the chapel. They paid an order of nuns to celebrate Mass each Sunday on behalf of their family.

Due to the involvement of a Lafayette, we were closely watched by secret agents until Napoleon learned that his own stepson was one of the subscribers to the fund that had purchased the property.

While in Paris Adrienne received a letter from Diane Simiane asking for a considerable loan to keep her creditors from harassing her. Despite our dire circumstances, Adrienne sent the money to Diane without telling me. I only found out about it from Anastasie who had learned about it in a letter from her sister. The nature and strength of the relationship between my wife and mistress was truly remarkable.

When the estate of Henriette was finally settled, Adrienne received the château La Grange-Bleneau. When the passports arrived, Adrienne sent mine and told me to join her at La Grange as soon as possible. I was relieved to at last have a country again, even though I was suspicious of Napoleon.

I had not been on French soil for seven years. George, Louis, and I loaded our paltry possessions into several carriages for the 300 mile journey. I had never been to La Grange, and was apprehensive. We had no problem at the border, and continued on to the small village of Courpalay. Townspeople directed us to a very narrow road covered with debris and fallen trees. The castle of La Grange, not far from the village, stood forlorn—a three-story, gray stone castle with dark circular towers at each corner. It was surrounded by a moat full of muck spanned by a drawbridge that led to the ominous entrance. The 400-year-old building, vacant for years, was immersed in thick vegetation and surrounded by dense woods. The thousands of acres of farmlands surrounding the castle, fallow for at least a decade, were overgrown with weeds.

But now La Grange was our home. Litter and cobwebs filled all three stories of the drafty building. We had to sweep a space in the entranceway so we could camp on the floor for the night. The next day we set about sweeping the rooms. After several weeks of camping, it was sufficiently clean to move in and begin restorations, including apartments for our children. We built cowsheds and sheep pens and hired locals to clear the fields for farming. Soon the rest of the family began arriving and contributing to the rehabilitation.

When Napoleon found out I had entered France, he sent agents out to La Grange to insist that I leave France immediately. I refused, and warned him of the public reaction and political consequences if he threw the "friend of liberty" in prison. Adrienne returned to Paris to deal directly with Napoleon, assuring him that he had nothing to fear because I was only interested in living peaceably in retirement with my family in the countryside. Imprisonment had impaired my health and the Jacobins destroyed my reputation, so I had neither the desire nor opportunity to get involved in politics. The consul admired Adrienne and agreed to let me stay as long as I kept a safe distance from Paris. But he refused to remove me from the list of enemies of the state.

Napoleon scheduled a referendum for February 7, 1800 to confirm a new constitution vesting power in the hands of the first consul—

which included no semblance to the Declaration of the Rights of Citizens I had prepared in 1789. However, just before the plebiscite, news arrived in Paris that George Washington had died on December 22. My family was heartbroken. All of France felt sad at the loss of the man who had led the world's first successful revolution. George and I received commiseration from sympathetic people throughout France who were aware of our close relationship with Washington. We wrote Martha, expressing our condolences and hopeful that we would have some role in memorial observances.

Napoleon ordered all flags throughout the republic to display black crepe for ten days, with a memorial service to be held at the Hôtel des Invalides. I was grateful that the consul had seen fit to honor him appropriately.

Napoleon, insecure in his recently acquired political role, took advantage of the tragic event to insure the outcome of the plebiscite by focusing attention on himself at Washington's service. Unwilling to share the limelight, he deliberately invited neither George nor me to the observance, barred my entire family from attending, and ordered all the speakers to avoid my name. He alone would give the eulogy.

George refused to be excluded from his godfather's memorial service by anyone, not even the most powerful man in France. He felt morally obligated to pay his final respects to his beloved godfather. Risking arrest and the wrath of Napoleon, he snuck into the service. I, older and taller than George and more recognizable by my limp and cane, was not so bold. My presence would have disrupted the service, caused chaos, and brought dishonor to the memory of my friend and mentor. George reported that Napoleon's eulogy barely mentioned Washington, but centered on himself and his Egyptian campaign, extolling his military feats.

In the election 99.9% of the voters confirmed the new Constitution and Napoleon as first consul, giving him executive powers above the other two consuls. At thirty-one, he had successfully plotted to rule the country and was effectively the dictator. More secure in his office, Napoleon signed a decree restoring the political and civil rights of all

244 LIVING A LIFE THAT MATTERS

those in the Assembly on the night of August 4, 1789, such as myself, who had voted for the abolition of the privileges of the nobility. The decree officially removed my name from the émigrés list and restored my citizenship.

CHAPTER 23

A Frenchman Once Again

1800

W ITH THE COALITION OF Austria and Russia advancing into northern Italy and preparing to invade France, George was eager to defend his country. In the spring of 1800 he joined the army. He was made a second lieutenant in the hussars, and in May crossed the Saint Bernard pass with one of Napoleon's many generals. Adrienne and I were concerned for our son's well-being, yet proud that he was serving his country.

By June Napoleon had secured a major victory against the Austrians at Marengo, and the "Second Coalition" of Britain, Austria, Russia, and Naples asked for peace, with the Austrians retreating as far as the Mincio River in northern Italy. While a treaty was being negotiated, Napoleon returned to Paris and left one of his generals in Italy to consolidate. On Christmas Day, General Brune led the French Army of the Reserve, including my son George, against the Austrians near the village of Pozzolo. Though the Austrians were forced back and an armistice declared, George was wounded on his birthday and sent home. A year later in March, France and Britain signed a treaty in the city of Amiens, bringing peace to Europe.

The French were delighted and the general plebiscite confirmed Napoleon as *Consul for Life*—though I was one of very few who voted against elevating him to a despotic office. To his credit, he began public works projects, and set up an efficient civil administration and four new legal codes. Trade prospered, wages improved, and provisions became cheaper. To secure his position, however, he began arresting his opponents and sending them into exile. I wrote to congratulate him on his defense of France, to thank him for promoting George, for allowing me return to France, and to request an audience.

The triumphant first consul and hero of Marengo seemed confident and assured, no longer concerned about me. He was surprisingly solicitous and friendly, and told me what a great soldier my George was. I told him that, with no income, I had come to ask him to reinstate me as a general, on the retired list, so I could receive the pension I was entitled to. I assured him that I wished only to take care of my family and remain in retirement at La Grange. He could hear from my wheezing and see from my limp that I posed no threat to him. There would be no harm in letting me receive the meager funds. He agreed to do whatever was necessary for me to regain my pension.

He was planning to restructure the French educational system, adopt a new Civil Code as well as a new constitution, and he needed people to administer a variety of new posts. He seemed eager to win my support and surprised me by asking me to become part of his administration. He offered me a senatorship, the position of minister to the United States, and even offered me the Cross of the Legion of Honor. I was sincere in hoping that he would improve French society, however I did not feel physically able to become actively involved, and wanted to take care of my severely ill wife. Though I refused on the grounds of poor health, it was to avoid insulting the first consul. He seemed irritated by my refusal and quickly became indifferent.

While George was recuperating at La Grange from his combat wounds, my old friend Antoine Destutt, comte de Tracy, came to visit me with his family. He had served with me in the National Assembly and briefly as a cavalry officer while I commanded the French army. George fell in love with his daughter Emilie and asked to marry her. The wedding was celebrated at La Grange in June and they settled in with us.

Shortly after the wedding, Adrienne received a letter from her sister Pauline about a suitable young man for Virginie, Louis de Lasteyrie—twenty-one, well-educated, charming, and handsome. Adrienne invited him to La Grange and they fell madly in love. Before their marriage, I went down to Paris on routine business and accidentally slipped on an icy sidewalk, breaking the upper part of my femur. Two young doctors convinced me to try a new procedure to set my hip, but they left me worse off than before the surgery. To repair their botched procedure, I had to wear a cast and was bedridden for a month. The treatment left me with a limp more severe than the wound I sustained at Brandywine.

My injury was so painful that I told Virginie I would be unable to stand with her and participate in the wedding, so they agreed to have the ceremony just outside my bedroom on April 20, 1803.

On May 17 the British navy began capturing all the French and Dutch merchant ships stationed in or sailing around Britain, took their crews as prisoners, and seized more than two million pounds of commodities. Then they declared war.

In response, Napoleon began assembling armies on the coast of France to invade Britain. But on learning that Austria and Russia were preparing to invade France, Napoleon invaded Austria and engaged the Austrian army in the Bavarian town of Ulm on October 16 before they could get organized.

The outbreak of war put pressure on Napoleon to raise funds to pay for his military and domestic objectives. Prior wars with Britain and Austria had been expensive, as had the cost of suppressing the slave revolt in Haiti beginning in May 1791 to protect the trade from

Haiti in sugar, slaves, and rum, worth more than all the trade from the French territory in western America. Napoleon decided to sell the entire 800,000 square miles of the worthless Louisiana territory, from Quebec all the way down the Mississippi to New Orleans. President Thomas Jefferson agreed to buy this unproductive land for the outrageous sum of three cents per acre, though quite a few members of Congress were irate and tried to block the purchase, calling Jefferson's unilateral actions unconstitutional. The acquisition doubled the territory of the United States and gave the country control of the Mississippi and the major port at New Orleans.

I wrote a letter to Jefferson congratulating him and telling him that I thought he had acted wisely. He responded by offering me the governorship of the new territory, assuring me that I would be welcome in America, and could make a fortune. I was honored, flattered, and tempted—but had to decline because both Adrienne and I were still in poor health. Adrienne could not survive the hardships of many weeks at sea, and I could not live away from Adrienne again. In spring of 1804, while I was still recovering from my hip injury I received the news that for the first time a slave army had conducted a successful rebellion for their freedom. The leaders of the triumphant uprising immediately replaced the French name *Saint Domingue* with their native creole name *Ayiti*, or *Haïti* (land of high mountains). I was joyful that there were now two independent nations in the Americas. Napoleon, however, suffering the loss of his most profitable colony—at the hands of blacks, no less—refused to recognize Haitian sovereignty.

Not long after the news of the loss of Haiti was received in Paris, Napoleon introduced a new constitution establishing the Bonaparte dynasty. 99.93% of the voters agreed. He quickly began taking on the accoutrements of royalty, choosing the Tuileries as his new residence. He set his coronation in an opulent ceremony at the Cathedral of Notre Dame in December 1804.

I was disillusioned by Napoleon's imperialist turn and assumption of royal powers—as were many people throughout Europe, including the young German composer Beethoven, one of his republican supporters, who tore up a symphony dedicated to Bonaparte. Not only powerless citizens like Beethoven and me were worried about his ambitions, but Britain, under constant threat of a French invasion, joined Austria and Russia whose armies were marching towards France through the mountainous Black Forest. George, recovered from his injury, and my new son-in-law Louis returned to the army, eager to defend France. Near the town of Austerlitz in Moravia the armies met on December 2, 1805 and Napoleon crushed this Third Coalition. Parisians were overjoyed—The Holy Roman Empire was ended, and France acquired Venice and southern Germany.

With constant threats to his power, the Emperor turned France into a police state, controlling the press, censoring books, spying on citizens, reviving the *lettres de cachet* to imprison people indefinitely without trial, and he appointed his family members to head various states in order to consolidate his power.

A new external threat emerged when Britain joined with Russia, Prussia, Sweden, Saxony, and Sicily to form a Fourth Coalition. British ships blockaded the French coast to hurt our economy.

In February 1807, my son and Louis were with Napoleon near the town of Eylau. A frontal attack by Napoleon failed with catastrophic losses. To retrieve the situation, the emperor launched a massive cavalry charge against the Russians. George was the aide de camp to Commander Emanuel de Grouchy, who was leading a charge into the flank of the Russian cavalry when his horse was shot and rolled on top of him. George pulled the general from under his horse and gave him his own horse, which saved Grouchy's life. The grateful general recommended George for a promotion. However Napoleon made known that out of vengeance for attending Washington's funeral—as well as for his father's refusal to support him—he did not intend to give George a promotion.

With no likely long-term career in the army, George resigned, as did Louis. I was happy to see the two boys return safe and sound to La Grange, but remorseful that Napoleon had chosen to punish them because of me. My well known opposition to Bonaparte associated my name with numerous plots against the emperor, though I had done nothing to warrant his animosity. I stayed at La Grange as promised—playing with grandchildren; walking with Adrienne; enjoying our flower gardens, farm animals, and wildlife; entertaining friends and visitors; and writing in my journal.

Soon after George and Louis returned, Adrienne began experiencing severe stomach pains. Blisters, sores, and abscesses developed on her arms and legs. We immediately traveled to Paris for the best possible medical care to diagnose and treat her. We found several highly regarded physicians whom we brought back to La Grange, but none were able to improve her rapidly deteriorating condition. Within weeks, Adrienne had developed a high fever and gone into delirium.

Our entire family had gathered together to celebrate her forty-eighth birthday on November 2. Although Adrienne was experiencing violent pain and fever, she appreciated the fact that her family was with her.

During one of those increasingly rare moments when her condition improved briefly, she spoke to me of things we had never addressed before. One night, after receiving communion, Adrienne turned to me and whispered weakly, "You are not a Christian?"

I was taken aback by the question. She smiled playfully. "Ah, I know what you are—you are a Fayettist."

I forced a smile. "You must think me very egotistical, but aren't you something of a Fayettist yourself?"

Adrienne grinned. "You are right. That is a sect that I would die for!"

I excused myself, pretending to need a glass of water when I only needed to hide my tears from her.

Christmas Eve was George's twenty-eighth birthday. Instead of a party, the entire family was hovering around Adrienne, keeping busy to mask our sorrow. I was leaning over to see her face when she put her frail arms around my neck and whispered weakly, "Je suis toute à vous" (I am all yours). She groped for my fingers, squeezed them, and was gone.

I could not accept the possibility. When it was confirmed, I forced myself to contain a scream of despair. But I was unable to dam the flood of remorse or stop my heart from breaking. I grieved to the deepest reaches of my soul. My soulmate, my protector, my love was gone. I regretted all the time I had taken myself away from her. I reproached myself for ever being unjust to her. I placed her picture in a medallion around my neck, and a lock of her hair in the small purse with her letter.

The short ride into Paris was very hard for me—I was physically drained and emotionally devastated. I was so weak I was barely able to speak at the funeral. I placed the wedding ring I had given her thirty-four years earlier around my neck in recognition of our love. I had witnessed death many times before—I was responsible for killing many people in battle—I had witnessed the death of wounded friends—I had lost my young mother and my dearest friend George Washington. But no death had impacted me like this. I felt lost and lonely. Hollow. Lifeless.

I ordered the cemetery to leave room for me to be interred by her side. I prayed—one of the few times in my life—that if there were a heaven, I might have the opportunity to see Adrienne once more.

After I returned from the funeral, I seldom left La Grange. I kept to myself for days. I couldn't sleep or eat, and lost all desire. I had the main door to her bedroom walled up so that visitors could not stray into it uninvited. Everything was left exactly as it had been when she was alive. Each Christmas Eve thereafter I have gone from my room into hers, alone, to spend the evening in her company.

The undeserved death of this extraordinary woman was the final proof for me that God did not exist. Or if He did, then that was proof that He was not a just, good God. At the very least it showed that leading a pious, good life celebrating all the rituals of the Church were of no help in this life—and I sincerely doubted their benefit for the next. Prayers were a waste of time—God was not listening.

I had left Adrienne and my family to kill fathers, brothers, and husbands, maintained a relationship with another woman over decades, and without doubt had committed numerous other sins, yet I had been permitted to survive.

In my despair the affairs of state no longer seemed important. Every day I thought about just how extraordinary she was. The only time the weight of her death lifted was when I forced myself to go outdoors and felt the warm sun on my face, watched soft scuttling clouds dancing through a pale sky, and heard birds calling in their mates, bees searching for flowers, and leaves blown by a breeze. The sights and sounds of life and renewal gave me my only pleasure. I found comfort in witnessing the birth of a lamb, inhaling the ripening scent of fruit. Still, I had to force myself to go outside to stroll aimlessly or putter about the flowers and trees and fields.

Gradually I recognized that I was finding pleasure in seeing things coming into existence and developing. I began to participate in creating them—planting seeds and watching them sprout and grow. Replacing life. Slowly I was drawn into the undemanding life of a gentleman farmer. Though unable to work hard, with help I began planting apples and pears and raising farm animals, watching them participate in the cycle of life. The sounds of the farm were a continuous symphony, adding melody to my shifting tempo, and always new.

Sun, fresh air, exercise, and fresh food were therapeutic. I put on weight. As I grew stronger, I became more deeply involved in improving my yields by breeding cattle, hogs, and sheep, as well as new varieties of fruits and vegetables. I introduced American corn to the French, and sold cider from my apples to pay off some of my debts.

Every morning I woke around daybreak, but remained in bed to write the friends of liberty all over the world—Charles James Fox in Britain, Simón Bolivar in Venezuela, Greek and Polish freedom fighters, and Spanish constitutionalists—then spent time on my knees in meditative devotion, holding the small portrait of Adrienne that I wore around my neck.

Life outside La Grange called to me. Despite our lack of money, Adrienne had established a school in the nearby village of Courpalay. I went into town to speak to the teachers, shopkeepers, and neighbors, and to catch up with current news. Though Napoleon dominated conversations, I was concerned that the life of the people was deteriorating with Europe in a perpetual state of warfare that drained not only the French economy, but resources all over the world, from European capitals to slave colonies.

Napoleon's police state monitored newspapers, censored books, controlled the theater, and spied on people. He had placed puppet rulers on the thrones of German states; attempted to enforce a Europe-wide commercial boycott of Britain; and invaded both Spain and Portugal. Most of Europe was either under his direct control, that of his allies, or under favorable treaties with rulers he had defeated. Spain, Portugal, and Russia were rebelling against his despotism. In April 1809, Britain formed a coalition with Austria, Spain, Sicily, and Sardinia. Again, Napoleon defeated the Austrian army to end the Fifth Coalition.

Tzar Alexander of Russia joined the Continental Blockade against Britain in 1810, but after only two years, his relations with Napoleon had deteriorated so badly that he signed a defense treaty with Britain to protect Russia from France. In response Napoleon marched 685,000 men (I cannot help but compare this to Washington's army that never numbered more than 18,000), artillery, supplies, and camp followers to Moscow in April to compel Alexander to remain in the Continental System and remove the possible threat of a Russian invasion of Poland.

After five months of marching 1500 miles to Moscow, the French army was looking forward to enjoying the fruits of their efforts. They arrived at the outskirts of Moscow on September 14, 1812. The inhabitants had abandoned the city and set their beautiful capital ablaze, rather than cede it to Napoleon. His men could only lie on hard ground and forage for survival. Napoleon's Grande Armeé had never lost a battle in Russia, but the march home was a disaster. The Cossack light cavalry constantly harried them and the Russian army burned crops and villages, destroying anything that might be useful to their enemy—food, shelter, water sources, farm animals. Men and horses died in droves, with disease, desertions, and casualties depleting the Grande Armée.

On November 5 they encountered heavy snow and temperatures below freezing. The emperor again abandoned his starving, frost-bitten men, and hurried to Paris. Only 40,000 soldiers managed to limp home. His defeat in Russia encouraged Prussia, Austria, Sweden, Great Britain, Spain, Portugal, and some Germanic states to bring together over a million men to oppose him.

Napoleon either had not learned the lesson, or his ambition over-rode reason. He soon repeated his folly by preparing for an attack on Prussia. Fewer men, however, were willing to die for him this time. 200,000 new troops did not have to walk so far to risk death, but they lacked both experience and a cavalry. At Leipzig Napoleon lost almost half his men and was forced to withdraw, hotly pursued by over half a million soldiers.

Coalition forces commandeered La Grange, forcing my family to flee to Paris. Soon they entered Paris, led by Tzar Alexander and followed by the King of Prussia. Napoleon had reached Fontainebleau when he heard that the capital had surrendered. Outraged, he called his most loyal and experienced generals to expel the Coalition. But even his closest comrades had had enough. With no choice, Napoleon abdicated.

The Coalition forces met with representatives of the emperor at Fontainebleau, and the terms of his abdication were spelled out on April 11. The madman was forced into exile on the island of Elba, thirty miles east of his birthplace.

I was relieved for France. Over a million French men had died in the Napoleon's wars, and perhaps another five million Europeans. Our economy was in ruins, and we were again with no government. I was concerned about who would move into the Emperor's vacuum.

PART V

Chamber of Deputies

1814–1824

CHAPTER 24

Monarchy Restored

1814

WITH THEIR EMPEROR FORCED into exile, the Senate unfortunately looked to restore the Bourbon dynasty. They invited the next in line to Louis XVI's throne, his middle brother Louis Stanislas Xavier, comte de Provence, who had been living in exile in Prussia, Russia, and the United Kingdom for twenty-three years. Suffering from a severe case of gout that confined him to a wheelchair, Louis sent his younger brother Charles, comte d'Artois, as his regent until he could get to Paris himself. Charles took the opportunity to create an ultra-royalist secret police that reported directly back to him without Louis's knowledge.

I had been at school with both brothers, and both had attended my wedding—though I was not friends with either, for they were aloof and reactionary, particularly Charles. I was not surprised that after Louis finally assumed the throne, he claimed that the new constitution was defective, and submitted in its place a charter he had prepared.

The first twelve articles ostensibly complied with the requirements of the Senate and protected the rights to the citizens. But the remainder of the document consolidated authority, making him head of state, commander of the armed forces, and the only one who could propose legislation and declare war. Although his charter provided for two congressional chambers, there was no real parliamentary system because legislators could not pass laws and had limited advisory powers.

Louis did his utmost to reverse the revolution—minor symbolic acts like replacing the tri-color with the white Bourbon flag, and major restorations like making the Catholic Church the official state religion and returning their land to émigrés and the Church. The Charter left only 90,000 citizens eligible to vote, which antagonized both liberals and royalists.

On May 30, Louis sent Charles to sign the Treaty of Paris, which allowed France to keep the 1792 borders, required no war indemnity, and made no provision for the occupying armies to remain on French soil.

Jefferson wrote to me his thoughts about this transition:

Monticello, February 14, 1815.

My Dear Friend

The newspapers told us only that the great beast was fallen.

A full measure of liberty is not now perhaps to be expected by your nation, nor am I confident they are prepared to preserve it. More than a generation will be requisite, under the administration of reasonable laws favoring the progress of knowledge in the general mass of the people, and their habituation to an independent security of person and property, before they will be capable of estimating the value of freedom, and the necessity of a sacred adherence to the principles on which it rests for preservation.

Unfortunately, some of the most honest and enlightened of our patriotic friends (but closet politicians merely, unpracticed in the knowledge of man) thought more could still be obtained and borne. They did not weigh the hazards of a transition from one form of government to another, nor the imprudence of giving up the certainty of such a degree of liberty, under a limited monarchy, for the uncertainty of a little more under the form of a republic.

From this fatal error of the republicans, from their separation from yourself and the constitutionalists, in their councils, flowed all the subsequent sufferings and crimes of the French nation.

In the end, the limited monarchy they had secured was exchanged for the unprincipled and bloody tyranny of Robespierre, and the equally unprincipled and maniac tyranny of Bonaparte.

You are now rid of them, and I sincerely wish you may continue so. But this may depend on the wisdom and moderation of the restored dynasty. It is for them now to read a lesson in the fatal errors of the republicans.

With us our thirty years of peace had taken off. This series of successes has been tarnished only by the conflagration at Washington.

Still, in the end, the transaction has helped rather than hurt us, by arousing the general indignation of our country, and by marking to the world of Europe the vandalism and brutal character of the English government. It has merely served to immortalize their infamy. And add further, that through the whole period of the war, we have beaten them single-handed at sea, and so thoroughly established our superiority over them with equal force, that they retire from that kind of contest, and never suffer their frigates to cruise singly. The disclosure to the world of the fatal secret that they can be beaten at sea with an equal force, the evidence furnished by the military operations of the last year that experience is rearing us officers who will probably raise a clamor in the British nation, which will force their ministry into peace. I say force them, because, willingly, they would never be at peace.

Their fears of republican France being now done away, they are directed to republican America, and they are playing the same game for disorganization here, which they played in your country. The Marats, the Dantons and Robespierres of Massachusetts are in the same pay, under the same orders, and making the same efforts to anarchise us, that their proto-types in France did there.

You once gave me a copy of the journal of your campaign in Virginia, in 1781, which I must have lent to some one of the undertakers to write the history of the revolutionary war, and forgot to reclaim. I conclude this, because it is no longer among my papers, which I have very diligently searched for it, but in vain. An author of real ability is now writing that part of the history of Virginia. He does it in my neighborhood, and I lay open to him all my papers. But I possess none, nor has he any, which can enable him to do justice to your faithful and able services in that campaign. If you could be so good as to send me another copy, by the very first vessel bound to any port in the United States, it might be here in time; for although he expects to begin to print within a month or two, yet you know the delays of these undertakings. At any rate it might be got in as a supplement. The old Count Rochambeau gave me also his memoire of the operations at York, which is gone in the same way, and I have no means of applying to his family for it. Perhaps you could render them as well as us, the service of procuring another copy.

I have sometimes indulged myself, of seeing all my friends of Paris once more, for a month or two; a thing impossible, which, however, I never permitted myself to despair of. The regrets, however, at seventy-three, of the loss of friends, may

be the less, as the time is shorter within which we are to meet
again, according to the creed of our education.

I salute you with assurances of my constant and affectionate
friendship and respect.

P.S. February 26th. My letter had not yet been sealed, when I
received news of our peace. I am glad of it, and especially that
we closed our war with the éclat of the action at New Orleans.

But I consider it as an armistice only, because no security is
provided against the impressments of our seamen. While this
is unsettled we are in hostility of mind with England, although
actual deeds of arms may be suspended by a truce. If she thinks
the exercise of this outrage is worth eternal war, eternal war
it must be, or extermination of the one or the other party. The
first act of impressments she commits on an American, will be
answered by reprisal, or by a declaration of war here; and the
interval must be merely a state of preparation for it.

Once more, God bless you.

—Thomas Jefferson

Not long after receiving Jefferson's letter I was shocked to hear that
that Napoleon had escaped from Elba. In February he and 1000 men
landed near Antibes and began walking towards Paris. He had 500 miles
to travel and there was ample time and enough men to stop him, but
Louis XVIII had failed to purge the military of its Bonaparists. When
they learned of his return, they deserted en masse from the Bourbon
armies. When Louis heard that Napoleon was getting close to the city,
he fled for the protection of Belgium, allowing Napoleon to walk into
the city on March 20 without a fight.

The United Kingdom, Russia, Prussia, Sweden, Austria, the Netherlands and a number of German states declared Napoleon an outlaw
and agreed to form a Seventh Coalition, pledging a quarter of a million
men each to end his rule.

Napoleon assumed power but realized that he would have to modify the constitution he had used as emperor to one more akin to a constitutional monarchy. He asked a liberal member of the Chamber of Deputies, Benjamin Constant, to prepare a new constitution. The Charter of 1815 established a parliament composed of two chambers—a hereditary Chamber of Peers and an elected Chamber of Representatives. The Charter ended censorship, guaranteed freedom of the press, and extended the franchise. It was adopted by a plebiscite a few months later. Napoleon was head of state once again, though his powers were theoretically restricted by the new liberal Constitution.

I decided to seek a seat in the Chamber of Deputies from the department in which La Grange was located, Seine-et-Marne. George chose to represent Chavaniac's department, Haute-Loire. The election was held in May. We both won and moved to Paris to claim our offices. My peers chose me as vice-president of the chamber. I wrote Jefferson in August to tell him the news:

La Grange August 14, 1814

My Dear Friend:

Your letter to me Nov. 30 is the last I have received. The newspapers and ministerial correspondence will have apprised you of the successive events which have overthrown Bonaparte, introduced the Bourbons, and once more thrown the dice for the liberties of France and of course of Europe. The strong powers and singular genius of Napoleon had been disharmonized by the folly of his ambition and the immorality of his mind. This grain of madness, not incompatible with great talents, but which is developed by the love and success of despotism, he trifled with, losing immense armies, sending abroad all the military stores of France, leaving the country defenseless and exhausted, and he seemed determined to have the last man the last shilling of Europe.

My wishes and just hopes had been different. . . . I wanted a national insurrection against domestic despotism. . . . I applied to military chiefs first in rank, to Senators, and principal citizens in the National Guards who all were well disposed but thought imperial tyranny too well organized to render it possible to shake up. . . .

I had no inclination to oppose measures tending to expel the able and professional destroyer of liberty in Europe, and giving to France a chance to recover constitutional freedom. There was no way to remove foreign influence and interior intrigue but in joining the desperate, destructive rage of Bonaparte. . . .

Meanwhile Talleyrand . . . felt no reluctance to act with the invaders of Paris, was abled to form a provisory government. . . . The Senate who had too long been the tools of Bonaparte, were led into selfish provisions for themselves which spoiled their constitutional decree and gave the king the means to evade it. Hardly was the imperial sun set, that the royal globe began to attract the hopes, and impress the fears. The engagements ended into a Charter not accepted, but given, by the king.

The Aristocratic Party is the same as you have known it. Constitutionals and Republicans are united into one brotherhood. The strength of Bonapartism wholly depends upon the conduct of this new government. . . .

The Ancien Regime ideas are uppermost. The pretensions of aristocrats are a compost of nonsense and madness. . . .

Ruin, vengeance, and redoubled folly would mark the return of [Bonaparte]. The mass of the people are fatigued and disgusted. . . . Bonaparte or the Bourbons have been, and still are the alternative in the country where the idea of a republican executive has become synonymous with the excesses committed under that name.

In the meanwhile you see the king of Spain, a vile fool, restoring inquisition after having expelled the Cortès, the pope reestablishing the old system, the King of Sardinia destroying every useful innovation in Piedmont, and Austria submitting her ancient possessions to the illiberal system of her cabinet.

Yet the advantages derived from the first impulse, the philanthropic intent of the revolution, notwithstanding all what has since happened, are widely extended, and deeply rooted. . . . I am convinced that those rights of mankind which, in 1789, have been defined under the encouragement of your approbation, and ought to have been the blessing of the end of the last century, shall before the end of the present one, be the undisputed creed and insured property not only of this, but of every European nation. . . .

I fervently hope there may be a peace. Should it be otherwise, I hope both parties in the United States will join to rise hand in hand against the invader—an union very necessary in the present crisis, which if I thought I might contribute to produce, I would, instead of this letter, smuggle myself in the cartel ship of the Commissioners.

My children and grandchildren to the number of sixteen are well and beg, such as can talk, to be respectfully remembered to you.

Receive the tender wishes and most lively affection of your old constant friend

—Lafayette

As a loyal Frenchman I could not help but support Napoleon in the defense of our country, but I opposed him on everything else. Unfortunately, even this limited support of Bonaparte caused the end of my friendship with Diane de Simiane. She was a royalist and despised Napoleon. She was very dear to me, and a good friend, but our continual difference of opinion came to an unresolvable head and we parted. I have not seen her since.

Coalition forces were again gathering troops, planning to invade France on July 1, 1815. Soldiers from the various countries were converging on holding camps, and the British and Prussian armies were camped just south of Brussels waiting for the Austrian and Russians troops to arrive.

Napoleon again attacked in advance. He hurriedly left Paris with only 70,000 troops, hoping that if he could defeat the Duke of Wellington's forces, the rest of the coalition would come to terms. Near the village of Waterloo in the Netherlands he overran British outposts. On June 16 he moved against the Prussians led by General Gebhard von Blücher who retreated northwards toward Wellington's army, creating a force equal to the French—until another 50,000 Prussian troops arrived. In one exceptionally brutal day of slaughter Napoleon lost two-thirds of his remaining soldiers and was forced to retreat hastily back to the shelter of Paris.

A few days after Napoleon's return, his younger brother Lucien stormed into the Chamber of Deputies and demanded the return of his brother's dictatorial powers. After years of silence, I rose to oppose him:

> By what right do you dare accuse the nation of want of perseverance in the emperor's interest? The nation has followed him on the fields of Italy, across the sands of Egypt and the plains of Germany, across the frozen deserts of Russia. The nation has followed him in fifty battles, in his defeats and in his victories, and in doing so we have to mourn the blood of three million Frenchmen.

The Chamber voted to deny his demand, and forced Napoleon to abdicate immediately. If I had some small role in achieving that, I would feel very proud. Napoleon fled to Rochefort intending to escape to America, but the Royal Navy was blockading every French port to forestall such a move. He surrendered on July 15, and was forcibly placed on a ship that transported the one time Emperor of France, King of Italy, Protector of the Confederation of the Rhine, and effective head of state of Spain and the Duchy of Warsaw a full 5000 miles from Paris to St. Helena, a remote island off the African coast where he would not be heard from again.

With Napoleon gone, the Chamber of Deputies and the Chamber of Peers elected a provisional government of five, and sent me to negotiate peace with the allies. We approached Wellington about putting a foreign prince on the throne of France, but Wellington insisted that Louis XVIII was necessary to preserve the integrity of France. I urged them to let us choose our own form of government, but Wellington would accept nothing but the Bourbon restoration. The provisional government, over my objections, capitulated. Wellington did acknowledge that Louis's initial government might have made mistakes—which he promised to correct before he would permit Louis to be restored. He directed Louis to fashion a new constitution, and he ordered the deputies in the Chamber to support the king.

The Chamber of Deputies arrived to resume our duties and found that Louis had dissolved the body, locked the doors to the meeting room, and posted guards to keep us from breaking in. In our place, Louis convened the Chamber of Peers, dominated by ultra-royalists. I was forced back into retirement, but La Grange had been commandeered by the Russians. I settled in alone at my apartment in Paris.

Louis resigned most of his duties to his council and appointed as prime minister Napoleon's chief diplomatic aide, Talleyrand, who had been chief French negotiator at the Congress of Vienna in 1815 that had brought peace to Europe on terms remarkably lenient, as Jefferson's letter noted.

Talleyrand intended to embark on a series of reforms and hoped that moderate deputies would be elected in August. However, for twenty-five years since the abolition of feudalism, the electorate had endured radical republicanism. As a result of manipulating electoral areas and changing the franchise laws, the citizens voted in anger almost exclusively for ultra-royalists. Talleyrand resigned.

Louis's government was forced to sign separate harsh treaties with Great Britain, Austria, Prussia, and Russia that reduced France's borders to their 1790 limits, forced France to pay 150,000,000 francs per year to the coalition to occupy France for at least five years, plus a war indemnity of 700,000,000 francs.

French people were unhappy, having already paid in men and economic suffering for Napoleon's ambitions, and foreign occupation was humiliating. Angry with the Bonapartists, they purged Napoleonic officials in a "White Terror." Officers in Napoleon's army and anyone suspected of ties with his several governments were arrested and executed without trial, ignoring the Constitution's regards for individual rights, so that the allied troops were forced to intervene. I was glad to have remained at home.

To stop further bloodshed, Louis issued an amnesty to the "traitors," but banned any member of the House of Bonaparte from owning property in, or entering, France. The ultra-royalists, led by the king's brother Charles, controlled the Chamber, which opposed any constitutional limits on the king and every liberal, republican, or democratic idea. They pressured the Bourbon government to be increasingly repressive, until even the king grew tired of them. To steer a middle course between liberals and the ultra-royalists, he dissolved the Chamber and called for new elections.

In 1817 I moved to Chavaniac. The people of the Sarthe district asked me to represent them in the Chamber of Deputies and elected me on October 30, 1818. I was past sixty. In the undeterminable time still available to me I wanted to lead a life that mattered to my descendants, the people of France, and even the world. To honor Adrienne's memory, I was determined to devote all my efforts to argue for people's liberty and rights.

My first act as deputy was to gain support for the people of Argentina in seeking independence from Spain. I was not unsuccessful. I also wanted all foreign soldiers out of France well before the five years stipulated under the treaty—a goal of all Frenchmen as well as my colleagues in the Chamber, both royalist and republican. With an agreement to pay over 200 million francs, the Coalition began leaving, and restrictions on the individual rights of Frenchmen began to ease. For the first time in 75 years, France was politically stable, had no war expenditures, and the economy was experiencing dramatic improvement. It was like a breath of deeply bracing mountain air.

I worked closely with liberals in the Chamber to expand constitutional protections, and spoke out regularly for freedom of the press, an independent judiciary, electoral reforms, support of liberal movements in Italy, Germany, Austria, Spain and England, and the end of slavery in the French colonies. Generally outvoted by the ultra-royalists, I took to working with liberals outside the Chambers.

I organized street demonstrations that demanded restoration of individual liberties and freedom of the press, and formed a new political club called the Friends of the Liberty of the Press. I joined the Constitutional Brothers of Europe to support pan-European communication among republicans, and supported liberal national movements in Latin America, Spain, Italy, Portugal, and Greece in their struggles similar to the American war for independence. People everywhere were seizing the opportunity, inspired by the American and French revolutions, to be rid of their oppressors. I hosted political refugees and liberal thinkers at La Grange, including English social reformer Jeremy Bentham. I had known him since the very beginnings of the French Revolution when I was a fledgling legislator. He had, at the early stirrings of our revolution, drafted a constitution for France advocating women's suffrage, and whose ideas were the foundation for the Napoleonic Code.

Jeremy, like me, was under constant scrutiny by his government for his liberal views, and he was aware that the public mails were not safe, and no longer private. When he had sensitive correspondence for me that he did not want to send by the normal carriers, he enlisted his trusted friend Fanny Wright who was going to Paris to see her publisher. He asked her to deliver a letter to me, and a letter of introduction. By chance we happened to be seeing the same publisher on the same day and met accidentally. She was with her constant companion Camilla, her younger sister. She gave me the letters and we adjourned to a café. We had previous corresponded about my offer to help translate her book about her travels in America in 1818 detailing the slave trade.

I quickly understood Jeremy's reference to Fanny as quite the "man of business." She was nearly six feet tall, had a commanding unfeminine presence, and was very direct. She dressed uniquely in bodices, ankle-length pantaloons and a dress cut to above the knee, with little feminine frivolity in style, makeup, or hairdo.

We discovered that we shared many attributes including a common birth date; losing our fathers at two and our mothers shortly thereafter; were unmarried; had gone to America at a young age and fallen in love with the country; and loathed slavery. We talked most of the morning, enjoying each other's company. To continue our conversation and get to know her better, I invited Fanny and Camilla to stay with me at La Grange.

They stayed for three delightful months. Fanny was most obliging, offering to help me work on my biography, and we discussed many issues. Adrienne had sensitized me to the inequitable treatment of women, and I had become increasingly concerned about the discriminatory practices that kept them from even an elementary education, forced them to endure abusive husbands, and disallowed their vote. Fanny educated me further and I began corresponding with a diverse group of women writers and political activists, including Germaine de Stael, the Irish novelist Sydney Owenson, Lady Morgan, and the Italian nationalist Cristina Belgiojoso—supporting their controversial books and political actions.

Fanny was interested in our experiment with La Belle Gabrielle, and discussed possible ventures to benefit the Negro, including the American movement to establish an African country where slaves could voluntarily go to escape their bondage, as well as our experiences in America with blacks. She was intrigued by James and wanted to know more about him. Unfortunately, I was ignorant about my friend, but promised I would try to find out. She also helped me broaden connections with networks of liberal activists in Europe, which was urgent because the reactionary monarchs in Britain, Russia, Prussia, Spain, and Austria were focusing their attention on halting the rapid spread of revolutionary ardor that was sweeping the world. With Napoleon disposed of, they were intent on building a bastion against democracy, revolution, and secularism throughout Europe and the Americas. They called their unholy collaboration the Holy Alliance.

Louis eventually joined them in order to contain the liberal and nationalist forces unleashed by the French Revolution. After his nephew, the duc de Berry, was assassinated on February 14, 1820 at the Paris Opera, the king tightened press censorship, permitted arbitrary arrest and detention without trial, and set about disempowering liberal voters. Legislation increased the number of deputies from 258 to 430, while requiring that they be elected by the wealthiest quarter of the population in each department to ensure that ultra-royalists remain in power.

He dissolved the Chamber and scheduled a general election. With his effective censorship, I and many other liberals were defeated. I was so discouraged about the prospects for legal reform that I plunged into conspiracies against Louis's government—and was concerned that I might be arrested.

Our *Amis de la Vérité*, a French version of the Italian *Carbonari*—a mixture of revolutionary political club, Masonic Lodge, and literary salon—was discovered. We better organized a new *Charbonnerie* among the leaders. We planned a revolt in eastern France for January 1822, with my arrival as the signal for the general uprising. But before I could arrive, my carriage was intercepted by a collaborator warning that the king had uncovered our cells. Meanwhile the political crisis and instability in Spain following Napoleon's invasion allowed wars of independence to break out throughout Central and South America.

With nearly all the Latin American colonies independent from the Spanish and Portuguese Empires, President Monroe, with less than a year left in office, was concerned that the Holy Alliance would invade the United States to stifle the birthplace of liberty. Meanwhile Britain was seeking economic interest in South America and had signed a trade treaty with Brazil granting the British a de facto monopoly. Worried that access to South America would be cut off if the other Alliance members regained their colonies, and to protect their colony in Canada, the British offered their navy and support to help Monroe. On December 2, 1823 Monroe warned the European powers that he would not tolerate their intervention anywhere in the Americas, and he delineated two different and incompatible political systems to be enforced by the British navy.

Monroe wanted this declaration protecting the New World against colonization to be publicized in Europe, in order to garner approval as well as to demonstrate his support for the liberal revolutionaries in Europe and South America. Since I was viewed by Monroe, Congress, and many in America and Europe as the principal opponent of tyrannical European monarchies, Monroe staged a highly visible tour of the republic for me during its celebration of fifty years of independence, with regular press releases to be sent to newspapers all over Europe.

The president contacted me at La Grange, inviting me to come as the Honored Guest of the United States, and offering to send a navy frigate to France to fetch me. Despite the disagreeable prospect of crossing the ocean again, I accepted his timely invitation. But not wanting to put his government to the expense, I turned down the frigate and booked a commercial packet, the *Cadmus*. I felt deeply indebted to Monroe and Elizabeth for helping keep Adrienne alive when she was imprisoned, for helping secure her release, as well as arranging George's travel to America and for providing passports that enabled our family to travel to Olmutz. And of course I was eager to see old friends and the changes of forty years.

I informed my secretary, Auguste Levasseur, of the purpose of the visit. He would accompany me everywhere, keep detailed notes, and send regular reports to the French and European newspapers to publicize the political significance of my visit.

With Auguste thus occupied, I invited George and his wife Emilie, as well as a few close aides and friends for companionship and assistance. This would be a fine opportunity for Fanny Wright and her sister, but to avoid any hint of scandal they thought it best to sail out of Dover, meet me in New York, ride and stay in separate accommodations, and not to be part of the official tour—yet attend all political and social events to which I was invited and meet my American friends.

When Monroe received my letter accepting his invitation, he must have informed his close friend and nearby neighbor Thomas Jefferson of my upcoming visit, because in January I received the following letter:

Monticello, November 4, 1823.

My Dear Friend,

Two dislocated wrists and crippled fingers have rendered writing so slow and laborious, as to oblige me to withdraw from nearly all correspondence: not, however, from yours, while I can make a stroke with a pen. We have gone through too many trying scenes together, to forget the sympathies and affections they nourished.

Your trials have indeed been long and severe. When they will end, is yet unknown, but where they will end, cannot be doubted. Alliances, Holy or Hellish, may be formed, and retard the epoch of deliverance, may swell the rivers of blood which are yet to flow, but their own will close the scene, and leave to mankind the right of self-government.

Whether the state of society in Europe can bear a republican government, I doubted, and I do now. A hereditary chief, strictly limited, the right of war vested in the legislative body, a rigid economy of the public contributions, and absolute interdiction of all useless expenses, will go far towards keeping the government honest and unoppressive.

But the only security of all, is in a free press. The force of public opinion cannot be resisted, when permitted freely to be expressed. The agitation it produces must be submitted to. It is necessary to keep the waters pure.

Who is to be the next President, is the topic here of every conversation. But the name alone is changed, the principles are the same. For in truth, the parties of Whig and Tory are those of nature. They exist in all countries, whether called by these names, or by those of Aristocrats and Democrats, Côte Droite and Côte Gauche, Ultras and Radicals, Serviles and Liberals. The sickly, weakly, timid man, fears the people, and is a Tory by nature. The healthy, strong, and bold, cherishes them, and is formed a Whig by nature.

To that is now succeeding a distinction, which, like that of republican and federal, or Whig and Tory, being equally intermixed through every State, threatens none of those geographical schisms which go immediately to a separation. The line of division now is the preservation of States rights as reserved in the constitution, or by strained constructions of that instrument, to merge all into a consolidated government. The Tories are for strengthening the executive and General Government; the Whigs cherish the representative branch, and the rights reserved by the States, as the bulwark against consolidation, which must immediately generate monarchy.

I thank you much for the books you were so kind as to send me by Miss Wright. Her 'Few Days in Athens,' was entirely new and has been a treat to me of the highest order._

After much sickness, and the accident of a broken and disabled arm, I am again in tolerable health, but extremely debilitated, so as to be scarcely able to walk into my garden.

You have still many valuable years to give to your country, and with my prayers that, they may be years of health and happiness, and especially that they may see the establishment of the principles of government which you have cherished through life, accept the assurance of my affectionate and constant friendship and respect.

—Th: Jefferson.

I sailed into the New York harbor on August 15, 1824. Though I was exhausted and dependent on a cane, my spirits were lifted considerably by the crowd waiting to greet me at the Staten Island docks—estimated by the papers the next morning as perhaps 30,000. I was amazed that the American people still remembered me forty-one years after Yorktown. I was touched and deeply appreciative of their warm reception—so different than forcing the door to America open at age nineteen.

Government officials transferred my party to a small ferry, and as we passed an island fortification off the southern tip of Brooklyn, I was informed that it had once been Fort Diamond, but was recently renamed in my honor Fort La Fayette, to celebrate the commencement of my tour. A welcoming salute was fired from the island. As the ferry approached the docks in lower Manhattan, another military salute was fired. On shore a crowd waved American and French flags. We disembarked to shouts of appreciation and were led over to Battery Park for a brief welcoming ceremony where a regiment of New York militia had taken the name of the *Garde Nationale* in my honor. I happily stopped to review them. I was greeted by a group of aging veterans wearing patched-up uniforms and standing on rickety limbs. Each old soldier snapped out his name, company, and the battle where he had served with me during the American Revolution: "Monmouth, Sir!" "Barren Hill, Sir!" "Brandywine, Sir!" My heart leapt to be remembered with such affection and in remembering each adventure of my youth.

Though I was exhausted, the day was not over. City officials had arranged elegant carriages with four large showy white horses to transport us to city hall. Along the route, New Yorkers waved hands and flags and shouted welcoming greetings over church bells and bands. The local dailies counted 50,000 lining the route. That night, 6000 attended a state ball. My host asked me how I wished to be introduced. With a moment to reflect I responded, "As an American General."

That day was an unimaginably magnificent beginning to fourteen months in the United States. Monroe had arranged my itinerary, and I did my best to maintain the schedule. After five days in New York recovering from the ocean voyage and seeing old friends, in Boston I laid the cornerstone of the Bunker Hill Monument, and was greeted on the Common in an occasion of special splendor, with a military review followed by a dinner for 1200 people under a marquee erected for the event. I attended commencement exercises at Harvard College, then went up to Quincy, Massachusetts to call on former President John Adams, now eighty-eight and very feeble.

From New Hampshire I returned to New York to visit Columbia College, and that evening attended a dinner held at the City Hotel in honor of my sixty-seventh birthday. The next day I celebrated the forty-seventh anniversary of the Battle of Brandywine with French residents, and saw a play at the Park Theater entitled *Lafayette, or the Castle of Olmutz* written by Samuel Woodworth—which re-opened barely healed wounds while generating pride in the impact my passage made on such powerful personages as the emperor of the vast Austrian empire.

I was treated to my first steamboat ride up to West Point with the widow of Alexander Hamilton. Her husband had been senselessly killed in 1804 by Aaron Burr, and I wanted to pay my respects to my close friend.

Five boats took us on the masterful Erie Canal to Troy, New York where a parade was led by members of the local Masonic Lodge. We paid a visit to the Troy Female Academy, the first school in the country to provide equal educational opportunities to girls, including an advanced curriculum in mathematics and the sciences.

I did not know Napoleon's eldest brother Joseph well, but I rode up to Bordentown, New Jersey to visit him. Napoleon had made him King of Naples and Sicily, and later King of Spain—roles he felt uncomfortable in, and was immediately opposed by both the Spanish populace and the Duke of Wellington, so that he had to flee Spain. He returned to France during the Hundred Days and was with Napoleon when he attempted to escape the United States. While Napoleon was captured and sent to St. Helena, Joseph had used a false name to board an American ship for New York.

Joseph was a good man—gentle, kind, and without the ambition of his brother, who agreed that France would be better off rid of Louis. I appreciated his keen sense of humor, his reasonableness, his kindliness of soul, and his humanity. He wanted a Bonaparte to resume the throne and I favored the Duke of Orleans. I told him candidly that I disapproved of Napoleon's dictatorship and of the aristocracy he had introduced. He responded:

> *Napoleon never doubted your good intentions; but he thought that you were judged too favorably of your contemporaries. He was forced into war by the English, and into the dictatorship by the war. These few words are the history of the Empire. Napoleon incessantly said to me, 'When will peace arrive? Then only can I satisfy all and show myself as I am.' The aristocracy of which you accuse him was only the mode of placing himself in harmony with Europe. But the old feudal aristocracy was never in his favor. The proof of this is that he was its victim and that he expiated at St. Helena the crime of having wished to employ all the institutions in favor of the people.*

In Philadelphia I was greeted by a long parade that included 160 Revolutionary War veterans. From there I went to Chadd's Ford to revisit the Brandywine battlefield. In Baltimore I was greeted by veterans of the War of 1812 and by old Revolutionary War soldiers. The band played "The March of Lafayette," composed in my honor.

I was excited to see the nation's new capital, a city planned by the Frenchman Major Peter L'Enfant, who had served with us at Valley Forge. I had commissioned my friend to paint a portrait of Washington years ago, and Washington had chosen the young engineer to design the city named in his honor.

I was escorted to the simple one-story house that served as the residence of the president. There were no guards in sight, and a single domestic servant took me to the Cabinet room where Monroe was sitting in a simple blue suit, so in contrast to the costumes worn at

Versailles. We talked of the issues distinguishing the candidates who would replace him, John Quincy Adams and Andrew Jackson. The Missouri Compromise of 1820 was threatening the collapse of the union over the issue of slavery—Adams representing the interests of the north, Jackson of the south and west. In the end Jackson won both the popular and electoral votes, but lacked a majority of electoral votes required by the Constitution, leaving the election to the House of Representatives.

Of course I needed to meet all the relatives of George and Martha Washington. Secretary of War John C. Calhoun escorted me sailing down the Potomac River on the steamship *Petersburg* to visit Washington's tomb at Mount Vernon. His step-son, George Washington Parke Custis, gave me a ribbon of the Society of the Cincinnati founded in 1783 to preserve the ideals and fellowship of the American Revolutionary War, whose membership included officers, American and French, who had served at least three years in the Continental Army. On the Cincinnati ribbon Custis had hung a ring with a lock of Washington's hair. To touch the hair of my friend long gone put me in an otherworldly mood, contemplating the relationship of time and physicality. Custis proudly pointed out the key from the Bastille above the main entrance.

Though starting to grow weary of travel and celebration, it touched me to revisit the dramas of men who had fought beside me, and those whose lives benefitted from our vision and efforts. It enabled me to see that we live our lives as our path unfolds, often unaware of the seeds we are sowing.

In Richmond on October 28 I was asked to attend a parade down the main street and, as usual, given the seat of honor in the center of the first row. I sat dutifully through the lengthy parade of marching townspeople, floats, and bands.

I stood up to express my gratitude to the town officials for their generous efforts in my behalf. I was shaking hands and thanking my hosts when an elderly black man with a weathered face approached the group of Virginia dignitaries. I had not noticed the gray haired man among the few black people in the back of the white crowd. He was in his well-worn Sunday best.

I recognized my friend James. Forty years and the meanderings of life had taken their toll on both of us. I was so glad to see him that I rushed over. I threw my arms around him, and started to cry in front of the bewildered crowd. My hosts and the onlookers were aghast at the Guest of the Nation, an elegantly clad French nobleman, friend to five presidents, affectionately hugging a poor black man. It bothered me that neither the dignitaries nor attendees knew about our relationship, nor what James had done for their independence and freedom, though it delighted me to demonstrate my appreciation and affection to one they so disdained. I vowed to rectify this shameful omission. I introduced James to all the dignitaries and guests, and to George and Fanny who had already surmised from my stories who this was. I insisted that James be my guest of honor at the municipal dinner.

Among dignitaries, politicians, members of Virginia society, military officers, and the Guest of the Nation, James was the only black man in the building, other than the staff waiting on us. I had intimated that I would not attend unless he were served and treated respectfully, as was his due. He was the first black man to be served there.

James sat beside me on the dais, uncomfortable though dignified as I spoke of his heroics during the Virginia campaign which had protected Governor Thomas Jefferson and saved Monticello and Charlottesville from destruction by the British. I told of his bravery in spying for the Continental army as well as pretending to spy for Cornwallis. The dignitaries nodded their appreciation, dutifully thanking James for his efforts. However, none made an effort to converse with him.

James and I spent several days together with my family and guests. The staff of the *Richmond Enquirer* followed us everywhere, reporting on our emotional reunion. This inspired James Ewell Heath to write a novel about James and me, *Edge Hill, or the Family of the Fitzroyals*. My meeting with James was so well publicized that several portraitists asked us to pose together. For one, we stood on either side of a large brown horse, I in my Continental Generals' uniform and James dressed in bright red and wearing a floppy, wide brimmed hat with two large bows—supposedly painted at the Battle of Yorktown. It was an unlikely outfit for a field slave whose success depended on being invisible, but at least it honored his contribution to defeating Cornwallis and achieving independence for the United States.

I learned that he had been free since 1787 when the Virginia House of Burgess emancipated him and let him select his free name. I was honored that he had chosen James Armistead Lafayette. He was granted a mule and forty acres in New Kent County, two days walk southeast of Richmond. He farmed, married, and had several children. Since 1818 he had been receiving an annual pension of forty dollars for his services in the Revolutionary War. Having not heard from me in over forty years, he risked coming up to Richmond—a risk because he was still treated with disrespect by most whites. He was apprehensive about being approached by any white man, even me. I was surprised when James proudly reported that he owned three slaves to help him farm his land. I restrained my urge to express disapproval. I wish there had been an opportunity for Jefferson—who owed his life to James—to meet him, and for us all to speak together about the issues of slavery and economics.

We embraced, acknowledging that it was unlikely we would see one another again—but that our bond of friendship would last forever.

Shortly before leaving, I received the following letter from Jefferson dated October 9:

> I have duly received, my dear friend and General, your letter
> of the 1st from Philadelphia, giving us the welcome assurance
> that you will visit the neighborhood, which, during the march
> of our enemy near it, was covered by your shield from his rob-
> beries and ravages. In passing the line of your former march
> you will experience pleasing recollections of the good you have
> done. It will be an additional honor to the University of the
> State that you will have been its first guest.

But what recollections, dear friend, will this call up to you and me! What a history have we to run over from the evening that yourself, Meusnier, Bernau, and other patriots settled, in my house in Paris, the outlines of the constitution you wished! And to trace it through all the disastrous chapters of Robespierre, Barras, Bonaparte, and the Bourbons! These things, however, are for our meeting.

You mention the return of Miss Wright to America, accompanied by her sister; but do not say what her stay is to be, nor what her course. Should it lead her to a visit of our University, which, in its architecture only, is as yet an object, herself and her companion will nowhere find a welcome more hearty than with Mrs. Randolph, and all the inhabitants of Monticello. This Athenæum of our country, in embryo, is as yet but promise; and not in a state to recall the recollections of Athens. But everything has its beginning, its growth, and end; and who knows with what future delicious morsels of philosophy, and by what future Miss Wright raked from its ruins, the world may, some day, be gratified and instructed?

Your son George we shall be very happy indeed to see, and to renew in him the recollections of your very dear family; and the revolutionary merit of M. le Vasseur has that passport to the esteem of every American, and, to me, the additional one of having been your friend and co-operator, and he will, I hope, join you in making head-quarters with us at Monticello.

But to all these things au revoir; in the meantime we are impatient that your ceremonies at York should be over, and give you to the embraces of friendship.

P. S. Will you come by Mr. Madison's, or let him or me know on what day he may meet you here, and join us in our greetings?

Attending our carriage train for Monticello were 120 mounted men of the Jefferson Guard and Virginia Militia. The road to Jefferson's home ascended through thick forests to his Olympian dwelling perched elegantly on the top of a hill, which he had had his slaves level prior to the construction. Meandering up the incline, we passed small slave houses on both sides of the road before entering the beautiful grounds of Monticello to a bugle announcing our approach. The mounted escorts that had preceded us during our ride lined up in a semicircle on one side of the front lawn across from 200 curious onlookers waiting in front of the neoclassical brick structure.

I had not seen Jefferson since Paris, thirty-five years ago. He was stooped with age, his temples hollow, and his cheeks lean. He passed between the white Greek columns, tottered down the steps, and walked slowly towards me. We fell into each other's arms, bursting into tears. He had been a great friend and mentor, and I valued his brilliant, elegant mind.

Dinner at Monticello was an occasion for lively, lingering conversation, and Jefferson did not want talk to be hindered by the presence of house slaves who might either interrupt or eavesdrop. Consequently, with the help of the dumbwaiters hidden in the fireplace, we served ourselves French wines and delectable victuals prepared by the slave whom Jefferson had had trained in Paris, James Hemings.

The next morning our entourage visited James Monroe at Highland, his thousand acre plantation adjacent to Monticello. After a couple of very pleasant days with Monroe, we traveled on to Montpelier to visit James and Dolly Madison. A small caravan, escorted by forty uniformed men wearing bright blue sashes, visited Jefferson's new university. The campus was picturesque, but the rotunda had not yet been completed. Yet sixty-eight students were already attending the first classes under a faculty of eight noted professors. The school's inaugural banquet was held in my honor with Madison and Monroe in attendance. The hall was beautifully decorated and a wonderful French dinner was served. Jefferson offered a toast, thanking me for helping him advance the mutual interests of both France and America:

I joy, my friends, in our joy, inspired by the visit of this our ancient and distinguished leader and benefactor. His deeds in the War of Independence you have heard and read. They are known to you and embalmed in your memories and in the pages of faithful history.

His deeds in the peace that followed that war, are perhaps not known to you; but I can attest them. When I was stationed in his country, for the purpose of cementing its friendship with ours and of advancing our mutual interests, this friend of both was my most powerful auxiliary and advocate. He made our cause his own, and in truth it was that of his native country also. His influence and connections there were great. In truth I only held the nail, he drove it. Honor him, then, as your benefactor in peace as well as in war.

I was touched and honored by his remarks. I in turn toasted Jefferson for his contributions to advancing the mutual interests of France and America, and acknowledging his help in drafting the Declaration of the Rights of Man and of the Citizen.

I was impressed by Jefferson's daring vision. He had mandated that the university have neither a divinity school nor a department of religion. He believed that higher education should be completely separated from religious doctrine, and that the school's center should be the library, rather than the church. This was a shocking departure for schools in America, and much opposed in Virginia by the majority of clergymen, politicians, and educators whose religious objections had made it difficult for Jefferson to attract the most highly qualified faculty. He had been forced to recruit in Europe—five of his faculty came from England. Two of the three Americans he had hired were not from Virginia.

We returned to Monticello, and two days later Fanny and Camilla arrived. Jefferson had known Fanny since 1818 when she sent him her play *Altorf* and subsequently *Views of Society and Manners in America*.

They had continued corresponding. When Jefferson heard I would be coming, he took the liberty of asking her to join us.

They were an odd couple—Fanny, twenty-nine, masculine, energetic, indifferent to dress, and Jefferson, eighty-one and meticulous. Yet Jefferson was fascinated by her radical beliefs—free public education for all children, universal equality in education, sexual freedom for women and birth control, women in medicine, and the threats of organized religion and capitalism—and he admired and respected her outspokenness, honesty, and passionate love of liberty, and enjoyed fencing with her sharp, witty mind. She admired his eloquence and brilliance, and his historic role in the colonists' revolt. Together we spent many hours in front of the dining room fireplace discussing poetry, literature, and politics. However, we mostly avoided the delicate issue of slavery to not offend our host—despite being constantly surrounded by his slaves. He had hundreds, living in shacks on Mulberry Row further down the hill, working as weavers, spinners, blacksmiths, tinsmiths, carpenters, sawyers, charcoal-burners, stablemen, and joiners. Hundreds of other slaves worked the four farms comprising Jefferson's 5000 acre plantation, living separately near the fields where they worked.

Then there were his elite household staff—sixteen who lived in better housing near the main house—all from one family descended from a black slave, Elizabeth Heming, and a white British sea captain. I had met two of the Hemings in Paris—Sally, whose duties at Monticello included being nursemaid-companion, lady's maid, chambermaid, and seamstress; and her brother, James, the chef. Sally lived close to Jefferson, and though she never married, had given birth to six children. I suspect that my host was their father.

Jefferson's house slaves were around us throughout the day and night, waiting on us, serving tea, preparing dinner, looking after the house and our clothes, and bringing basins of hot water for our morning baths. All the water we drank and washed with was carried by slaves from the streams that flowed at the base of the mountain on which Monticello was perched. Their days were filled with hauling heavy containers nearly a thousand feet uphill and discharging the contents into cisterns near the house.

During my six week stay, Jefferson asked that we speak only in French to assure the privacy of our conversations, and he ensured an abundance of good wine. After I departed he noted, jovially I thought, that he had had to replenish nearly all of the red wines in his cellar. Each day included a carriage ride to see friends or take in the beauty of the countryside. On one when George was with us, I remarked that I had been motivated to come to America by the Declaration of Independence to fight for noble principles—the freedom of mankind, the inalienable right to liberty, the pursuit of happiness—and yet throughout Virginia and much of the United States, slaves were still being held in bondage.

I knew that Jefferson had refused to teach even the Hemings family to read or write. Since he was focusing on education now, I suggested how he would profit if his slaves were educated. He replied that he had no objection teaching slaves to read, but was concerned about teaching them to write, for that would enable them to forge papers. I did not know what papers a slave would want to forge, other than a document authorizing their own freedom, so I did not respond. I was disappointed in my friend's callous contempt toward fellow humans.

Jefferson's views regarding blacks made both Fanny and me uncomfortable, and after several glasses of a particularly fruity wine, she said she was not pleased with his excuses for maintaining slavery on his own plantation, as well as his general attitude toward Negroes. She accused Jefferson of treating his slaves inhumanely, merely as property and investment. I had shared similar views with Jefferson on many previous occasions. I wished again that Jefferson could have met James.

After I returned to France, I received a long appreciative letter from Fanny, explaining to me why she had not rejoined the tour. She and Camilla had stayed at Monticello long after I was gone. She became increasingly upset with Jefferson's views on slavery. Their arguments caused Fanny to leave both Monticello and the tour. She decided to prove to Jefferson that he could emancipate and educate slaves without serious personal or financial consequences, so she devised a plan following the model of La Belle Gabrielle.

Without any protective male escorts, she and Camilla immediately left Monticello for the west, in search of cheap land. Near the small village of Memphis, Tennessee she bought 2000 acres of mosquito-ridden wilderness and named it *Neshoba*, the Chickasaw word for wolf. She arranged for thirty slaves to clear, fence, and farm the land, and promised to pay them for their work, educate them, and when they were able to purchase their freedom, she would pay for their transportation to Liberia or Haiti. I happily agreed to be a trustee of the enterprise. Three years later Fanny contracted malaria and was forced to return to London. I did not hear from her again until I received a letter from New York inviting me to be best man at her wedding to a French physician.

I went on to see Monroe again for a brief visit. He told me that while I was at Monticello, Jefferson had spoken discretely to him about my financial difficulties, leading Monroe to urge Congress to award me a grant for my service to the country: 23,000 acres in central Florida, as well as the generous sum of $200,000. Monroe told me that when I returned to the District of Columbia, the House of Representatives requested that I address them.

I met with President Monroe several times during my winter stay in Washington, D.C., met again with George Washington's relatives, and made official visits to the Senate and the House of Representatives where I was officially awarded the money and property that Jefferson and Monroe had suggested.

In late January I set off toward Richmond for a tour through the south and west. By inauguration day for John Quincy Adams I had reached Raleigh, North Carolina, where I was happily reunited with colonel William Polk who had fought and been wounded with me at Brandywine. I had missed Charleston, South Carolina during the Revolution, so I enjoyed three days of balls, fireworks, and reunions with their gracious hospitality, and met Doctor Francis Huger to personally express appreciation for his efforts to liberate me from Olmutz.

In Camden, South Carolina I visited the tomb of Baron de Kalb to pay respects to my mentor, colleague, and friend. In Savannah I laid the cornerstone of a memorial honoring Nathanael Greene in Johnson Square. I followed a circular route through Alabama, New Orleans, the new state of Kentucky, and up to Pennsylvania and New England, then down the coast to Mount Vernon once more for a brief visit.

The thirteen separate and separated colonies I had known back in the 1780s were twenty-four states united into a nation doubled in size and population, with new roads and institutions linking them into a true union which now reached across the Mississippi River. Disparate states had agreed to a single written constitution, a president, a national judicial system, a two-house Congress, a professional army and navy, and had achieved its own strong currency. I felt such pride in holding faith that a peoples could achieve so much. I hoped that France might eventually stabilize for a similar accomplishment.

On September 6 I met John Quincy Adams and addressed a joint session of Congress, the first foreigner to be so honored. It was attended by Monroe, Adams, and Jackson, who also joined us for a splendid birthday party at the White House to celebrate my sixty-eighth birthday and the conclusion of my tour.

Monroe arranged for the American warship *Susquehanna* to take me back to France. As a gesture of the nation's affection, he had the frigate renamed *Brandywine* to commemorate the battle in which I shed my blood for American freedom.

On September 7 George, Emilie, and our staff boarded the steamboat *Mount Vernon* which took us down the shallow Potomac to the *Brandywine*. We were carrying numerous gifts and a large chest of topsoil from the field in Brandywine where I had first distinguished myself in battle. I hoped it would someday cover my body. The *Brandywine* raised anchor and sailed into Chesapeake Bay and open ocean.

CHAPTER 25

Constitutional Monarchy Succeeds

1825

S HORTLY AFTER ARRIVING IN New York at the beginning of my tour, I had learned that Louis XVIII had died. The following month he was succeeded by his younger, conservative brother Charles-Philippe who tried to restore the political and social system of France prior to the Revolution of 1789. He restored the divine right of kings and absolute rule, bolstered the power of the nobility, returned control of schools to the Church, passed the Anti-Sacrilege Act prohibiting blasphemy and sacrilege with penalties from perpetual forced labor to decapitation.

When I arrived home I was appalled by the reactionary policies. During my tour I had tried to influence events back home, with my secretary Levasseur sending clippings and copies of my speeches in America to French periodicals. However, government censorship had kept much of it out at the press. But Levasseur had kept a detailed journal which he published serially and as a book. The monarchist minister to America, Baron de Mareuil reported to his superiors in Paris that my words were less "homage to America than an appeal to the revolutionary passions in Europe, a wish for their success and for the complete triumph of democracy." And indeed my tour had helped regain some of my political prestige in France. There could be little doubt that Charles was not pleased to see me triumphantly return to France a liberal hero.

To avoid travelling during the winter months, I took an apartment in Paris at 6 rue d'Anjou where each Tuesday evening I held a reception that attracted liberals from America and Europe. My soirees in Paris, like Adrienne's salons and my dialogues with guests at La Grange, facilitated contact between different generations, contributed to connections between politicians and writers, and brought together my French friends and foreigners.

In 1827 I decided to re-enter the political sphere to work against the policies of Charles X. I was elected to the Chamber of Deputies where I became, effectively, the leader of parliamentary opposition to Charles' programs to restrict liberty in France.

In January 1830, Charles sent a military expedition to Algeria to end Algerian pirates' damage to Mediterranean trade—as well as to play the ever-effective card of increasing his popularity with a military victory. When we voted to require Charles to consult the Chamber for authorization, he dissolved the newly elected chamber. In July he suspended the Constitution, censored the press, altered the electoral system, and called for elections in September. When the newspapers published these ordinances, protests began in the streets of Paris. I urged the people to "make revolution, because without it we shall have made nothing but a riot."

In the Chamber of Deputies I urged that we depose the king and name as his successor Louis-Philippe, Duke of Orleans who, though related to the Bourbons, had fought as a republican in 1789. We needed every vote to depose the king, so I sent an urgent message to my old colleague Benjamin Constant. Though his legs were swollen and his feet and tongue paralyzed, I informed him of the stakes, and demanded, "A game is being played here in which our heads are all at stake. Bring yours!"

With great effort the courageous Constant made it to the Chamber of Deputies, and we were able to pass a motion of no confidence against the king and his ministry. Charles ignored our motion, and dissolved both Parliament and the National Guard. But the election returned an overwhelming liberal majority. On August 2, Charles abdicated in favor of his nine-year-old grandson Henri, and he named Louis-Philippe, his Lieutenant General, as regent. When Louis refused to serve, Charles and his family were forced to flee into exile in London.

The people of Paris wanted neither Bourbon nor Bonaparte to replace Charles, but rather a new republican government run by the people. I was confident that I could win, but at 73, I was too infirm to consider declaring myself a candidate to be the country's first president—I was beyond taking on such a monumental challenge. The Chamber of Deputies created a Municipal Commission to defend Paris and maintain order, which installed itself in the Hôtel de Ville and asked me to look for a successor to Charles.

I was concerned about a new republic becoming a terrorist Jacobin regime, but Louis-Philippe had impeccable credentials. His father, Louis Philippe Joseph, had been a republican supporter of the Revolution of 1789 whom the Paris Commune referred to as "Citoyen Egalité." Louis-Philippe had also joined the Jacobins and commanded a republican division at the battle of Valmy. After the Convention he plotted to guillotine deposed Louis XVI. In his twenty-one years in exile, four had been spent in America. With his background, I thought he would make an excellent choice for the throne of France. A group led by the banker Laffitte promoted his candidacy and urged the Commission to establish a liberal constitutional monarchy along the British parliamentary model.

I asked Louis-Philippe to meet me at the Hôtel de Ville, but when he entered the building, the crowd was clearly not interested in another monarch, much less a Bourbon. I took the duke by the hand, placed a tricolor flag in his other hand, and led him onto a balcony in view of a vast gathering. I threw my arms around the duke's neck in an affectionate embrace saying, "You know that I am a Republican, and that I regard the Constitution of the United States as the most perfect that has ever existed."

"I think as you do. It is impossible to have passed four years in the United States, as I have done, and not to be of that opinion. But do you think that in the present state of France a republican government can be adopted?"

"No. That which is necessary for France now is a throne, surrounded by republican institutions. All must be republican."

He announced before the crowd that he agreed, which immensely strengthened his position.

My colleagues and I drew up a plan to reconcile republican institutions with the forms of a monarchy. I personally took it to the Palais Royal and submitted it to Louis-Philippe. He agreed to it, and a week later the people chose him as their new king.

To show his appreciation for my help, Louis-Philippe appointed me president of the Council of Ministers and Honorary Commanding-General of the National Guard of the Kingdom. I gratefully, but unwisely, accepted the honor despite my poor health and age. As the new leader of the National Guard, I led 30,000 strong in review before him, as the crowd cheered their new king.

Word of the uprising in France sparked an uprising in Brussels and the Southern Provinces of the United Kingdom of the Netherlands, leading to their separation and the establishment of the Kingdom of Belgium. It also inspired revolutions in Italy and Poland, however unsuccessful. In October the Belgians sent a delegation asking me to accept the chief magistracy of the proposed republic. Though honored to be invited, I had to decline. The Belgians proceeded to form a constitutional monarchy—then offered me the crown. Wisdom required that I turn it down. It had quickly become apparent to me that I was too infirm to continue carrying out even my duties as commandant of the Paris National Guard. I resigned.

Louise-Philippe began his rule unpretentiously, avoiding the pomp and lavish spending of his predecessors. He was much loved by the people who called him "Citizen Smith" and the "bourgeois monarch." He abolished press censorship, returned education to the state, and lowered the voting age. Parisians did not forget, however, that he was by birth an aristocrat and a Bourbon; that he had taken no part, either by word or deed, in the conflict for the overthrow of the despotic throne; that concealed in the recesses of his palace at Neuilly, he had not shown his face in Paris until the shedding of blood was terminated; and that he had come to Paris merely to assume a crown. Also, despite this outward appearance of simplicity, his support came from the wealthy bourgeoisie—and soon Louis began catering to them. He grew increasingly conservative and monarchical. I realized that despite all his assurances, he was not nearly as democratically inclined as I had hoped. As conditions of the working class deteriorated and the income gap widened, his popularity began to suffer.

Elected a deputy once again, I urged the king to take a principled stand for a variety of just causes. I continued to stir up opposition, demanding that he: put an end to hereditary seats in Parliament, as he had promised; extend voting rights to all French citizens; and abolish the slave trade. When in November 1830 there was an uprising in Warsaw against their Russian occupiers, I urged the Chamber of Deputies to enact favorable legislation. I gave endless speeches as well as financial support, and housed and entertained many exiled Polish refugees at La Grange. We raised money, provided refuge, sent volunteer fighters, and bought arms.

Unfortunately, in December 1 I lost my dear friend and valuable colleague Benjamin Constant with whom I had worked closely for fifteen years in supporting liberal causes. I spoke at his funeral four days later at a Protestant church on rue Saint Antoine, and praised him to those in attendance:

Love of liberty, and the need of serving her, always ruled his conduct. To say this is a justice due him, over his grave, by a friend who, less trusting and temperate than he, was nevertheless the confidant of his most intimate thoughts.

I continued serving as a delegate in the Chamber of Deputies to try to improve conditions, but I was increasingly ineffective. I had turned 74 and was unable to accomplish what I had in my youth.

In June 1832 Louis-Philippe's government brutally put down public demonstrations at a cost of 800 lives. Shocked by these counter-revolutionary actions, I resigned from all my government offices, including the post of mayor of my local community, because they were based in a regime that had gone back on its democratic promises. I came to believe that the fight for liberty would never be won as long as a Bourbon occupied the throne of France.

Then in March, I did a very imprudent thing. A good friend of mine, General Dubourg, was killed in a duel. On a damp and very chilly day I followed his bier to the gravesite and spoke at his funeral. I caught a cold which turned into bronchitis, and eventually into pneumonia. My children have come to attend me, and I'm now lying in bed on the rue d'Anjou writing my memoirs, which I hope to finish with the help of large amounts of quinine and rest. I trust I will be well soon.

I am beginning to feel that it's time for me to retire for good so I can spend my months or years with my children, grandchildren, and great-grandchildren. Even if I am able to recover fully, I know I probably don't have much longer to live and hope that my memoirs will prove interesting and even useful to my children, friends, and scholars.

I must acknowledge that though my intention had never been to be important, for the last years I have had reflection from many quarters beyond family that my life has mattered. I have tried to lead a good and productive life, and I do have much to be proud of.

I have come to realize how fragile freedom is, that we will never be more than one generation away from extinction. Our children will not inherit it—they will have to fight for it, protect it, and teach their children to be vigilant and active in preserving it. I have risked my life and spent my fortune fighting to protect freedom against the regimes of five monarchs—King George III in the American revolution, King Louis XVI in the French revolution of 1789, Charles the X, Louis XVIII, and in the end even Louis-Philippe whom I promoted. I opposed and often clashed with many formidable adversaries including Cornwallis, Danton, Robespierre, Francis II, and Napoleon. Unfortunately, as Mr. Jefferson so eloquently said, the tree of liberty must be refreshed from time to time with the blood of patriots and tyrants.

I have supported revolutions in America, France, Poland, Italy, Spain, Greece, and South America, and efforts by slaves, Indians, and women to obtain their freedom. I take pride in my efforts if they have been helpful in gaining freedom for some people, and especially for providing James his emancipation, a small gesture when weighed against the impact of his brave actions that encouraged the British to admit defeat—an accomplishment which inspired so many to take up their own fight for freedom. Had I helped liberate even a single person in my lifetime, my descendants should be proud of me, and I would, contented, abandon this fragile vehicle and station.

Not that I will not carry regrets to Picpus cemetery. I deeply regret that I could do nothing to stop the Reign of Terror that killed so many of Adrienne's and my family and friends, and so many other decent visionary people. I was unable, though I tried, to prevent Napoleon from wreaking havoc across Europe, destroying millions—including his countrymen whom he sent into battle not for their own better-ment, but merely to prove and gain more power. I was also not suc-cessful in ending slavery in America, though it was my unrelenting commitment. And I most regret having supported any monarchy, however limited it might have been by constitutional restraints, even on the British model. I acted out of repulsion by the excesses of the Jacobins and wariness of their brand of republicanism.

I am proud of the fact that when I was affluent, rather than partici-pating in the hedonistic lifestyle like so many of my peers before the revolution, I risked everything I had in the cause of liberty, even taking on enormous debt to pursue my principles. I want my descendants to know that the greatest happiness does not depend on the conditions of life which we are born into, but is the result of good conscience, good health, a rewarding occupation, and the blessing of freedom in all just pursuits. I believe that it is important to try to lead a life that matters, if only to a single other person.

Despite the grand gestures of squandering my fortune, reputation, and body in efforts to force the removal of wealthy, armed, powerful rulers of mighty countries, my biggest regret is my inability to convince my wife to leave her voluntary confinement in Olmutz prison. I watched her disintegrate and weaken, and I am convinced that I have lived so many years without her companionship as a result of her confinement. I have missed her wisdom, warmth, support, and compassion every triumphant day of my twenty-six years without her.

I am now facing oblivion. I am skeptical—with only the faintest hope that the Catholic Church has been truthful in preaching that there is a heaven. I have seen them lie, deceive, and willfully burden the poor, side with the corrupt, and condone slavery. Again Mr. Jefferson said it most germanely: "In every country and every age, the priest has been hostile to Liberty," to which my friend Patrick Henry would add his refrain, "Give me liberty, or give me death." For my own epitaph I would say: "I loved liberty with the enthusiasm of religion, and with the rapture of love." I hope my grandchildren and their children will be fighters for liberty, because protecting another man's freedom is the only way to protect your own.

My ultimate freedom will come shortly. I have studied many beliefs relating to an afterlife and can only hope that whatever form it may take, if any, I will be with my beloved Adrienne again, and say belatedly, "Je suis tout à toi."

Epilogue

I was born to be a soldier. And a major part of my life was set in that context. In the end I see that the vicissitudes of circumstances have at least as strong a role as the intentions of kings and generals and revolutionaries. Our grand ideals—or our enormous lust for power and wealth—are as fragile as a slave's life, being subject to the phenomena of this mysterious earth. An unpredictable squall can scatter ships of battle and send them to the bottom of the sea without so much as a cannon aimed at them. Swamp disease or interminable winter can claim more lives in camps than all our bullets, sabers, and cannon balls on the fields of engagement. The foibles of one man or the treacheries of another or the cleverness of a slave or the blinders of an aristocrat can temper the course of millions of lives for generations.

Given these vicissitudes, it strikes me that only a deeper wisdom can be driving the course of events. Despite happenstance and good intelligence, liberty has still managed to rise out of the smoke and dust stirred up by human hearts smitten with a vision.

❧

Lafayette died on May 20, 1834. Louis-Philippe, fearing that Lafayette's memory would cause a huge crowd of grieving mourners to rise up against his royal rule, forbade a public funeral and lined the funeral route with a triple row of armed soldier, with loaded cannons placed at strategic locations. In spite of this conspicuous show of might, tens of thousands of people turned out to see 3000 National Guards, members of the Chamber, government ministers, and representatives of foreign governments accompany Lafayette's coffin to the humble Picpus cemetery. His body was interred next to Adrienne and covered with soil from both Brandywine and Washington's grave at Mount Vernon. In death, as in life, Lafayette was bound together with his wife and his friend George Washington.

The relationship between Washington and Lafayette—which resulted in both men becoming known throughout the world as soldiers, politicians, and diplomats—has been honored since 1890 with an American flag flying eternally over Lafayette's grave.

The capital of the United States of America is named for George Washington. As President, Washington signed the act of Congress authorizing the construction of the White House within the district of the new federal city, and he chose the site for the building that stands for the symbol of the presidency. Directly across from the White House a park was built in honor of Washington's closest friend—the Marquis de Lafayette. Between the White House and Lafayette Square runs Pennsylvania Avenue, named for the state where Washington and Lafayette first met and the site of battles where both risked their lives in the cause of freedom.

Washington is buried nearby at Mount Vernon, next to his wife Martha. Near his grave is the key to the Bastille—a gift from Lafayette symbolizing the start of the revolution in the country of his birth.

As a further sign of the love and respect America has for Lafayette, he was formally made a citizen of the United States—one of only six people granted that honor. Throughout America, from Lafayette, California to Lafayette, Louisiana to Lafayette, New York over sixty cities are named in his honor, as well as numerous counties, parks, public schools, and streets, and even a college.

•—◆—•

In 1818, author Madame Germaine de Stael, daughter of the famous liberal Swiss banker Jacques Necker, wrote in her famous book on the French Revolution:

M. de la Fayette ... must be considered a true republican; none of the vanities of his class have ever entered his head; power, which has such a great effect in France, has no influence on him; the desire to please in salons does not alter his conversation in the least; he has sacrificed his entire fortune to his opinions with the most generous indifference. In the prisons of Olmutz as at the pinnacle of influence, he has been equally unshakeable in his attachment to the same principles.

In 1832 the German poet Heinrich Heine wrote:

Lafayette established for himself a more stately column than that at Vendôme, and a better statue than that of marble or metal. Where is the marble as pure as his heart, and where is the metal as firm as the devotion of old Lafayette? Of course he was always partisan, but partisan like the needle of a compass, which always points to the North, and not once deviates to the South or to the East. And so Lafayette has daily said the same thing for forty years, and always points toward North America. For that is where the revolution began with its universal declaration of human rights. Still in this hour he persists in this declaration, without which there can be no healing—that partisan man with his partisan heavenly Realm of Freedom!

Maps and Illustrations

Metz

Paris
Château de la Grange-Bléneau

F R A N C E

Chavaniac in
the Auvergne

Major Battles of the American Revolution

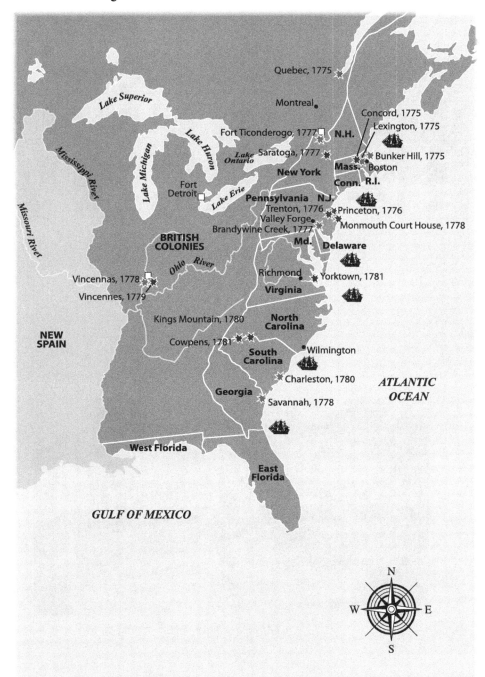

Quebec, 1775

Montreal

Concord, 1775
Lexington, 1775

Lake Superior

Fort Ticonderogo, 1777   N.H.

Lake Michigan   *Lake Huron*

Lake Ontario   Saratoga, 1777   Bunker Hill, 1775

Mississippi River

New York   Mass.   Boston

Conn.   R.I.

Fort Detroit   *Lake Erie*   Pennsylvania   N.J.

Trenton, 1776   Princeton, 1776

Valley Forge   Monmouth Court House, 1778

Missouri River

BRITISH COLONIES

Brandywine Creek, 1777

Md.   Delaware

Ohio River

Vincennas, 1778   Richmond   Yorktown, 1781

Vincennes, 1779   Virginia

NEW SPAIN

Kings Mountain, 1780   North Carolina

Cowpens, 1781   Wilmington

South Carolina

ATLANTIC OCEAN

Georgia   Charleston, 1780

Savannah, 1778

West Florida

East Florida

GULF OF MEXICO

N
W   E
S

Hôtel de Noailles, Paris

Château de Chavaniac

ATTRIBUTION: MARY MACDERMOT CRAWFORD

ATTRIBUTION: TROYE OWENS

Château de la Grange-Bléneau

Washington and Lafayette at Mount Vernon, 1784

Engraved portrait of James Armistead Lafayette (c. 1759–1830)."
After the painting by John B. Martin, ca. 1824.

Lafayette and James Armistead Lafayette in Virginia, 1825

About the Author

As a trial lawyer for 30 years David Weitzman specialized in the defense of individuals arrested for political reasons, or in violation of their civil liberties. He is now retired and wanted to tell the story of one of the world's champions of liberty and his own personal hero, the Marquis de Lafayette. As an attorney for the American Civil Liberties Union, and Chairman of ACLU chapters in Northern Virginia and Berkeley, California, Mr. Weitzman was personally involved in trying notable civil liberties cases, representing the late Abbie Hoffman when he was arrested for wearing an American flag shirt, and representing the writer Norman Mailer when he was arrested for demonstrating against the war in Viet Nam at the Pentagon. For over 30 years Mr. Weitzman worked diligently trying to protect the Constitutional Rights of demonstrators, war protestors, garment workers, farm workers, and U.S. Marines.

Made in the USA
Las Vegas, NV
15 August 2024

93885605R00177